My Roman History

My Roman History

ALIZAH HOLSTEIN

VIKING

VIKING
An imprint of Penguin Random House LLC
penguinrandomhouse.com

Grateful acknowledgment is made for permission to reprint the following:

p. vii: C. P. Cavafy, "The City," from *C.P. Cavafy: Collected Poems*, translated by Edmund
Keeley and Philip Sherrard. Translation copyright © 1975, 1992 by Edmund Keeley
and Philip Sherrard. Used with permission of Princeton University Press.
Permission conveyed through Copyright Clearance Center, Inc.

Image on p. 100: "American Girl in Italy," Florence 1951.
Copyright © 1952, 1980 by Ruth Orkin.

Excerpt(s) from *Purgatorio* by Dante, translated by Allen Mandelbaum, translation copyright
© 1980 by Allen Mandelbaum. Used by permission of Bantam Books, an imprint of
Random House, a division of Penguin Random House LLC. All rights reserved.

Excerpt(s) from *Inferno* by Dante, verse translation by Allen Mandelbaum, translation copyright
© 1980 by Allen Mandelbaum. Used by permission of Bantam Books, an imprint of
Random House, a division of Penguin Random House LLC. All rights reserved.

Excerpt(s) from *Paradiso* by Dante, translated by Allen Mandelbaum, translation copyright
© 1984 by Allen Mandelbaum. Used by permission of Bantam Books, an imprint of
Random House, a division of Penguin Random House LLC. All rights reserved.

Images on all pages except pages 61 and 100 from the collection of the author.

Library of Congress Cataloging-in-Publication Data

Names: Holstein, Alizah, author.
Title: My Roman history / Alizah Holstein.
Description: New York : Viking, an imprint of Penguin Random House, 2024. |
Includes bibliographical references.
Identifiers: LCCN 2024003500 (print) | LCCN 2024003501 (ebook) |
ISBN 9780593490082 (hardcover) | ISBN 9780593490099 (ebook)
Subjects: LCSH: Rome (Italy)—Civilization. | Rome (Italy)—Description and
travel. | Holstein, Alizah—Travel—Italy—Rome. | Dante Alighieri, 1265-1321—
Influence. | Americans—Italy—Rome—Biography. |
Rome (Italy)—Study and teaching.
Classification: LCC DG807.6 .H657 2024 (print) | LCC DG807.6 (ebook) |
DDC 937—dc23/eng/20240207
LC record available at https://lccn.loc.gov/2024003500
LC ebook record available at https://lccn.loc.gov/2024003501

Printed in the United States of America
1st Printing

Designed by Alexis Farabaugh

*for the people we have been
and for those we will one day be*

Keep Ithaka always in your mind.
Arriving there is what you're destined for.
But don't hurry the journey at all.
Better if it lasts for years,
so you're old by the time you reach the island,
wealthy with all you've gained on the way,
not expecting Ithaka to make you rich.
Ithaka gave you the marvelous journey.
Without her you wouldn't have set out.
She has nothing left to give you now.
And if you find her poor, Ithaka won't have fooled you.
Wise as you will have become, so full of experience,
you'll have understood by then what these Ithakas mean.

CONSTANTINE CAVAFY, "ITHAKA"
TRANSLATED BY EDMUND KEELEY

CONTENTS

Part I

Part II

Part V

Part I

1.

ROMANA

Italian, like most Romance and Germanic languages, does not differentiate between "history" and "story." Both concepts are contained in a single word, storia. *What follows is both history and story. It is a* storia.

‿⊙⌒

The first place I ever wanted to go, independently and of my own volition, was Rome. When I was seventeen, my brilliant senior-year English
teacher introduced our class to Dante. While the medieval poet likely did
not write *Inferno*—the first part of the trilogy known as *The Divine
Comedy*—to appeal to teenage girls, it nevertheless worked on me some
kind of dark magic. Dante, a middle-aged man meandering through a
landscape of perdition, led me to Italian history, and the history led me to
the language. It was the language, I think, that led me to the place.

One evening that fall—it was late 1992—I decided I would go. Not
that summer, or the following year, but that very night. My parents and
brothers had already gone to sleep. Our house, located alongside the tracks
of the Green Line on the Boston trolley system, was quiet but for an intermittently passing train. Rumbling along on their steel tracks, the trolleys

had become such a familiar background to my thoughts that I hardly noticed them any longer. That night, though, the passing train suddenly seemed a signal of opportunity. Like a vein leading to the beating heart of something.

I stuffed a backpack with some extra clothes and picked up the bank card that gave me access to my collected savings. I took a last glance at the poster on my wall, a gift from a friend in my class, depicting a young American woman striding down an Italian sidewalk, then crept down the stairs and slipped out of the house. I'd buy the plane ticket at Logan Airport, I thought. Could you really do this? Or did it just happen in movies? I didn't know. I didn't concern myself too much with the details.

Standing under the dim lights at the deserted Beaconsfield trolley stop, I imagined waking up the next morning in Rome. I didn't have a clear sense of what that might look like, but I envisioned a saturated kind of sunlight, chirping birds, the *click-clack* of shoes on cobblestone. I would listen to people speaking words that Dante had spoken. I would touch, with my hands and the soles of my feet, the history of a place I knew only from books. Paper and ink would miraculously turn to soil.

This was the first of many moments in which Rome exerted its pull on me. I had never been to Rome, nor Italy. I knew, in a vague way, that my grandparents had spent time there after the war, but they had rarely spoken of it in front of me. I wasn't Catholic, didn't have an Italian name, a beloved *nonno*—none of that. All I had—that night, that year, very possibly all my life—was desire.

From where, people have asked, did this desire arise? Such is the hunger for rational explanations. Such is the thirst for believing that everything can be accounted for. And although I know it's a fool's errand, although I know that what lies at the center of love, at the center of desire, is not a checklist but an impenetrable black box, I still want to hazard an answer. Surely there were multiple points of origin, not just one. Every so often a new one would unfold, a new track leading me to Rome rather than anywhere else in the world. For much of my life, I have been trying to get there.

And yet I never quite have. Not in the way I first envisioned, anyway. I haven't had a real life there: no long-term lease or mortgage, no births, no funerals, no bank accounts, no job, at least, not in the traditional sense. Several times I have set Rome behind me, thinking I was done with it forever. And just as many times, I have raced back. My to-and-fro has been at times unaccountably happy, and just as often, irredeemably sad. Within the city's walls, and in the countryside surrounding it, I have been gifted remarkable moments of friendship, coincidences that border on magical, and access to a history that grounds me.

There is a downside. Of Rome I am jealous the way some are of their lovers. When friends visit, and, upon returning, tell me stories of their five or seven days there, I don't listen well, but rather wait patiently for them to finish. When it comes to Rome, I seldom want any story that is not mine. This is a fact that embarrasses me, for I am the first to acknowledge that Rome belongs to everyone. In human love, I am not the jealous kind. But when it comes to Rome, I am all teeth.

With Madrid, my husband's birthplace and a city I have come to savor, I experience none of this. There, I don't hesitate to ask for directions, or fret when I bungle a verb. There, the *charcutero* in the central neighborhood where we once lived for seven months calls me *guapa* as he retrieves a small present—fruit-flavored Popsicles—for my boys. As with him, my relationship with the city is blithe and effortless. I am happy in it, at ease. "Tia Ali!" my nieces shout as they run toward me on the playground. I scoop them up unabashedly in my arms, flip them upside down as they squeal and reach for the ground. But what has come so easily to me in Madrid—love, family, a portal into a culture different from my own—in Rome has come to me in small droplets, and with great effort. And yet while Madrid comes and goes, Rome is always in the background of my mind. The map of its streets is as familiar to me as the lines on my own hand. I have pored over its history—its stories—and imagined my bones scattered among the ancient bricks and tufa stones, the miniature marine mollusks and pine cones that form its soil. I have sifted Rome's speckled earth, bottled it, boxed it, brought it home in cans. I cannot know if I will chase after Rome all my life, or whether at some point I will earn a pardon, a reprieve, wave my white flag and say enough is enough. I'm an American asunder, a New Englander out of sorts, a Bostonian, born in the bend of the Charles, who is not from that city on the Tiber, but who has found in it an essential part of her story. *Romana*, some who care for me have called me. Roman, though I know I am not, and never will be.

That night in the late fall of 1992, I did not get on a plane. I had been on the trolley for twenty minutes when it occurred to me that I would need a passport. Of course. And so I got off at Kenmore Square, walked the distance home, slipped quietly back into my house, and went to sleep. But that night the dream, and the possibility of attaining it, had become real.

2.

ROME AT A GALLOP

A college professor told our seminar that although we'd be studying medieval history, we would not be able to understand it until we were at least thirty. To understand the past, he told us, you have to know what it means to live in time.

I was twenty-one then. I thought I knew very well what it meant to live in time. Now over forty, and a historian myself, I realize that whatever I do know about time, it is only the tiniest, most obscure fraction of the truth.

❧

In the beginning, Rome does not exist.

Then out of Troy migrates Aeneas (heroic, destitute), who rides the pink-tipped waves to the mouth of the Tiber. His line begets the wolf-suckled twins Romulus and Remus (fratricidal, innocent), which leads to the succession of kings (strange, primitive), which leads to the Roman Republic (militant, honorable). For the first time—but not the last—the city is sacked, this time at the hands of a Gallic tribe. Civil wars ferry the republic into empire (voracious, golden). From the east, slaves flow in.

Within a handful of generations, one in three people on the globe lives under Rome's laws.

At the height of this Pax Romana, one million people call the city home. The rich dwell in houses (fragrant, luscious), while the poor cram into apartments (flimsy, fire-prone), some of which climb nine stories high. But almost everyone has running water.

In the first century, Emperor Vespasian builds the Colosseum (grisly, gorgeous) as a gift to the Roman people. Soon after, the Pantheon is completed. Its portico bearing sixteen granite columns, each weighing 120,000 pounds and brought by ship from distant Egypt. Marcus Aurelius, cast in bronze (stoic, weaponless) atop his horse, leads his empire calmly into the future. But after him the tide begins to turn. Wars multiply. Foreign mercenaries fill the ranks. Expansion turns to retraction. New walls are erected to protect the city's seven hills. In the empire's farthest reaches, the subdued shake the soil from their shoulders. The stream of slave labor dwindles to a trickle. Slowly, inevitably, the empire unravels. For the first time in eight hundred years, the city is sacked (astonishing, astounding), this time by the Visigoths. Those within earshot watch as their world turns on its head.

Hush.

The city (forsaken, frondescent) gives way to villages. Visigoths and Romans duke it out, then others: Ostrogoths, Byzantines, and Franks. One day in Rome a pope crowns Charlemagne *emperor*, and with him the ghost (nascent, tremulous) of the old empire rises. From now on all the emperors will say: the authority we hold (divine, brittle) is inherited from the ancient emperors (dusty, transmogrified).

Rome's power is in ashes, but its name alchemizes into legend.

Over generations the papacy (crusading, strident) prospers and establishes itself as a secular power. Inquisitions abound, leaving southern

France, northern Italy, in flames. Meanwhile, Rome's noble families (besieging, besieged) raise their fists—against the papacy, against one another—jostling for rank and power. Just after 1300, Pope Boniface VIII (jubilant, irascible), himself a Roman nobleman, is kidnapped and beaten, and soon dies. Some contemporaries gasp; others look on. The papacy gathers its cassocks and flees to southern France, where the Avignon papacy (corpulent, flatulent) is born. Rome (abandoned, weeping) reels. Pilgrims visit, marvel at the bones of martyrs (gruesome, sanctified), at the ivy climbing the aqueducts, many of which, miraculously, still run with water. Poets—Dante, Petrarch—visit, too, and stumble (lost, found) among the ruins.

Rome stands alone. Free of emperor, free of pope. Shorn of power. Forlorn. Clutching nothing but its own name.

The city becomes a town becomes a village. One million souls have withered to eighteen thousand. Within the city walls, nature blooms. In the Colosseum, cows graze. Chickens peck at the tombs of emperors.

In this landscape of ruins, a man named Cola di Rienzo says he will revive the empire, says he will bring down the Roman noble families. Cola reminds the populace, reminds Petrarch, that the authority of emperors is derived from none other than the Roman people themselves. When he fails, when his ashes are dumped into the Tiber, the dream (fabulous, far-fetched) of *Roma caput mundi*—Rome, capital of the world—vanishes.

The Black Death sweeps the land. The scythe swings (ashes, ashes), the apocalypse looms, and in the ensuing silence (tragic, sublime), we close the book on the Middle Ages.

Hush.

We know that's not the end. Decades lie quiet, then stir. Out of this dustbin rises the Renaissance papacy (velvety, nepotistic), back in Rome and fueled by money. It redesigns, rebuilds, replaces; artists rejoice, compete. The pope's army grows. Then Martin Luther nails his theses to the door of a church in Wittenberg, and, in the north, the Reformation takes hold. A whirlwind ignites. German, French, and Spanish mercenary armies (codpieced, lustful) descend on Rome in search of booty, prestige, sunshine, women. The pope prevaricates. The walls are breached. The troops pillage and plunder, torture and rape. Corpses pile up in the streets, libraries burn, art vanishes, plague sweeps, the fields lie fallow, and the city, great city, lies in smoking embers.

Hush.

Gradually, gathering from the dust, a new strength. The Counter-Reformation (dyspeptic, macabre) brings the Council of Trent, the Inquisition, the Index of Prohibited Books. In the seventeenth century, the Baroque (tenebrous, sumptuous) explodes, angels and saints descending from on high. But not only. Straight lines curve sinuous. Artists, Caravaggio, Artemisia Gentileschi, exult in struggle (light, darkness), the flesh (sensuous, wounded), compassion and brutality turned twins on the canvas.

Young adults (amorous, chaperoned) arrive in the city to admire its ruins (seductive, senescent) and its new buildings (earthbound, soaring) and to hear the composer Palestrina's divine counterpoint. Not long after, someone hoists the Tricolore in the name of unification, and the Risorgimento (glorious, terrible) is off and running. Then on to Mussolini, Fascism (sloganed, suffocating), war, and colonialism (arrogant, annihilating), during which that old ghost *empire* (hungry, delirious) again claws its way out from its grave. On its heels, a penitent postwar republic (film: grainy; teeth: crooked) leads to the film studios at Cinecittà (Vespas: shiny; teeth: straight) and the manufacturing boom (automobiled, televisioned) to domestic terrorism in the Years of Lead (explosive, grisly) to Berlusconi (bunga bunga) and finally to Eataly (consumerist, abundant), an empire of a new variety.

❧

The past is enormous. We are dwarfed by it. Like a tsunami risen behind our backs, its shadow lengthening over our breathless footfalls. Exhausted, we know it will claim us. Is there any sense in looking?

3.

DANTE LED ME HERE

In 1337, two men ambled down the via Lata—the wide, straight street that since ancient times has split the city of Rome in two. One was Francesco Petrarch. In his early thirties, he was already on his way to becoming one of Italy's most famed poets. This was his first visit to Rome. The other man was seventy-two years old and the scion of one of the city's oldest and most powerful families. He was Stefano Colonna, and his brother was Petrarch's patron. To visit the Colonna family, the poet had made the long trip down from the papal court at Avignon. As the two men walked along the via Lata, Stefano recounted the matters weighing on his heart.

Principally, he lamented the chasm between him and his seven sons. What he thought of as war waged among the city's noble families for the goal of peace, they saw as vendetta and jockeying for power. But his sons understood little of war, he complained, and consequently, little of him. Rome was changing, everyone was saying so—his sons clearly saw him as a vestige of a time gone by. They leveled accusations: he was nothing but an old warmonger. Their only inheritance, they claimed, would be a legacy of hatred and discord, endless strife with other Roman noble families.

But Stefano found even this too optimistic. Pay close attention, he said to Petrarch: to his own great sadness, he expected to leave his children no legacy at all. Deep in his heart, he knew he would in fact outlive them. The old man turned away from Petrarch, his eyes brimming with tears.

We know about this conversation because, more than a decade later, Petrarch would write Stefano a letter in which he recounted it in detail. Penned in September 1348, the letter was meant to console the old man on his losses. One of Stefano's sons, Cardinal Giovanni Colonna, had recently succumbed to the Black Death. Just ten months earlier, Stefano had suffered an even greater loss when three other members of his family were taken from him—not by plague but by war, in a battle just outside the Rome city gate then known as Porta San Lorenzo. At eighty-three, the aged lion of the pride of noble families, Stefano had now buried his wife, five brothers, at least four of his seven sons, at least three nephews, and a grandson. His losses must also have counted daughters, of which he had six, but the records on them are silent.

In his letter, Petrarch recalled the portentous vision that the old man had had ten years prior: that he would outlive all his male heirs. If their conversation on the via Lata was the first time the historical record shows Stefano Colonna in tears, the second and last time was on the day he received Petrarch's letter. That nearly a year had passed since the event that had pierced old Stefano's heart seems not to have dimmed its emotional power. Reading the letter, he collapsed into a torrent of grief, weeping for so long and with such intensity that the messenger who delivered it reported that he feared Stefano would die of sorrow. When he was finished, the old man wiped his tears and vowed that in all his life, he would never cry again.

Leading the force that had decimated Stefano's family in that November 1347 battle was not a rival nobleman but an idealistic young Roman, much given to literature and poetry, who had built a movement of followers based on an ambitious, if unlikely, idea: that Roman citizens might restore their city's position in the world. His name was Cola di Rienzo, and as leader of Rome's revolutionary government, his plan to build a new Rome based on the ideals of the ancient Roman Republic had just gone wildly off the rails. The rule of law that he had envisioned and that he had built over months had, in the space of a few hours, unraveled into a bloody mess, reaching a paroxysm of violence in which the powerful Colonna family was brought to its knees. This had not, as far as we know, been Cola's intention. But it was the outcome, and Cola would in good time pay the price for it.

For a short while during his life, this man was seen as the greatest transformational figure of his day. Though most today no longer remember his name, as a historical figure he has in fact enjoyed a very long afterlife. Machiavelli, writing in the early sixteenth century, saw Cola as an "agent of both Italian unity and the Renaissance," and the soldiers of the Risorgimento—the nineteenth-century movement for Italian unification—saw him as a protonationalist visionary. Richard Wagner made Cola into a Romantic hero in his first commercially successful opera, *Rienzi*, while Hitler appropriated elements of Cola's image as a populist leader anachronistically to his own evil designs. Mussolini was warned by a childhood friend that he would end up just like Cola—and he did.

Though the reality turned out to be messy, in his ideals Cola was not alone. Long before Colonna blood was spilled beneath the city gate, Cola's greatest supporter, and possibly his closest and longest-held friend, was none other than Petrarch. This tangle of affinities perhaps explains why Petrarch waited so long to write to Stefano following his great loss. On the one hand, the poet was indebted to Stefano and maintained deep ties to the Colonna family. On the other, Petrarch and Cola shared a vision for Rome's future, a vision that had come to define them both—and whose realization would have inconceivably tragic implications for Stefano. So it was that these three individuals—the poet, the revolutionary, and the nobleman—formed a triangle that illuminates both the aspirations and the strains of Roman society in a decisive moment of the city's history.

I came across this story in September 2003 during the first few weeks of my doctoral research trip to Rome. I was holed up in the Istituto Storico Italiano per il Medioevo, the Italian Historical Institute of the Middle Ages. Founded in the late nineteenth century, shortly after Italian unification, it acts as a publisher and repository of published medieval Italian texts, and as a seat of study for those connected to the world of that history. In those first weeks in Rome, I was making use of its library the way a sailor, before setting sail, might sit in the ship's hold studying a map: to figure out where I was going.

More specifically, I was planning how to make use of Rome's archives over the coming year. My objective was to assemble enough archival material about fourteenth-century Rome to write a dissertation once I returned to Cornell, where I was a graduate student. I knew it would not be easy—the surviving primary-source documentation for Rome in the 1300s is scarce, as is sometimes the case for periods of political or social unrest. But in this tumultuous period I saw the opportunity to ask a provocative question: What is Rome without the papacy? For between about 1305 and 1376, the pope had removed the entire papal court—not just the religious hierarchy but all its judges and notaries and assorted bureaucrats—to southern France. Those seven decades were the first time in a thousand years, and as yet the last time, that Rome would find itself for so long a city like any other, head of neither the papacy nor an empire. What was Rome, and what was it to the Roman people, I wondered, when cleaved from the power and prestige that had long been associated with its name?

During those early weeks at the *istituto*, when searching indices and catalogs for relevant archival materials became cumbersome or overwhelming, I would open an English-language biography of Petrarch that had caught my eye. Reading it was a respite from Latin and Italian, from big tomes with systems of reference that were foreign to me. It was here that I read the story of Petrarch and Stefano Colonna. After reading it, I opened my journal, a red suede hardcover that my mother had gifted me on my twenty-fifth birthday more than three years earlier and that I had waited until then to use. "Petrarch Stefano Colonna—good story," I wrote, unaware of the significance the story would one day hold for me.

The academic year, unblemished by obligations, meetings, or deadlines, stretched out before me like a road to nowhere. As I began charting my course, I knew I was in sole charge of my progress. It would likely be months before any of my professors reached out to check on me. And I was not even certain they would. By this point, I had been to Rome many times, but never for months on end. Never with an extensive research plan to fulfill, or with a dissertation to write. And never had I come so alone, with neither friend to accompany me nor institution to host me.

It is the odd lot of the humanities graduate student to fall into a foreign location so alone. Who else does it? Backpackers, maybe, though they tend to be nomadic. And migrants, of course—those seeking better lives or fleeing troubles, and to whom my situation was in no way comparable. In the sciences or math, people go to research institutions or foreign universities. They leave their colleges, their jobs, their homes, to go be a part of something somewhere else. But I was simply here to use Rome's archives and libraries. No one was expecting me. There was no one to greet me with a sign, check my name off a list, or show me the way to dinner.

As an American, as a foreigner, I stood outside the culture around me—whether you call it Roman or Italian or by any other name. I was not really, in the true sense, part of any community at all. There was not a door in all the city behind which resided a familiar face. My first name is foreign, and my last name begins with the letter *H*, a sound that in Italian does not exist. At night I would stand before my window in my nightgown, looking out over the rooftops and into the distant glowing boxes of people's homes, wondering when, if ever, I would know someone here.

Amid this solitude, the *istituto*'s reading rooms came to feel as much like home as anywhere. Of its several rooms, there was one I liked best. It was lined on all four sides, and up to the high ceiling, with rows of books housed in cabinets of honey-colored wood. A narrow gallery, on whose lustrous planks a slender person might gingerly tread, was suspended above this first level, forming a second, vertiginous tier of shelving above. Never did I see anyone up there, though. In those days, I appeared to be the *istituto*'s sole visitor. Its reading rooms were so quiet that I could hear the librarian, three rooms away, as she opened a drawer, unwrapped something—a piece of gum, maybe, or a mint—and once again gently pushed the drawer closed. On successive days, she would demonstrate no sign of remembering me. Each morning as I entered the institute, I stepped over the mosaic of a white-eyed, open-mouthed Medusa inlaid in the hallway floor and handed her my ID. Every morning, she checked it with precisely the same level of diligence, wrote my name down in her visitor log, checking once and then twice its unfamiliar spelling, and then handed my card back with a tilt of her head, indicating that I was free to enter.

I spent these days thumbing through card catalogs. Long, narrow wooden drawers lined with thousands of index cards that over the course of a century had been meticulously typed or handwritten. Each drawer extending its curved brass knob, inviting a finger to pull it out and leaf through its contents. Those days, I encountered few computerized catalogs. Most of my searching was done just like this, flipping through index cards, or—even more antiquated—through handwritten, leather-bound books that listed materials accumulated over centuries in the collections of this or that family. These were very old systems of organizing knowledge that followed logical systems entirely different from those I had grown up with in American libraries. Even to locate the basic materials for my research, I needed to learn a new pattern of thinking—one that I had never been taught, and that no one in this library, or any other, had the time or desire to help me learn.

But although I was still on the outside, being a student of history granted me remarkable access—to archives and libraries, and sometimes monuments, sites, and museums, too. Once I accepted that outward amiability on the part of librarians and archivists would not be part of the general bargain, this access came to feel like a great gift.

Over the course of my research year in Rome, the work of hundreds of hands—of notaries and scribes—would pass through mine. As I turned one manuscript page to the next, the velvety parchment, made from animal hides, slid across my fingers. I could see the pores, in some cases even the tiny hairs, of an animal that ate and slept seven hundred years before I was born. The handwriting of a person whose palm once rested on this very page. The ink that pooled when their hand, for a moment, paused its progress. This type of work—reading the handwriting of another being on a sheaf that has itself been worked by hand—offers, when it comes down to it, a kind of intimacy. I had not realized how much I needed that intimacy in those early months until the archive, in its peculiar way, extended it to me.

❧

The bathroom of the *istituto* looks out over a small air shaft where a jumble of windows meets dark ocher walls. On a metal cabinet beside one wall, someone has stuck a sticker depicting Dante, with a worm peering out of an apple in his laurel crown. He looks up at the worm, his eyebrows furrowing deeply.

The sticker feels uncanny because it was Dante who led me here. Dante Alighieri, a native of Florence who lived from 1265 to 1321, remains the first and only poet who inspired me to learn a language. Perhaps this is fitting, in that Dante is often spoken of as the father of the Italian language. Although he composed some of his works in Latin, Dante wrote the trilogy known as *The Divine Comedy* (*La divina commedia*) in the Tuscan vernacular—an unusual choice given that, at the time, most poetry was still written in Latin. Because the poem was so influential, and because the vernacular dialect in which he wrote it went on to become the foundation of modern Italian, Dante is widely considered essential to the development of Italian as we know it today.

In *The Divine Comedy*, Dante (the poet) narrates the fictional travels of a character, also named Dante, who closely resembles the poet himself, into the afterlife. *Inferno* (Hell), the first of the *Comedy*'s three canticles, tells the story of Dante the traveler's journey through the underworld. Guided through Limbo and the rings of hell by a fictionalized representation of the classical Roman poet Virgil, Dante bears witness to a catalog of human sins as he meets the tortured souls of real people, some his contemporaries and others historical or literary figures, who in their lives erred from the "straight path." The second and third canticles of the *Comedy*—*Purgatorio* (Purgatory) and *Paradiso* (Paradise, or Heaven)—continue Dante the traveler's journey out of hell and toward divine grace. Ascending the mountain of *Purgatorio*, he meets souls who, while still in conflict with themselves, must reflect on their deviations of character. What they discover, or recover, through this laborious process of interrogation is the capacity to love "rightly"—that is, in just measure—and to receive the love that is God.

When Dante reaches the uppermost terrace of *Purgatorio*, Virgil, who lived before the advent of Christianity and so cannot access heaven, hands him off to Beatrice, who will guide the poet through *Paradiso*. The character of Beatrice in *The Divine Comedy* was based on the real-life "girl next door" with whom Dante (the poet) had become enamored when he was still a child, and who later became his muse. Simultaneously a historical, flesh-and-blood woman and an allegorical representation of divine love and intellect, Beatrice guides Dante the traveler through much of *Paradiso*, where he meets the souls who have entered the realm of the heavenly spheres. Over the five days of his journey through the afterlife, Dante bears witness to the spectrum of the human condition, and by its end, he has perceived the divine love that, according to his vision, sets the universe in motion. And so while Dante is sometimes remembered, especially by those who have read only *Inferno*, as a curmudgeon who banished his enemies to hell, it is the pursuit of love and its divine manifestation that I see as the central impulse of the *Comedy*.

Ever since the high school literature class where I first encountered it, I have struggled to understand why this beautiful, perplexing text has assumed such a central place in my life. How does a middle-aged, Catholic poet who writes in rhyming tercets about an imagined journey through the afterlife speak so powerfully to a teenage girl of mixed religious background who speaks no Italian, and who lives half a world away and seven centuries down the river of time? Why would a young person—or anyone living, really—bother with the words and the world of someone so long dead?

Before reading *Inferno*, I did not pursue history outside my schoolwork. I did not think about why or how history could be important, or on what levels it might speak to us. I was not even certain that I would go to college. Reading Dante changed that. Something in his poem made me want to know all about the world it depicted—not so much the particularities of medieval Christian theology but the people in it, the history, the literary web from which it had sprung. I had the feeling that if I could read and understand this text, if I could *feel* it, I would gain the keys to some kind of gleaming city of the mind—and even, perhaps, of the heart.

To this day, the beginning of *The Divine Comedy* remains one of the few poems I have memorized. It is the only one I ever took the time to write out, in calligraphic hand, and illustrate. I own various copies—an Italian version that includes copious notes and a CD, and a variety of translations and editions, some old and some new, some illustrated and some not. And I still have the edition of *Inferno* that we read in high school—Allen Mandelbaum's translation. It is dog-eared and smooth with wear, its pages populated with the purple ink of my comments, questions, notes to self—a chart of my seventeen-year-old mind as it strived to make sense not only of the poem but also of the alien world it described. The beginning of *The Divine Comedy* is one of only two poems I recite when I cannot sleep, when I am unsure of myself on a mountainside or having unpleasant dental work done.

> *Nel mezzo del cammin di nostra vita*
> *mi ritrovai in una selva oscura*
> *ché la diritta via era smarrita . . .*

> When I had journeyed half of our life's way
> I found myself within a shadowed forest,
> For I had lost the path that does not stray . . .

These lines have grown, I realize now, into a kind of prayer.

⌒∕०

Reading Dante was not an end in itself but a beginning: a gateway to the Italian language, to Italy, and to medieval history. When, about a decade after my first contact with *Inferno*, I came to the point in my graduate studies when I needed to choose my dissertation topic, it was the period in which Dante had lived—the late thirteenth and early fourteenth centuries— that called me.

The fourteenth century held particular fascination. For Rome, it had started out so well. The year 1300 marked Rome's first Jubilee, or Holy Year, which brought countless pilgrims—and their much-needed money—to

Rome, on the promise of full absolution for a lifetime of sins. The event was such a success that Pope Boniface VIII, who had organized it, decreed amid great fanfare that the event would have to be repeated in 1400. As pope, he was at the height of his powers, and he was leading a papacy that had recently burgeoned into the most sophisticated institution of its time. Clerics, pilgrims, government officials, and money poured into and out of Rome. Dante, who was otherwise highly critical of Pope Boniface, condemning him in *Inferno* to suffer for eternity among the fraudulent, was one of the visitors at this first Jubilee, and he commented with awe on the number of pilgrims crowding the city.

In 1303, however, Pope Boniface VIII died following a violent altercation with a member of the noble Colonna family. Boniface's successor remained in office only eight short months, and the next pope to be elected, Clement V, resided in France. Instead of remaining in Rome, the papal retinue left the city to join Clement in France—eventually, in 1309, settling in Avignon, which was closer to, but not under the jurisdiction of, the increasingly powerful French king. The papacy would remain there for about seventy years, a period termed by Petrarch the "Babylonian Captivity."

During that long absence, Rome was routinely depicted in literature and art as a widow in mourning. As the city population dwindled, Romans and non-Romans alike conjectured about what kind of city Rome could be. Some, like Dante, Petrarch, and Cola di Rienzo, harbored ambitious dreams for the city's future. As these and other ideas were pursued, political upheaval became the norm. Socially, the city was changing quickly, too. The powerful Roman families that had dominated city life for the past century found themselves challenged by an emerging commercial class. Larger forces, too, were at play. At midcentury, the bubonic plague devastated Italy, and Rome, too, felt the havoc of its destruction. By the century's end, the optimism and expansion that had characterized its beginning gave way in Rome to a pervasive retraction and sense of failure. The dreams of early century were, by its end, mostly dust.

Part of what attracted me to this rather gloomy period of Roman history was how little studied it appeared to be. Few people, and certainly none of my professors, seemed to know very much about it. What work there was on the topic was written by scholars who were themselves Roman and, more often than not, living in Rome. For American medieval historians, Florence was the place to be. Venice, too, had panache. Everywhere else—even Rome, the great *urbs*—felt like a backwater.

One of my professors at Cornell was a scholar of Renaissance Florence. When, after my second year, I decided to pursue Italian history, he was the person with whom I studied most. That he characterized my decision to study Rome as "brave" should have been a good indication that the road ahead was one I would walk mostly alone. My adviser would be of even less help. "Wouldn't we all like to spend time in the sun," he said to me on the phone, when I told him I had received a grant to conduct additional research in Rome—when, of course, what I had been curious about all along was the darkness. Looking back, perhaps part of me wished to distance myself from these older male professors and their trodden turf. In Rome I would stake out something I could call my own.

When it comes to medieval Rome, most history books either devote a few scant pages to it or, more commonly, jump right over it. At the time I chose my dissertation topic, I could count the number of studies in English about the history of medieval Rome on one hand. Had I been willing to focus on art history or on architecture, I might have doubled that count. But I had never been trained in art history. I did not want to start anew. Rather, I wanted to explore what Rome was when it was neither the head of an empire nor the seat of the papacy. I wanted to know what becomes of a city, what happens to its people, when it endures its lowest of times. When the optimism retracts, when the climate shifts, when war

and pestilence begin to take their toll, when we feel we might be on the edge of a precipice, and the darkness yawns.

In October 2005, two years after charting my course at the Istituto Storico, I was selected to participate in a medieval history seminar hosted by the German Historical Institute. Seven German graduate students and seven Americans, plus two faculty from each country and two representatives of the GHI, would spend three days in a Venetian palazzo overlooking the Grand Canal. The seminar was, delightfully, all expenses paid. I was abuzz with anticipation. The month before, I had finished my dissertation and defended it before a panel of three professors. Though I did not yet have the diploma in hand, I was essentially a PhD, just waiting for the academic calendar to catch up and for the university registrar to issue the degree.

The airline lost my luggage and, being the first presenter, I had to scramble in a single morning to find an appropriate outfit that went passably well with the knee-high Spanish riding boots I had foolishly chosen to wear on the plane. Nevertheless, I arrived at the seminar bright and eager. It was a pleasure to be back in Italy, to feel years of academic work come to fruition in the form of a paid trip. I was thirty now, and finally starting to feel like a professional.

At one point during the seminar, Patrick Geary, an eminent American scholar, asked us why we had chosen to pursue medieval history. The German students were the first to respond, articulating reasons that spoke to their cultural identity, or to the roots of the modern European Union. The reasons they gave showed that their motivations for pursuing medieval history went deep into their personal and family backgrounds, and into the questions they had about the world around them. As for the American students? We hesitated. Someone tapped the table nervously; others coughed lightly or reached suddenly into their bags, ostensibly looking for something. In many cases, such as my own, I imagine we had never been asked this question before a group of peers. Why was *this* a lifelong commitment for *us*? Had I had the courage to speak the truth, I would have said, *Because I love it. Because I loved Dante, and Dante led me here.*

In the wake of our long silence, Geary resumed speaking in his thoughtful, southern manner. "This is often my experience," he told us. "American students in general struggle to find the deeper reason they are studying history, and medieval history in particular. One answer Americans often give is 'Because I love it.' But why do you love it? I wonder. And is loving it enough? When I teach in Eastern Europe, by contrast, the students are passionate. They argue and engage. There is something at stake for them. What is at stake for you?" he asked, looking at us one by one. "Why are you devoting your lives to this?"

I looked deep within myself in that moment, and I discovered, to my dismay, that I did not have any single answer that I would feel confident enough to put before that table. When undergraduates asked me the similar—but not identical—question of why they should care about the Middle Ages, I would offer them the usual, if passionately delivered, reasons from my arsenal of responses: that in the West, the Middle Ages are the link between the ancient and the modern, that many institutions that we take for granted and that underpin U.S. society—such as the university or the postal service—were born in that age, and that many of them have lasted over a thousand years, which is a mind-boggling expanse of time. I would summon, as well, the flourishing of vernacular languages and literatures around which whole cultures have formed, the newly global horizons for merchant travel and the growth of religious tourism, the growth of the papacy as an international bureaucracy founded on a sophisticated body of legal thought still in use today, the emergence of polyphonic music, and the explosion of innovative architectural forms. This list tended to convince students that their time would not be entirely wasted in a medieval history course. But as I understood him, Professor Geary was not asking for intellectual motivations. He wanted to know, on a personal level, what was at stake for us.

That conference was almost twenty years ago. I am no longer a professional historian. And yet it is only now that I have begun searching for the answer to his question.

4.

A FAMILY STORY

When I was a child, my grandparents kept a small fragment of statuary in their northern New Jersey living room: a marble hand, it sat just right of the fireplace, on a shelf too high for me to reach. I knew little about this object other than that my grandparents had brought it from Rome, where they had lived for some time when they were young. My grandparents didn't say much about their years there, but I was aware that Italy had been important in their lives in much the same way that one is aware of sunlight—something immaterial that nonetheless fills the room. As for the marble hand, well, it was unattainable, and as a child I was far more compelled by what stood just below it: a glass jar as tall and wide as my torso. This jar held a bounty of hard salted pretzels, the thick kind that are difficult to bite through. After retrieving a pretzel, I would brush the salt from the top and bite into its loops using my molars. *Crack*. It cut the roof of my mouth, and the salt burned.

It is only now, after my grandparents have passed away, that I have taken interest in the marble hand—which now stands on the mantle in my father's living room—scanning it for clues about their time there.

One afternoon when I am visiting my father, I take the time to really look at it: its curved, dimpled fingers, its white marble streaked with rivulets of gray. In form it is slightly masculine, although I suppose it could conceivably be a woman's. Its fingers are wrapped gently around a thick stick or baton. Picking the hand up, I consider its heft and weight. I place my own hand over it, note how much larger, heavier, it is than my own. Its smooth, matte surface is cool to the touch. The form is robust, and yet its lines are soft. It exhibits no sign of existential struggle—no attempt to grasp or strike. On the contrary, it is a relaxed kind of hand, serene, without worry for the future or resentments about the past.

And yet traumas it bears. It has been broken off at the wrist from a sculpture that may have depicted the entire human form. The index finger, which once extended along the length of the baton, has been chipped off at the first knuckle, where the baton, too, now abruptly ends. The thumb, too, has suffered the same casualty.

Were it a document, a text, I would know better how to interrogate it. Years of graduate school have taught me how to look at premodern texts, to think about words on the page and what they tell us about the society that generated them. But this, an actual three-dimensional object, a piece of the past, a simple, serenely executed hand, I feel ill-equipped to evaluate.

Soon thereafter, I ask one of my uncles about it.

"Your grandparents lugged that thing all the way back from Rome!" he replies.

I ask him where in Rome they got it. Did they find it on the ground, or buy it? Or was it perhaps given to them? He shakes his head. He does not know. And the hand—resolutely silent—offers no answers.

My grandfather was stationed in Rome immediately following the end of World War II. Working for the U.S.-led international organization known as UNRRA (United Nations Relief and Rehabilitation Administration), a forerunner of the Marshall Plan, my grandfather was among the first American civil servants sent to distribute aid throughout postwar Europe.

My only Jewish grandparent, and a Unitarian through lifelong practice, he arrived in Italy in the fall of 1945, when tanks were still rolling up and down the peninsula. Poverty abounded. "Inside the isolated city, sacked and besieged," Elsa Morante would write in her novel of Nazi-occupied Rome, *La Storia*, "the true master was hunger." My grandmother followed in the spring of the following year. In tow were my father, Ned, who was two, and his older brother, Frank, age five. They would live in Rome for two years.

As a child, I knew this story in only the barest of outlines. Strange as it may seem, it is only now that I have begun to ask myself whether there might have been any connection between my choice to pursue Italian history and the fact that my father, uncle, and grandparents spent a formative period of their lives there. That when my father came home to the United States, he was a four-year-old who spoke Italian better than English. That my grandmother would beam whenever someone mentioned those years. That my father's sister, who was born after the family returned to the U.S., ended up marrying a man from Verona, and that I have cousins who have long, mellifluous Italian names and who sometimes speak Italian at home. It is only now that I have begun to ask whether it was not only Dante who led me here but whether somewhere in our family, perhaps, there remained a yearning for that place, and for a time gone by, that had lain dormant in me, waiting to be awakened.

When I ask my uncle and father about the family's experience living in Rome, they both say the same thing: *It was the greatest adventure of our parents' lives.* When I ask for their recollections of postwar Rome, my father, especially, summons the memories of a very young child—hazy, uncertain, poignant bordering on fantastical. About their parents' lives, the arc of their stay, they recall little.

When my grandparents passed away, they took *the greatest adventure of their lives* with them—and with it, a part of our family history. The historian in me is accustomed to mourning the losses of history. I am less used to mourning the loss of stories, especially those I consider in some way mine. When Grandmother got sick, I had just written a hundred pages about medieval Rome for my graduate exams. I was wading knee deep through the history of that city on a daily basis. Its stories flooded my bookshelves, cascaded across my keyboard, filled my notebooks to their brims. But I knew next to nothing about my family's history in Rome. How could it be that when it came to *the greatest adventure of their lives*, the family storyscape was so parched?

I have spent time scratching in this soil. Looking for the well of stories that links me to the place my grandparents lived, apparently so happily, and where my father learned Italian, essentially his first language. I think of the things we might have shared. But I have found, too, that silence speaks. At least as loud as words, and sometimes louder. Their story will never be known to you, the marble hand tells me. Grandmother and Grandfather will never be known to you.

I probe this conclusion, crack it between my teeth. It cuts the roof of my mouth and the salt burns.

❧

There is only one story that I remember Grandmother telling me.

"Your father," she would say. "When we came back to the United States, he was four years old. There was a poem he liked to recite, and he would say it like this: *Poosy cat, Poosy cat, vair have you bean? I ave bean to Lahndan to veeseet da Qveen. Poosy cat, Poosy cat, vott you do dare? I found a leetle mowfie undairrr dee chair.*"

She would laugh. "Can you imagine? Your father spoke with an Italian accent! We thought it was so funny, we wrote it down. And after we came home, for a year, maybe, your father and Frank went on speaking in Italian to each other, to say things they didn't want the adults to understand."

Now it occurs to me to ask, Is this even a story, or just a vignette? And yet I still relish that image: my father and uncle, mischievous children equipped with a superpower—a secret language they reserved only for one another.

Recently I learned that Grandmother kept a journal during the early part of their stay in Rome. In addition to the marble hand, a few photos, and my grandparents' ceramic espresso cups, it is the one other piece of primary-source material—the historian's bread and butter—that I have seen.

For about the first five months of their adventure, my grandmother, Rosa Lee Holstein, summarized her days with a sentence or a single phrase.

MARCH 28, 1946:

143 W. 49th St., Plymouth Hotel. Ship Vulcania, Pier D. Jersey City, NJ . . .

MARCH 29:

Sailed for Italy at 6 o'clock after 4 horrible hours on dock. A cabin and 4 bunks for children and myself.

MARCH 30:

Life on shipboard very strange to us. Ned sick with fever tonight. All frightened by strangeness.

APRIL 1:

Children and I sea-sick. Very miserable.

APRIL 2:

Still sick.

APRIL 3:

Improving.

APRIL 4:

Storm disappeared. Sunshine. Well and beginning to enjoy superb food and deck.

APRIL 5:

Enjoying good friends aboard—children happy.

APRIL 6:

Anticipating arrival and union with our beloved Woodie.

APRIL 8:

Sailed into breath-taking harbor of Naples—sunny, wisteria hanging over all. Capri misty. Woodie boarded from pilot boat—lunch in Naples, auto, truck convoy to Rome. Arrived new home, maid Louisa late tonight.

APRIL 9:

All getting acquainted again. Children upset by travels a bit. Struggling with the new language. Very, very happy with Woodie.

In these pithy entries, I can narrowly discern my grandmother's voice. And when the ship pulls into Naples and she spots Woodie, my grandfather, coming out to meet her on the pilot boat, my throat catches. I can see her, smiling and radiant. I can even *feel* her a little—the triumph she must have felt. At first "frightened by strangeness," she had just crossed an ocean. Having known her to be frightened of travel, I cannot help but marvel in this instance at her bravery. What must it have been like to board that ship? To see the ocean stretch out before her that gray day on the New Jersey pier? To hug and kiss her parents goodbye, take her children in her arms, and walk across that gangplank? Like a shard of pottery unearthed, the journal fills in one small facet of my family's experience. I keep going, see if I can reconstruct—or imagine—the rest.

I ask Uncle Frank what it was like living in Rome in the late 1940s. When he begins to talk, it feels as if he is exhuming something large and unwieldy from deep in the ground. He looks into the distance, squinting, as if trying to make out something on the horizon. He speaks slowly.

He remembers the topography of war.

> *There was a racetrack nearby where we lived. It was full of bombed-out and shot-up tanks—the whole field was just wall-to-wall tanks. We would go over there and play, but it was also a very grim reminder of what war is.*

He remembers the toll on lives.

> *We saw these things. And although Rome suffered minimal damage, there had been bombings. We saw many apartment buildings split right down the middle, so one side survived and the other didn't. There would still be people residing in those that were intact. But it was scary to see what a bombing looked like up close, with people involved.*

He remembers the hungry mouth of poverty.

> *The poverty was overwhelming. The urchins would figure out where the British and the Americans lived, and they were aware of when mealtime was. They'd fight over the scraps that were taken out to the garbage cans.*

He remembers the spirit of ingenuity.

> *Many people couldn't afford a newspaper, so therefore in the parks you would find somebody who had cut out different columns of the paper.*

They would paste these columns to the back fenders of their bikes and they would ride down past the benches and stop for anybody who wanted to read. The people on the benches would give them a small tip to read the paper or the article that was pasted to the fender.

He remembers the taste of lost things.

All the milk was canned. We didn't have fresh milk the entire time that we were in Rome. When we came back into New York harbor, while we waited to disembark we were able to order fresh milk for the first time in years. We just kept ordering it and ordering it—like it was ice cream. We had a feast on fresh milk.

He remembers beauty.

We became friendly with the nanny. Her name was Teresa. I had a tremendous crush on her. One time she dyed her hair blond and I thought she was a movie star. I was six years old.

Dad, who has been listening quietly, weighs in. He acknowledges the fragility of memory.

The earliest memory of my life probably didn't happen. Meaning I don't think this happened. In my memory we had a car and we had it loaded on the ship to go back to America. It's probably a dream, a complete fabrication. Of watching a yellow car being hoisted by a crane in something like a net or a grappling hook of some kind and swung over and lowered into the hold of the ship. Whether it happened or not I have no idea.

Uncle Frank nods in agreement.

It did happen.

Dad looks up.

It did? You remember it too?

Uncle Frank nods.

Yup. It was pretty dramatic.

Now my dad has questions.

Was it a yellow car?

Uncle Frank nods again. I begin to grow suspicious of the easy con-currence of their memories. But Dad's memory, perhaps encouraged, begins to open up. Now he remembers a voyage.

And then I remember on the way back, on the ship, I think we had some rough seas and there was some seasickness, and we weren't allowed to go up on the deck.

Uncle Frank, too, remembers storms.

We also had really rough seas on the way over, from the U.S. to Naples. The porthole in our stateroom began to leak seriously. There was water all over the floor and the beds, and it was kind of a grim situation. There was nothing luxurious about these ships. We were all sick. They had these things around the dining room table to stop the plates from crashing to the floor.

He remembers a harbor blighted by destruction.

We came into Naples—that arrival was very melodramatic because the Germans had sunk a huge number of Italian and other ships in the harbor, so our ship had to anchor down. You couldn't get into the piers, and you had these launches taking the people in, weaving through the sunken ships. Dad came out on a launch, with flags flying, like the king of England! We even have pictures of that. We just thought it was something else—there's Dad, wow!

He tells of searching for the past.

Your aunt and I made the mistake of going back to look for the old apartment. We had the address, via Flaminia, and oh my god, we walked and walked and walked, and finally we got there. I don't know what we were thinking—of course it wasn't the same. It was a new, modern apartment. And I wanted to find this park I was talking about, the one with the bicycle newspapers, but I couldn't find it, and I wanted to find the racetrack and I couldn't find that. There was a stadium over there, but it's all hodgepodge. So we tried—but it was anticlimactic.

With that, my father and uncle have exhumed their history; they have told me a story.

～⌒つ

I imagine the drizzly March afternoon in 1946 when my grandmother and her two boys stepped off the Jersey City pier to board the ocean liner. I see the ship's glossy black hull slicing the green-gray water and, near the bow, the name—*Vulcania*—in bold block letters. I notice sparkling-white balconies overlooking the sea that promise plush, private cabins. And three rows of dark porthole windows below deck that promise much less. Droning loudly is a state-of-the-art, ten-cylinder Fiat engine—one of the largest and most powerful of its day. The pier below is thronged with the departing, and with loved ones waving goodbye, their upturned faces glistening with rain.

I watch my grandmother, Rosa Lee, from far away across the channel of time, as if though binoculars, her image refracting through its prisms. I see her holding Frank by the hand and carrying my father, a toddler, in the crook of her arm. All three shiver on account of the cold. As they step onto the gangway, Frank slips his hand from his mother's to peer down at the seawater frothing against the hull's steel plates. I see him imagining the sea life hidden beneath the water's surface, smell his damp wool sweater letting off the smell of sheep. My father, meanwhile, stares up with wonder at the two tall masts, the prominent smokestack painted red, white, and green, the rows of identical white lifeboats lined up like toys on a shelf. He curls his arm around his mother's neck.

Rosa Lee hesitates, retrieves Frank's hand, glances down at the pier, and manages a strained smile for those she is leaving behind. Her every fiber tells her to go back, to flee this ship and its dangers. She revolves her body, leans lightly against the railing as she feels her way backward across the gangway. The scent of diesel wafts on a gust of wind. A storm is beginning to blow. She feels it propel her, against her will, onto the ship, into the future to which her back is turned. In all her life, she will never feel as dreadfully alone as she does now. The ship is enormous, she is five stories above the earth, and yet in the vastness of the ocean they—she, her two little boys—will be specks of dust on the wind. She reminds herself to control her imagination, to rein in her visions of tempests and *Titanics*, of incapacitated engines and terrible fires, of U-boats rising inaudibly from dark waters, of slick con men and drunken captains and children who, chasing a gull, plummet into a voracious sea. Frank looks up at her in confusion, wondering why his mother is backing onto the ship, why she does not want to crouch beside him and summon the sea creatures skimming against the ship's bottom. She senses his confusion and gathers herself. With effort and resolve, she turns herself around, steps over the pile of her mental debris, and no longer looks back.

∽⌒⌒

Rosa Lee is not the first to board this ship uncertain of what the voyage might bring. By now, 1946, the MS *Vulcania* is already an old hand. Built in Trieste in 1926, it has already traversed the globe north and south, east and west. For most of its life it has been Italian; now, for a brief stint, it flies under the American flag. But these feel like technicalities, for on board a certain cosmopolitanism prevails. It can be felt in the ship's aesthetic—the classical columns in its first-class dining room, the wooden bas-reliefs by Italian sculptor Marcello Mascherini lining the tourist-class bar—which reflects the mixed influences of its Italian, Austrian, and British designers. But this international flair is not present just in the ship's decor. After two decades of service, the *Vulcania* has already served far and wide. It has carried the rich and the poor, the privileged and the deprived, the adventurous and the desperate, the courageous and the meek.

In the early 1930s, when Rosa Lee was still a teenager, almost two thousand Jews, those prescient or fortunate enough to leave Europe just before the rise of the Third Reich, had crowded the *Vulcania*'s decks. The ship ferried them from Trieste—point of exit from a rapidly darkening Europe—to sunny Haifa. At almost 24,000 gross tons, it was the largest ship ever to have entered Haifa's port. The *Vulcania* made transatlantic voyages in that period too, shuttling between North America, Italy, and Palestine. In 1934, the ship carried the notorious swindler Charles Ponzi back to Italy after his deportation from the U.S., fourteen years after the collapse of his disastrous financial scheme. With less fanfare, the ship also sometimes ferried the dead to their resting place of choice, as when it took the bodies of a deceased Jewish couple from Brooklyn who wished to be buried on the Mount of Olives near Jerusalem. Similarly transported was the body of decorated Neapolitan aviator Francesco de Pinedo, who in the 1920s had piloted to every continent except Antarctica, and who dreamed of a future in which the masses commuted to work by seaplane. "Civilization is built on water," he observed, making the case for why planes ought to land on seas, lakes, and rivers instead of at costly airports. In 1933, he was done in by an asphalt runway: his plane crashed during takeoff at a Brooklyn airfield, and de Pinedo perished in the flames. His body was ferried back to Italy in the hold of the *Vulcania*—water, not air, lofting his body on its final voyage.

In 1934, Rosa Lee married Elwood, my grandfather, known to most as Woodie. Not long after, in 1935, the winds of war began to blow and the *Vulcania* was transformed into a military ship. Requisitioned by the Italian government for colonial efforts in Eritrea, Ethiopia, and Somalia, its decks vibrated under the boots of Italian soldiers. For three months, the ship ran Naples–Massawa–Mogadishu, tracing the axes of Italy's imperialist ambitions, then was decommissioned, resuming its Trieste–New York route. Now the *Vulcania* would ferry European and Levantine emigrants—Italians, Germans, Lebanese, Swiss, Hungarians, Poles, Spaniards, Liechtensteiners, Lithuanians, Portuguese, Belgians, and many described as "stateless"—to the ports of Brazil and Argentina. Among them, the ship's registers list diplomats, musicians, housewives, doctors, tailors, journalists, high school and university students, children, technical workers, scholars, barbers, engineers, businessmen, carpenters, merchants, farmers, locksmiths, and fishermen—a broad swath of humanity. Such humanitarian endeavors would be short-lived: the Italian government soon re-requisitioned the ship for its conflicts in Africa.

In 1940, Rosa Lee and Woodie welcomed their first child, Frank, into the world. The *Vulcania* was busy, now painted white with a red cross, bringing thousands of Italian women, children, and elderly back from East

Africa while ferrying doctors and nurses out to tend the wounded soldiers whose task it had been to prop up Italy's colonial invasion. On the long trip home around the African continent (the British denied Italian ships passage through the Suez Canal), the *Vulcania*'s decks and halls served as venues for activities and propaganda designed to reinstill Fascist values, especially among the children.

In September 1943, Italy surrendered to the Allied forces. Two months later, Rosa Lee gave birth to her second child, my father. Fleeing Nazi capture, the *Vulcania* sped to the Americas. For the remainder of the war, it would sail under the American flag, carrying troops, war brides, and military dependents.

At the war's end, Woodie was assigned to Rome. Rosa Lee agreed to join him six months later. She would travel alone, and bring the children.

❧

The day before the *Vulcania* set sail for Naples, Rosa Lee gathered her boys and their belongings, and together they left their home in Washington, D.C. Her parents, knowing her fear of travel, accompanied them to Manhattan. From the Plymouth Hotel, which at that time stood on Forty-Ninth Street, it would be an easy trip to the pier the next morning. I recently found a matchbook from the hotel, dating to about that time, the mid-1940s, on eBay. In the illustration, the Plymouth resembles any number of Manhattan buildings, square and brick and chiseled at the top like a ziggurat. A solid, stalwart twenty stories or so. The matchbook advertises four hundred rooms, each with a bath, a radio, and circulating ice water. *Newest Times Sq. Creation.* MOST LUXURIOUS *and* ULTRA MODERN. And also, MODERATE PRICES. At the bar and restaurant, you can get a *Telephone at your Table.* Rooms start at $2.50.

In 1946, aboard the *Vulcania*, grandeur was no longer on the menu. When Rosa Lee and her sons boarded it, the ship still felt like a troopship, its former luxuries pared down. Their room came with bunk beds, not four-posters. But the *Vulcania*'s military days were gone for good. For another quarter century, until the ship ran aground near Cannes and was towed to Taiwan for scrapping, it would carry civilians. They would play tennis and shuffleboard on the decks, sun themselves in bathing suits, smoke and play cards in wood-paneled smoking rooms. In contrast to the *Vulcania*'s earlier passengers, exile, displacement, or war would be something most of these travelers had to search to find. War would be as foreign to them as the sea creatures brushing up against the hull beneath the water's surface.

As Rosa Lee watched the New York City skyline recede until it blended with the ocean on a nebulous gray horizon, her country was still on the heels of war. And yet the March rain carried with it the first whiff of optimism and prosperity. For the next six months, until Italian president Alcide De Gasperi visited the U.S. to advocate for the return of the *Vulcania* and three other formerly Italian ships to Italy, American Export Lines would run its operations. And this day, March 29, 1946, was the inaugural day of its newest passenger route: New York–Naples–Alexandria. As Rosa Lee and her boys walked the length of the ship to find their sleeping quarters, they added their footsteps to those of the many who had come before: European, Slavic, and Levantine emigrants, American tourists, Jewish refugees of myriad nationalities, deported felons, Italian soldiers, nurses, doctors, and colonists, American soldiers and sailors, and the casketed bodies of those who dreamed of a better afterlife in a far-flung land. Among all those moments, I imagine one most clearly: Rosa Lee, my grandmother, bracing herself against the wind and holding her children with firm resolve. Lightly shaking, she crosses the gangway. All the rest is future.

~~~

When my grandparents returned to the U.S. in the spring of 1948, my four-year-old father spoke Italian better than English. But as an adult, he has retained no Italian at all. Where does a language go when it is forgotten? Does it end up in a heap with all the other forgotten memories? Does it crumble to dust, get shepherded out of our bodies while we sleep? Does it sink, lingering lifelong like an atrophied muscle or a leathery strip of dried fruit? Or does it have a chamber all its own in some quiet cul-de-sac of the brain? Maybe you could open the door to it, shine in a flashlight, and there it would be, lying on the floor like a rope, just waiting to be uncoiled.

My father likes to think that one day, were he to relearn Italian, his memories from early childhood could come flooding back. He conjectures that his memories, now lost, could well be tied to his Italian vocabulary, wherever it may be. As if the two, memory and language, had gone astray together, like two lost children holding hands in the woods. If he could lure one back, the other might follow. But this is a theory he has not tested. Perhaps I, in his place, have assumed the task of remembering, of accumulating memories—and languages—that are not mine. It strikes me, for instance, to think that it is easier for me to imagine the Rome of 650 years ago, in which Petrarch and Stefano Colonna ambled up the via Lata, than it is for my uncle or father to remember the Rome of their childhood. And is that not what historians do—make it their job to remember what is not theirs?

There is another possibility. Perhaps the Italian is still there, embedded deep in my father's brain. And so, when my father dreams dreams he does not remember, I like to think he dreams them in Italian. Our minds do not always tell us all they know.

5.

ANCIENT HISTORY

I once asked my friend Niall what made him become a historian. "I had some really good teachers," he replied. He told me about the art class he took in high school, how his teacher exposed him not only to art but to art history as well. Niall is now a tenured professor of art history at a top-tier American university. "Do you think the path you took in life is a consequence of the teachers you happened to encounter, or because of an innate interest or ability within yourself?" I asked. Niall thought for a moment, then answered: "All I know is that what I learned about art history in high school, it blew my mind."

❧

Training the question on myself, I try to reconstruct what the word *history* meant to me, as far back as I can remember. History was the fifth-grade classroom where we first learned about ancient Egypt. The classroom had a floor-to-ceiling glass wall that faced the fluorescent-lit interior hallway, on which teachers' shoes clicked as they walked. The pyramids were born to me in that class, and even now when I imagine them, I see them rising up from between our student desks like volcanoes from an ocean floor. In that class we learned, too, about Romans and Aztecs and Greeks and Maya. I associated these ancient peoples with enormous blocks of stones, with barefoot workers pulling eternally on ropes, with the misery of their toil and the resplendence of their accomplishments.

From sixth and seventh grades I remember little of history. Except for in Hebrew school, where it was made clear to us that history was important. Crucial, even. Hebrew school was two afternoons a week, which was two too many, and Sunday mornings, a tragic blight on the otherwise wide-open landscape of weekend freedom. As I perched on my stool, we were shown maps of Israel, Palestine, Syria, Jordan, and Egypt. Lines were drawn, some solid and some dotted. Wars were named, and the dotted lines moved. Our teacher, a dull-eyed, squat woman fond of sequins, and whose name I have forgotten or repressed, told us that the tide of history was against us. Intermarriage, she warned, would be the end of the Jews: Arabs were reproducing faster. History, I came to understand, was an awful game of numbers. It was *Diplomacy* and *Risk* and any other board game where you assembled armies, navies, and populations on or near borders. Where your objective was to crush, to squelch, to overrun, and to hold. It was multiplying your people in an effort to move the dotted lines from here to there. I scanned the faces of the boys in the room—awkward Jared, arrogant David—repulsed at the idea of having to marry and multiply with any of them. History was a menacing obligation, a personal threat, a moral void.

But history was also our eighth-grade teacher, Mr. Kelly, who in addition to teaching us about World War II instructed us in making detailed maps on large sheets of Mylar. Through him we learned the geography of the world, the map on which all the history we would ever learn played out. (Except the moon landing, of course, and we never did make a map of the moon.) But South America, yes, and the USSR, which was falling apart as quickly as I was pulling it together with my markers on the Mylar sheet. I questioned how to draw a border that was dissolving, or one that was just going up, while the mountain ranges I traced with confidence, sure that they were not going anywhere anytime soon. Mr. Kelly was tall and lanky, wore boot-cut corduroy pants with a wide belt like a hippy. As he spoke, a perfect sphere of spittle would collect at the center of his lower lip. He taught us that naming things, and knowing what is where in the world around us, is a source of both empathy and power—even as that world shifts and changes, which to me, still a child, was in itself a novel concept.

In the ninth grade, new to our big public high school, we sat in a circle and listened to our teacher, young Mr. Lansdowne, expound on *The Epic of Gilgamesh*. As he did, he paced the center of the room, gesticulating wildly, his curly hair bouncing. You could tell the subject meant something to him. Ancient Mesopotamia was cuneiform tablets and a wash of beige over everything: sand, maybe, or stone, or both. Deserts and oases. Symbols and secret languages. To me, it also meant a fear of body odor but being too shy, even at fourteen, to ask my mother for deodorant. Mesopotamia was formed by the Tigris and Euphrates Rivers and was the cradle of civilization. Some of the earliest trade in human history was floated down the Tigris, Mr. Lansdowne explained, while I chewed my pencil and worried that I was getting my period.

In tenth grade, history started—maybe—to add up to something. Mr. Dudley, who taught European history, was our most formal teacher, dressing in khaki pants, blazer, and tie. He did not often laugh or respond to our teasing, our giggling, our minor provocations. Mr. Dudley seemed like a machine that ran on tracks. The students he connected with most were the teacher pleasers, those boys—and they were always boys—we already knew were smart. They sat in the back, toward the center of the classroom, eagerly waving their hands in the air. Even though I excelled in Mr. Dudley's class, I knew full well that the molecular weight of the classroom rested with those boys. Their cluster was where Mr. Dudley's eyes landed most frequently and where his occasional jokes were invariably directed. My seat, by contrast, was beside the windows overlooking the school's quadrangle, its center courtyard.

Elsewhere in Brookline High School, we hardly ever sat in rows. In fact, Mr. Dudley's was the single humanities class I remember not arranged in a circle. He had a fondness, too, for the multiple-choice tests administered on bubble sheets that many other teachers openly disdained. And in Mr. Dudley's class, we had to memorize. Although that method was, and is, out of fashion, it gave me the skeleton on which to hang the cloth that made up my later studies of history. After Mr. Dudley I could say what happened when the Roman Empire fell, who the Goths were, why we should care about Charlemagne, where the modern university was formed, what Copernicus said about us and the sun, and why the French Revolution might matter to those of us living in Massachusetts in 1991. Having this knowledge at my disposal gave me a sense of confidence. The world around me—newspapers, novels, and even my parents' conversations with their friends—began to make more sense. Some things that Mr. Dudley taught us have never left me.

"Look at that tree," he told us once, pointing outside into the school quadrangle.

"Aristotle would see that tree and say, 'It's one tree of many,' and we need to look at all trees individually and come up with unique identifiers to decide what is a tree and what isn't a tree."

I considered the tree. It stood maybe two stories tall, its leaves full, shiny, and green. For some reason I remember it as a maple. On that day, the sun was shining, and the leaves were gleaming, rustling with passing breezes. It was a pretty tree. A tree that made you feel good about being alive.

"But Plato," Mr. Dudley went on, "Plato would have looked at that tree and said something very different. He would have said, 'Now there we have an approximation of the ideal of tree.' What does that mean, 'ideal of tree'? Plato believed that every concept, like tree or desk or pencil"—he waved a pencil before us—"is a representative of a single ideal form that exists not in the world but in our minds. And that, my friends, is the difference between Aristotle and Plato."

Now, decades later, when I close my eyes and think of "tree," that single specimen—leafy, sun-dappled, swaying in the breeze—is the one I see. The remaining trillions of trees on earth, including all those I have ever seen since, are simply replicas. Maybe this is what learning is—a teacher, a book, or our life experiences toss an idea into that fire, and just before it is consumed, an image of that idea is thrown up against the wall of our minds. There it remains, flickering and shifting, becoming the artwork and architecture of our mental living space.

6.

· ALL HUNGERINGS

Rome began for me not as a physical destination but as words arranged into lines of text. Those lines of text were like roads, trolley tracks, flight patterns leading my eyes from left to right. Eventually, left to right became west to east, and I went through the same motions on the world map: Boston to Rome, Boston to Rome.

⤳

Our senior-year English class began reading Dante's *Inferno* in early October. In the first canto, it is just before dawn when Dante, the traveler, realizes he is lost in the woods. A leopard-like creature, a hungry lion, and an emaciated she-wolf (*la lupa* in Italian) appear before him, blocking his path and causing him to tremble with fear. The third creature, *la lupa*, prevents him from ascending toward the morning sun, which is just beginning to rise over the distant mountain of Purgatory, and instead nudges him deeper into the shadowed forest, where he is soon to meet Virgil, his guide. But *la lupa* was not just *any old* wolf, I discovered in the footnotes. This was the same *lupa* who had suckled the twin infants Romulus and Remus, mythical founders of Rome, after they washed up on the shores of the Tiber River, and she was therefore a—if not *the*—symbol of the city. That the simple appearance in the text of *la lupa* could summon with such immediacy the myth of Rome's earliest history astounded me. What symbol did Boston, my own home city, have that even came close to matching the fiercely self-possessed, majestically teated she-wolf? The answer was: nothing I could think of.

Inferno was the first piece of literature I read that felt like a riddle— which perhaps explained the fervor with which I was now reading footnotes, and the fact that I was soon seeking out scholarly studies of Dante to read on weekends. Strange animals and landscapes appear right off the bat, and you must decide whether to take them literally or as metaphor. Not that it was necessarily one or the other. Our teacher, Mr. V, explained that the work could be read on four levels—the literal, the allegorical, the moral, and the anagogical—and he challenged us to apply them to *The Divine Comedy*'s first canto. Hunting for symbols and metaphors was new and exciting. It felt exhilarating to decipher what they meant. But to do so, you had to know something—and in some cases quite a lot—about history.

Mr. V pushed us to take our interpretation of *la lupa* further: she appears before Dante famished—"*di tutte brame*"—"with all hungerings." So not only does the gaunt she-wolf literally block Dante's path, and not only does she symbolize Rome, but she is also an allegory of civilization's appetite for conquest. She is avarice in its broadest sense, a lust for money, power, or pleasure so all-consuming that violence and corruption are legitimized as means to an ever-receding end. It surprised me later to learn from my reading that, on a moral level, Dante did not consider the "hungerings" that drive *la lupa* bad or sinful in themselves. Quite the opposite: he saw them as essential to the human condition and necessary to every endeavor worth undertaking. But because that hunger lacks moderation, because it lacks the restraint of reason and is therefore insatiable, *la lupa* surpasses the productive hunger that seeks nourishment and instead represents its state of excess, cupidity, which harms rather than nourishes. She is desire unbounded, ravenous and ravaging. Dante shivers at the sight of *la lupa*, but I knew from that very first canto that I wanted to follow her.

Or was it my teacher I wished to follow? There appeared to be no end to the threads one could pursue in *Inferno*, and in Mr. V's classroom, any one of them might tomorrow be the subject of an intense discussion. Or, alternatively, of a debate carried out in the margins of our essays. I had never before taken much interest in teachers' comments on my work. Reading them was a chore to be hurried through or, better yet, skipped entirely. But Mr. V's were different. Instead of check marks or single words like *vague* or *explain*, his comments prompted a conversation.

I filled the margin of one of my essays with scribbled drawings depicting the tortures of Dante's *Inferno*—sad, elongated forms that constituted my offhand visual reflections on the text. My essay came back with his looped red writing at the end: "Your marginalia remind me of the etchings of Gustave Doré." What? During free block, I ran to the school library and looked up *marginalia* and *etchings* in the dictionary. Then, in an encyclopedia, I looked up "Doré, Gustave." Though the French artist made etchings depicting many other subjects, it so happened that the article displayed a small image of one of his woodcuts of the *Inferno*: the proud Florentine Farinata degli Uberti rising stiffly out of a lit and smoky grave, demanding of Dante and Virgil, "Who were your ancestors?" This was a question, I learned, that was intimately connected to the medieval Italian experience, but one that, for myself, I had hardly the tools to answer.

Other comments verged on banter. When I loosely interpreted an assignment and wrote it in a kind of logically organized gibberish, Mr. V wrote in the margin: "HEY! Non scherzare!" That my English teacher would reply to me in Italian with the invocation "Don't joke!" was both a joke in itself and, as I read it, an invitation to learn Italian, sending me rushing to a bookstore in search of an Italian-English dictionary.

Now, as I feel around the edges of that impenetrable black box, the origin point, or points, of my longing for Rome, I think that somewhere in those tightly scribbled comments must lie a clue to the early stirrings of my heart and mind. And although I know that chronology is a bastard and, more often than not, a lie, maybe, just maybe, this point of origin was among the first: "Reading your essay is like having a tartufo cioccolato at the Tre Scalini cafe in Piazza Navona in Rome."

A sentence to make you pause. To make you decode each foreign word and savor it like the delectable thing that it was. I wrote an essay. In return my teacher offered me the knowledge of a *tartufo cioccolato*, a chocolate truffle. And of the Tre Scalini, a name you skip up one-two-three-four and when you reach the top of it you turn around, smile into the sunlight, and the world is yours for the taking. And of Piazza Navona, which, I was sure, must be a place like no other. I quickly forgot the essay. But the Tre Scalini, Italian, and Rome—these were my teacher's gifts.

Within a month or so of beginning *Inferno* in class, I checked out a set of beginner Italian audio cassettes from the public library. Night after night I sat at the desk in my bedroom, parsing the basic structure of the language and trying to apply what I had learned to the text of *Inferno*. It bore some structural similarities, I discovered, to French, which I had been studying since the seventh grade. But where studying French raised in me a mild curiosity, learning Italian felt like turning the key to a room that, with every passing day, I wished more fervently to enter. Every phrase I learned felt like progress—toward a text, toward an ongoing conversation with my teacher, toward a world beyond the confines of the family home.

Before I could even string together a sentence, I began memorizing the opening lines of *Inferno*, reciting them, while my family slept, like some kind of incantation. I soon shared my undertaking with Mr. V. At this news, his lips formed a tight, almost conspiratorial, smile. He did not, as I read it, want to look too pleased. But from then on, he wrote many of his comments to me in Italian. Sometimes I understood them. When I didn't, I scurried to my Italian dictionary, recently acquired at Brookline Book-smith, until I had gotten the gist. I was breaking the code.

My own home was full of other codes, adult conversations that I tried to understand. My parents were highly educated professionals—my father was a doctor and my mother, who had earned a master's degree in Islamic art in the 1970s, worked in development and communications at large, mostly nonprofit organizations such as the New York Public Library, and later, after we moved back to Boston, the Isabella Stewart Gardner Museum and Harvard University. Though they would not have described themselves as intellectuals, to me, they seemed to know so much. On those occasions when they asked for my opinions—about art or music or politics—I either didn't want or didn't know how to answer. The phrase "kind of" was among my favorites then, and I drove my father crazy with it.

"Did you like the movie?" he would ask.

"Kind of," I would answer.

"Kind of yes? Kind of no?"

"Just kind of," I'd say.

At that time of my life, this was about as articulate as I got with him.

What I thought, generally speaking, was that I didn't know enough to say. In fact, that is one of the single recurring thoughts I remember most clearly from that period: *If I just read more, maybe I'll know enough to have an opinion on things.* Until then, I didn't. The newspapers that landed with a thud on our doorstep each morning—*The New York Times* and *The Boston Globe*—offered daily proof of how little I knew. I read them, trying to piece together the many enigmas of the world and its problems, trying to comprehend the systems that held it together, about which I felt I knew so little. First world, third world . . . Was there a second? Parliamentary democracy, constitutional democracy . . . What was the difference? It felt like trying to fill a crater with a teaspoon.

Upstairs in the "computer" room—we had an early-model Macintosh whose function seemed limited to primitive, unsatisfying games—lived our giant *Encyclopedia Britannica*, my main source of information about the world. It was bound in dark leather, or what looked like leather, and took up two whole rows of a massive bookshelf. We had bought the set when we lived in New Jersey, about seven or eight years earlier, from a salesman who rang our front bell.

Though at seventeen I didn't yet know it, for me, the *Britannica*'s status as an intact compendium containing the whole of the world's knowledge was to be short-lived—not only because the computer, or really the internet, would soon take over and render the printed encyclopedia a vestigial artifact of a bygone age, but because my parents, six months later, would announce their separation and, soon after, their divorce. With the divorce, the question of who would get the thirty-volume set would be answered not by my parents but by an arbitrator, a person my parents hired to help them divide their lives. Her solution: the *Britannica* would be cleaved down the middle. I was familiar with the story of Solomon. I knew that splitting the baby down the middle was foolhardy and cruel. But here we were. At the direction of a professional, my mother got one half while my father ended up with the other. It made a kind of sense, though only through the twisted logic of divorce.

⌒⌒

Mr. V was a man of old-world proportions, and though his long face and prominent chin were slightly pocked, he was handsome in his own way. He was probably, I guessed, in his late forties, and he dressed well, always wearing a suit when he taught. On his right hand he wore a ring with an explosion of silver needles protruding from a round base, not unlike a sea urchin. He was cagey about where the ring came from, allowing our imaginations to run wild. I could perceive even then that Mr. V was a skilled cultivator of his own mystique. The boys in my class liked to speculate on his Mafia connections; to them it made perfect sense that he wouldn't be able to talk about it.

This theory was helped along by his name. The *V* stood for *Viglirolo*, an Italian name apparently considered by some to be impossible to pronounce. Long before I reached his classroom, he had settled simply for *V*. But this, too, had the effect of amplifying his mystery—his unpronounceable last name, his spiky ring, his vague connection to the south of Italy, the high, even old-school standards that he held for us. It was an image that Mr. V curated, and one that spurred some of us to work harder for him and aspire to win his approval.

Mr. V was demanding in his pedagogy and probably slightly eccentric in his person. His class, which covered European literature from the Middle Ages to the twentieth century, was as ambitious, if not more, in scope than any college course I would later take. His syllabus came with a detailed time line of European literary and artistic production spanning from the fourth to the sixteenth century and an article by Sven Birkerts on the difficulties of teaching writing to students who don't read for pleasure. He paired these with a page-long letter to prospective students warning that his class might be one of the most challenging classes we would experience at Brookline High. I would soon discover this for myself. Mr. V was a demanding grader, and my first quiz in his class earned a C+. Any higher grade than that, and also any lower, his letter explained, we would have to work to attain.

You got the sense in Mr. V's class that he wanted no less than to transform us. Once, when we were reading Molière's *Tartuffe*, he began to recite by heart the scene in which the play's antagonist and title character, Tartuffe, attempts to seduce Elmire, the married lady of the house in which Tartuffe has become a trusted guest. As Mr. V arrived at the height of Tartuffe's declaration of love, there was a knock at our classroom door. In walked another English teacher, who handed Mr. V a piece of paper. She was about to leave when she surprised us all by spinning around and continuing the dialogue, assuming the role of Elmire. Before we knew it, the two teachers were locked in an embrace, Tartuffe dipping Elmire backward over his desk, their faces nearly touching. They held the pose a moment before breaking out in laughter. Our class erupted into wild applause. It never occurred to me at the time that such a moment might have been planned. In my eyes, Mr. V was a master, a living embodiment of the transformative power of books.

Perhaps what felt to me like transformation was actually, in Mr. V's view, self-realization. The end of the letter accompanying his syllabus read in part: "This course offers you the chance to discover what it is that you can do." Every day on the chalkboard he would write out four or five quotations about literature or philosophy from the likes of Marguerite Yourcenar, Immanuel Kant, Joan Didion, or Cervantes. We had to copy them in our notebooks, the hope being, I suppose, that something might sink in. We had the sense that if we worked very hard, we might bear a chance of pleasing him, but only if we imbued our work with some kind of independent, authentic effort. And I think I already understood that the goal was not ultimately to gain his favor but to connect with the works he taught and to learn how to "see" a text—*saper vedere*, as he always said. He aspired to show us nothing less than the beauty, power, and meaning of literature.

Mr. V took less interest in the high achievers than he did in the struggling, moderately troubled kids, with whom he was often successful at connecting on a personal level. I was used to getting good grades, but high school had also brought out in me a penchant for low-grade mischief. The Scantron attendance sheets that teachers relied on were distributed on Mondays. One friend and I had figured out that, if we slipped them from our teachers' desk drawers on Monday afternoons, those teachers would have no way to record our absences for the rest of the week. We pulled this stunt for the classes we liked least and, in so doing, found ourselves scot-free to take the T during school days to Copley Square, where we'd roam the hallways of the Westin and Marriott Hotels, making off with dozens of miniature pots of jam and honey that guests had left untouched on their room service trays.

I brought this minor rebellion into the classroom, too, where I tested Mr. V as I might have a parent. As I grew more confident in his class, I wrote the occasional obtuse essay on purpose. I ignored directions or failed to hand in an assignment and offered no explanation as to why. At the end of an exercise done relatively well, I tacked on a gibberish sentence. I wrote an essay in the form of a comic. I was being playful, but I think I was also casting the line for a response. I wanted more of his comments, more of his attention. I preferred praise, of course ("I want to keep your journal!"), but I would settle for any response I could get ("Aside from the crucial error of not fulfilling the assignment as I outlined in class, your entries are nonetheless engaging").

I wasn't too worried about the consequences of these small acts of defiance, in part because before Mr. V's class I had not even been sure I wanted to go to college. I dreamed at one point of being a forest ranger and at another of exploring the world on foot—either of which would provide necessary life experience for my ultimate, inevitable (as I saw it) career as a writer. But the one class I never skipped, even despite my tangled ambitions, was his. On the spectrum between rejecting Mr. V's authority, as I had that of many other teachers, and trying to leap through every hoop he set before us, I emphatically chose the latter. Even if that sometimes meant refusing to leap and instead engaging in a dialogue—cherished attention!— about that refusal. I think now that what differentiated me from those of my classmates who resented Mr. V's tough-love style of teaching was that I actually wanted to be transformed: not into a scholar but into someone whom grown-ups would take seriously, someone possessed of knowledge and languages, of concerns and pursuits, that would crack open the gate to a universe beyond my home.

And so, under Mr. V's tutelage, I threw myself into the study of the *Inferno* as I had never done with anything before, visiting the Brookline Public Library and checking out books on Dante and Italian history and literature that our high school library didn't own and that were, candidly speaking, far above my level. My mother pitched in, too. She agreed to buy me a tweed jacket, which I saw as a solid investment for the kind of person I was becoming, the kind who attends public lectures. (My mother surely saw the jacket as a hedge against my other fashion choices of the moment, which included anything I could find at Rags—the warehouse in Boston's North End that dumped used clothing in eight-foot-high piles and sold it by the pound—as well as a necklace I had fashioned from a rubber chicken strung by its feet. Red plaid pants played a role as well, and steel-capped Dr. Marten shoes, and a skirt that would close only with a dozen safety pins.) She also acted as an energetic researcher, scouting out university talks and readings about Italy or Italian literature, while I aided the effort by scanning the *Brookline TAB* newspaper for other upcoming events I or we might attend. Public lectures became something we occasionally did together. It was also in this period that my mother gifted me the black bust of Dante, its visage based on the poet's death mask, that has for decades looked down with apparent disdain on my living space.

The pinnacle of these outings, for me, was the seminar on Dante we attended at Harvard's Center for European Studies. One early-spring afternoon, we tiptoed into an austere, wood-paneled seminar room and, without a word, seated ourselves around its oval table. For the next two hours, my mother and I listened as the academics in the room—colleagues, I now realize, who surely all knew one another—threw around a number of arcane points regarding Dante. Taking notes in my tweed jacket, I felt serious and sophisticated. When the time was up, I closed my notebook and my mother and I quietly left the room. No one had spoken to us. Nor had we spoken to anyone else. Surely, I realize now, they must have been scratching their heads: *Who were those people?* But going to that seminar made me feel as if at seventeen I were already starting down my life's path—which, as I saw it then, would be about either Dante or writing. Escorted, of course—for I doubt I would have had the courage to set foot in that solemn room without my mother by my side.

❧

Through Dante, I discovered a new kind of reading—"literary criticism"; it exhilarated me to take a text and plunder it for all the meanings you could find. During this period, in a Beacon Street bookstore, I chanced upon Italo Calvino's *The Uses of Literature*, which I underlined and marked up with notes and definitions of words—*execration, agoraphobia, abnegation*—previously unknown. Knowing that Calvino was a monumental literary figure, I was struck all the more by the questions he asked, which were so simple and elemental: How does writing happen? Why do we read? Why do we read "classics"? What *is* a classic? I did not yet know that the most difficult, and captivating, questions are often the simplest.

Reading Calvino's essays, I was still caught by surprise when I stumbled across the name *Dante*. In my young mind, Dante still seemed like *mine*, like some gem I had unearthed in my own backyard. It took me a while to perceive—to really understand—that Calvino and Dante formed part of the same universe. And so I sought out Calvino's stories, novels, and folktales, as well as other stars and moons circulating in that same galaxy: works by Alberto Moravia, Primo Levi, Natalia Ginzburg, and Umberto Eco—writers who were widely translated and available to me. I also found works by English-language writers who wrote about Italy, such as Barbara Grizzuti Harrison, whose short stories would color the way I perceived Italy for years to come.

One thing that this reading impressed on me was that my cassette method of home Italian study was far too slow. That January I signed up for an adult education beginner's Italian course that met several evenings per week. Young and impatient, it seemed to me that my adult classmates could not possibly have been more sluggish, but nonetheless, over the next few months, my knowledge of Italy and Italian began to expand. In Mr. V's class we read stories from Boccaccio's *Decameron*, as well as poems by Petrarch and the private letters of Machiavelli. We learned, too, about the relationship between languages. Mr. V was the first teacher in my life to mention translation: when we read Michelangelo's sonnet about Dante, he handed out two English versions and asked us to pinpoint the choices and trade-offs each translator had made. When, later that spring, we read the twentieth-century Sicilian poet Salvatore Quasimodo, we received his original text in Italian and an English translation. Mr. V read the Italian out loud so we might hear its cadence. *Ognuno sta solo,* he read. Each alone . . .

> *Ognuno sta solo sul cuor della terra*
> *trafitto da un raggio di sole:*
> *ed è subito sera.*

> Each alone on the heart of the earth,
> impaled upon a ray of sun:
> and suddenly it's evening.

I quickly memorized the poem, and it joined the opening lines of *The Divine Comedy* as an Italian refrain that hummed at the back of my mind—always there, always retrievable when I needed a poem or a lullaby or a mantra to soothe my thoughts, or calm my nerves, or remind myself that in this big world I at least knew something small. Memorizing Quasimodo's poem gave me the feeling, for maybe the first time, that knowing something was akin to possessing it. That all I needed in order to make it "mine" was a little bit of concentration and time.

The center and the source of all this remained Dante. Unlike the world around me, which was infinitely large and about which my parents would always know more, Dante was at the center of a different universe, one with its own laws, its own terminology. I could have my own opinions about *Inferno*, I discovered, and I could back them up. It didn't matter if my familiarity with it was still relatively superficial—*The Divine Comedy* had shown me the way to a new world, one that was both fictional and historical and yet also inextricably connected to an actual place on earth. In this universe, I could already stand on my own two feet.

7.

SEARCHING FOR DANTE

DANTE ALIGHIERI

As a seventeen-year-old, of course, I had a different sense of my reasons for delving so deeply into *Inferno*, if I gave much thought to them at all.

"Don't I look like Dante?" I asked my close friend Joanne one day, holding up a portrait of him beside my own face.

It had become clear to me, if not to anyone else, that Dante and I shared some marked physical similarities. Namely: wide cheekbones, a large nose with a signature bump, and a penchant for scowling.

Joanne looked at me skeptically, then at the portrait—the frontispiece of Lawrence Grant White's 1948 English translation of *The Divine Comedy*. It was my first copy, not counting the cheap paperback edition of Allen Mandelbaum's translation of *Inferno* that we had received in class. I had found White's edition in a used bookstore and snapped it up when I saw that the illustrations were by none other than Gustave Doré. Holding Doré's portrait of Dante up with one hand, I looked at Joanne straight on, then rotated slowly to the side.

"Maaaybe," she said, her eyebrows arching the way they always did when she thought I was full of it.

"And now?" I asked, pushing the corners of my lips down into a deep frown and furrowing the space between my eyes. "Now what do you think?"

"Oh yes, *now* I see it, definitely," Joanne replied, laughing at me more than with me. "You two might as well be twins."

Joanne's sarcasm aside, I took heart in the idea that I might resemble the father of the Italian language. My pursuit of Italian had *obviously* been preordained.

～⁘～

One problem with thinking you look like Dante is that no one really knows what he looked like. The illustrations in my used-bookstore edition of *The Divine Comedy* were made by Doré in the 1860s. Like artists before him, Doré depicted the poet as he imagined he ought to look, and he used earlier portraits such as those by Giotto, Andrea del Castagno, Botticelli, Raphael, and Bronzino as models.

Many depictions of Dante were based on a description given by Boccaccio, who was a boy when Dante died. His face was long, Boccaccio attested, with an aquiline nose, rather large eyes, a large jaw, and an upper lip that protruded over the lower one, and he was always, in his expression, melancholy and pensive. In short, a typical perception of the aged by the very young, especially the detail regarding the lips, which paint the portrait of a toothless old man. In these early depictions, Dante's clothes are variations on a theme: a vermilion gown or tunic, most often with a mandarin collar, sometimes open like a keyhole at the neckline and sometimes not; and also a red cap, sometimes long and pointed, other times fitted, with white ear flaps. (Is there any historical figure, I have long wondered, more closely associated with their outfit than Dante is with that red tunic and funny hat? Among his many other accomplishments, the man was a fashion maven.)

The earliest portraits of Dante, including that by his contemporary fellow Florentine Giotto, depict him bareheaded, without a crown of laurel leaves—the traditional honor bestowed on poets of stature, which Dante, in his lifetime, never received. But from the middle of the fifteenth century, when Domenico di Michelino painted Dante presenting *The Divine Comedy* to the city of Florence in the cathedral of Santa Maria del Fiore, the poet would rarely go without his wreath. By the time Doré made his etching four hundred years later, it was unthinkable to depict Dante without his laurel crown. So Doré stuck with the laurel, while elongating the ear flaps on Dante's cap, which lent the poet the air of an indignant springer spaniel. In place of the medieval tunic, however, Doré chose an outfit he must have considered more appropriate, more manly, or more of his time—a jacket with padded shoulders, lapels, and buttons—while also turning the poet's already dour look into a formidable scowl. In his nineteenth-century jacket, Dante looks as if he just might run off and fight for Garibaldi.

Which in a way, he did. Or rather, his words did. Dante had been among the first to write epic poetry in the spoken language of his Italian city-state rather than in Latin. When, in the nineteenth century, Italian nationalists sought a single language that could unify the peninsula, Tuscany's long literary tradition—whose prestige derived in part from Dante, Petrarch, and Boccaccio, as well as renowned Renaissance humanists such as Pietro Bembo—made it the obvious choice as a model and resource for a new, modern "Italian" language. It helped, too, that Florence's vernacular tongue was, linguistically speaking, positioned between north and south.

But even following the 1861 unification, Italian would remain largely a literary language. Since most of the population was illiterate, and would remain so for the next half century, the sense of unity created by the new language was limited largely to the upper class, who might read their newspapers or favorite books in Italian, while in ordinary homes and communities, Italy's more than three dozen regional languages continued to flourish. From the 1920s into the 1940s, the Italian language was so heavily promoted by the nationalist Fascist prime minister and Hitler ally Benito Mussolini that foreign words were banned and regional languages relegated to folk status. And yet, despite those efforts, it wasn't until decades later, in the 1950s and beyond, with the diffusion of mass media and compulsory state-sponsored education, that Italian gained real ground as a widely spoken language. Today, although more than thirty indigenous languages are still spoken throughout Italy, news, television, film, and technology have spurred a homogenized Italian to grow and dominate.

Such is the tide that Dante, seven hundred years ago, helped to set in motion. So as for precisely what his face looked like, does it really matter?

It seems to—at least, to some.

In 1921, six hundred years after Dante's death, two physical anthropologists, Giuseppe Sergi and his former student Fabio Frassetto, were granted permission to open Dante's tomb and study his remains. Sergi and Frassetto's wider interest lay in their spurious search, based on their measurements of bones, for a distinctly Mediterranean racial identity. In Dante's bones, the two men, not surprisingly, saw "the most glorious and authentic representative of the Mediterranean race." And true to the Fascist environment in which they lived and worked, they claimed that Dante's measurements proved not only his "high intelligence" but also his "masculine temperament."

Frassetto embarked on a yearslong project to reconstruct Dante's likeness, with the aim of featuring the team's specious conclusions in a film. After taking more than one hundred detailed measurements of Dante's cranium, he located a skull that approximated Dante's measurements, fabricated a plaster model of it, and then painstakingly whittled and sanded and plumped until the model conformed, as closely as he could make it, to Dante's skull. When finished, Frassetto teamed up with the sculptor Alfonso Borghesani to re-create Dante's likeness in a bronze bust based on that reconstruction. The "true face" they created was a bit longer and thinner than many previous depictions, but Dante's aquiline nose and jutting chin, his most salient features, remained little changed.

More than eighty years later, in 2006, a group of Italian anthropologists and scientists, eager to apply new technologies to the perennial question of Dante's appearance, attempted a second facial reconstruction. They made a 3D digital model of the cranium constructed by Frassetto and then fabricated a new physical model of the skull by means of a rapid prototyping system. To this they applied the facial reconstruction techniques currently employed in forensic anthropology to reimagine the soft layers of muscle, fat tissue, and skin. As always, many details remained speculative and subject to interpretation. But the result was surprisingly different. With a still-crooked nose but a newly fleshy face, and relieved of his characteristic furrowed brow, Dante went from looking like a stern aesthete to a man of the people. One lead scientist feared that the new model would cause a scandal. But the opposite happened: many were relieved that their beloved poet had turned out to look like the guy next door.

There remains one significant problem. No one in recent memory has had access to Dante's entire skeleton. When the poet died, he was famously buried not in Florence, his home city, from which he was bitterly exiled, but in Ravenna, where he lived the final years of his life. Over the centuries his bones and sarcophagus were moved multiple times to protect them from danger. But somewhere in the shuffle, Dante's jaw went missing.

This is a fact I find almost too poetic to be true: the skeleton of the father of the Italian language is missing one of the few bones required for speech.

We will never know exactly what Dante looked like. Unless the jaw resurfaces, and there is very little reason to believe that it will, we will never know Dante's face with precision, not without making part of it up, without imagining and speculating and inserting ourselves into the process. It's as if the poet's skeleton itself were telling us to give up. When Frassetto supposedly summoned his spirit through a medium at a 1929 séance in Trieste, Dante apparently said as much. "Don't search for my mandible," he snapped. "You won't find it." Dante—or his spirit—knew of what he spoke. For what matters is not his face but his written word and the language, spoken every day by more than sixty million people, that it helped to beget. It is only there that we will find him.

8.

DOLLAR BY DOLLAR,
WORD BY WORD

It takes money to get from Boston to Rome, even more if you would like
to stay there awhile. I pull a sheet of paper from my desk drawer and try to
figure out how much. There's the plane ticket, of course, but there will
also be trains, hotels, museums, meals, and at least one *tartufo cioccolato*. My
mother looks it over. Eight hundred and fifty for the plane, forty a night
for hotels.

"What?" she says, her eyes wide with alarm. "Fifty dollars a day for
food?"

"Too much?" I ask. I am seventeen. I have little idea how much food
costs when you're not at home.

"I'd say! In my day, we had a travel guide called *Europe on Five Dollars a
Day*. Imagine, fifty on food alone!"

I remind her that that was thirty years ago.

"True," she says. Still, her furrowed brow reveals her disapproval. I'm
not certain if it stems from the number fifty or from the number ten (my
clothing size) compared with six (hers).

I admit that fifty might be a lot. So I scratch it out and scribble "$15"
in its place. My mother nods in approval.

Later that night, I erase "$15," blowing off the shredded eraser bits and brushing the area gently with the side of my palm. In its place, I pencil in "$25."

I regard my work with satisfaction. Italy is a series of line items on the page, each just waiting to be devoured.

⁓

To save up for a plane ticket, I take a job working weekends and school vacations at a smoothie joint called the Monkey Bar. It's one of many establishments lining the marketplace of Boston's Faneuil Hall. On New Year's Eve, the corridor is packed shoulder to shoulder. Throngs of people flow through the narrow channel of fast-food establishments. I listen to, try to latch on to, their many languages.

I slice fruit, toss it in blenders. My shoes stick to the black plastic floor mats splattered with pulp. Sometimes I must use one foot to hold down the mat while peeling off the other sole, as if I had stepped onto a sheet of cooling caramel. I try not to think of the roaches that, that very morning, were lying belly up on these same floors, their legs still twitching. At six dollars an hour, I figure I will have to spend 150 hours chopping bananas and washing out blenders before I can buy my plane ticket.

While fruits whirl and settle, an unwieldy mass of bodies lurches by. It reminds me of a river after a mudslide, choked with sediment. I pour and serve. "Next!" I say. Some tip generously. A man buys himself a smoothie for three dollars, winks, and stuffs two twenties into my tip cup. Forty whole dollars.

Eight hundred and twenty-ish more to go.

⁓

Grandmother and Grandfather give me a whopping five hundred dollars to help cover expenses, a gesture so generous it unmoors me. "Take all the trains you want," Grandmother says, while Grandfather sits beside her with his usual reserve.

An old friend of my parents gives money, too. "Spend it frivolously," he says with delight. *Frivolously*—the word spills from the upturned corners of his mouth.

"Your father," Mom says gravely, "thought we should give you condoms to take along." Her eyebrows knit with disapproval.

Instead, she pins a brass angel to the suitcase handle. "A guardian angel to watch over you," she says.

❧

Work at night. When your parents and brothers are sleeping, when the only noise is the halogen lamp buzzing in the corner of your room.

From your desk drawer, retrieve the plastic box. Crack it open and regard the six cassettes, three on each side. The black film of each one rolled entirely to the left, waiting for you to pick up where you left off.

Read the title: *Living Language All-Audio Italian.* Assure yourself of the promises its cover makes: "Learn Anywhere." "No Reading Required."

Say the words out loud. Imitate the vowels, the rhythm, the intonation of the chirpy woman whose voice leads you where you want to go. *Buonasera, signora. Le posso prendere la valigia?* Read the translation: "Good evening, madam. May I take your luggage?" Yes, the lessons are formal and seem to belong to another era. They are not phrases you can imagine saying out loud. But this doesn't dampen your enthusiasm. Each phrase is a plank set on the bridge between you and the other world. The more you collect, set together, the farther out you can venture.

A few months before your trip, get out your drawing book, a mechanical pencil, a large eraser, a ruler, and a fountain pen. Across each page, using your ruler and a pencil, draw parallel lines, delicate and straight, a quarter inch apart, leaving a two-inch margin on the outside edges. When finished, find your copy of Mandelbaum's translation of *Inferno*. Press it under your left hand and, using your fountain pen, begin transcribing the text with your right (vice versa if you are left-handed).

> *When I had journeyed half of our life's way*
> *I found myself within a shadowed forest*
> *For I had lost the path that does not stray . . .*

Imitate, to the best of your ability, the calligraphic scripts you have seen. Try to make your letters equal in size, balanced, pleasing to the eye. Now and again you will fail, make spelling errors, inadvertently skip a line. When you pause to rest your hand, segments of your words—your work—will languish under puddles of ink. Notice how much ink gets sucked into the thirsty page. Think that you are performing the labor that all those monks once did, hour upon hour, by sunlight and by candle.

It might seem that each page takes an eternity. Try to relax your hand, keep it from cramping. Write only one page per night. Acknowledge how weak you are, how quickly the muscles in your hand have begun to quiver, how your body has already registered in a dozen small ways its rising protest.

Empty your head of everything except the phrase you are writing. Think not about meaning. Instead, focus exclusively on how that phrase, that assembly of words, that march of glyphs, advances across the page. Maintain the correct amount of white space, evaluate the slant of ascenders and descenders, regulate your letters' height, observe where punctuation intervenes. The words will enter your eye and exit your hand—you are the medium, present but vacant, through which they flow.

> *Ah! It is hard to speak of what it was*
> *that savage forest, dense and difficult,*
> *which even in recall renews my fear . . .*

At the end of the tercet, take a breath and read the Italian aloud: *Ahi quanto a dir qual era è cosa dura / esta selva selvaggia e aspra e forte / che nel pensier rinova la paura.* Imagine Dante writing these lines with his own hand, as he once did. You will feel a small spark of kinship with him, almost as if you had put your ear to his chest and heard the pounding of his heart. Imagine how his shoulders, under the scratch of his red wool tunic, must constrict as he recalls his fear that evening in the wood, and how his belly must relax and warm to the touch as he recounts to you his long story, word by word.

9.

WAITING TO BE REALIGNED

Over the nearly thirty centuries of its existence, Rome has been many things. It has been the sacred ground of pagan gods, the home of emperors, the seat of a small city-republic, the fictive underpinning of a "holy" federation of states, the birthplace of the international bureaucracy known as the papacy, a playland of politically powerful popes, and, most recently, the capital city of a united Italian state. In addition to the varied roles it has played on the international stage, Rome has also occupied, for at least a thousand years, a central place in the imaginations of both East and West. Its name has been synonymous with political power, with legal authority, with holy investiture; it has been a place where the rich go to seek power, and where the poor go to have a shot at salvation. The sheer number of lenses through which Rome has been examined is mind-boggling: there is the Rome of Livy and Tacitus and Suetonius; the Rome of Ovid, pervaded by myth and lovelorn cares; the Rome of Saints Peter and Paul, Perpetua and Felicity, and on and on through Constantine, granting visions by the wagonload. There is Rome the oppressor, the colonizer, giver of laws and legions; and Rome the victim—trophy Rome—the prized plunder of peripatetic peoples. There is the Rome of the medieval pilgrim, already teeming with ruins and the haggard spirits of the holy; and the Rome shorn of popes in the age of Saint Birgitta, whose visions in the fourteenth century led to her newfound order of cloistered nuns, and whose entreaties that the papacy return from Avignon helped to bring the pope back to his original home. There is the Rome of Michelangelo, dominated by big money, powerful patrons, and the mischief-making artists whose names we remember; the Rome, romanticized and sublimated, of Keats and Shelley and Byron, the golden ring on the Grand Tour; of Edith Wharton, city as backdrop and foil of its aristocratic Anglophone residents; and that of Giuseppe Gioachino Belli, whose sonnets in the Romanesco dialect satirized the vulgarity of life under the popes. There is the Rome of Antonio Moravia, a city invisible but for the malaise and alienation it provokes; the Rome of Roberto Rossellini and Anna Magnani, a blinking black-and-white pastiche of gritty lives and fleeting loves against the backdrop of international power plays; the Rome of Fellini, a voluptuous mother with too many children to count; the Romes of Natalia Ginzburg and Elsa Morante, with their small satisfactions gleaned amid the obliterating tragedies of war. Of Pier Paolo Pasolini, for whom Rome's stupendous, wretched soul was laid most bare in its peripheral neighborhoods. More recently there is the Rome of Paolo Sorrentino's *The Great Beauty*, nostalgic, decadent, and hollow; the Rome of immigrants, migrants, and the otherwise dispossessed, sidling up against its shores in flimsy boats with dreams of a bed and a paycheck; the Rome of Amara Lakhous, in whose novels Egyptians, native-born Romans, Somalis, Neapolitans, Tunisians, and Bangladeshis are inextricably bound in a web of common need and misunderstanding. Of André Aciman, in whose city, still bright with hidden promise, we might alight at any moment upon some past self, and in so doing free ourselves of the ennui that we fear has come to define us; and that of Igiaba Scego, to whom Rome's landscape of monuments still seethes with the living past of the city's colonial crimes. There is Jhumpa Lahiri's Rome, beautiful but often hostile, in which natives and newcomers alike strive in vain for an ever-receding sense of belonging. And there is the Rome of *Suburra*, a multi-ethnic *Roma capitale* pervaded by corruption, scandal, and violence. Rome has been so much to so many—who is any one of us to say what Rome is?

※

June 14, 1993. At the airport, I pose for photos with my brothers. High school graduation was only a month ago, and all of a sudden I'm so much taller than they are. My parents put their arms around me, squeeze my shoulders, check my suitcase to make sure all the zippers are closed. I wear a broad smile, pants with a wide belt cinched at the waist, bought just for this trip. Annie, my friend and traveling partner, stands beside me, nervous and giddy. Our backpacks tower over our shoulders.

Along the wall, just before the boarding gates, is a multifaceted mirror, its myriad small panes tilting off in every which direction. This was before there were lines for security. As we pose, smile, hug goodbye, I catch sight of myself in that mirror. I entered the departures area whole, and already, not even on the plane yet, there I am in a hundred pieces: random, scattered, waiting to be realigned.

※

I never considered, when I first went to Rome, that part of me might get lodged there, like a chip of nail between two teeth, and never get free.

I never considered that Rome might plant a thread in me, the way a fish gets caught on a line, and that from then on, no matter where I was in the world, I would still feel tethered to that one fixed point.

I never considered that Rome might be so much that everywhere else could become too little.

Part II

10.

ARRIVAL

The stillness of waiting.

As if the faster we are moving toward a destination, the more imminently it is upon us, the more still we must become. The runner for whom the wider world goes silent, for whom nothing exists except the finish line. The infant who spirals down the birth canal, arms folded, subject to forces beyond her control, in a daze, in a trance, in the throes of becoming.

Stillness. When I wake, the cabin is dark, thick with splayed legs, drooping heads, a haze of dreaming. Cracking open my window shade, there is a sudden peeling back of night, a tear of light. And by chance, at that very moment, the coastline of Italy slides across the pane.

My first glimpse.

Somewhere north of Rome.

A strip of sand and a long breaking wave. The sand, golden; the wave, dipped in pink. More than a quarter century later, that single, pink-tipped wave still crests, frozen in time, in my mind's eye.

My quickened breath leaves ringlets of moisture on the oval window.

❦

I put all my energy into figuring out how to get to Rome. But I thought little about actually arriving. I might have arrived like a Greek soldier, guiding his boat over the chop of waves. Or like a Carthaginian general, spurring an elephant, against all odds, across the snowy Alps. Or I might have neared the city at a snail's pace, like a blistered pilgrim limping southward along the via Francigena. I might have been an enemy held captive, dispossessed of personhood but ripe with muscled body, bound at the wrists and carted off to a life of servitude in a villa on the Aventine. I might have first flown over it, an Allied pilot in 1943, gazing down on the city spread out like a dream. Or arrived as a corseted lady swaying sidesaddle on her horse's lathered withers. I might have rowed up the Tiber in a leaking rowboat, banking in the sun-shot reeds and clambering out, wet-footed, onto a muddy embankment beneath a grove of willows. Or slumbered, lightly snoring, as my night train from some far-flung city slid smoothly into Termini Station.

If I were not a person? I could have been a sandstorm blown over from North Africa—a sirocco—my body sieving dust over the mosaics in the Baths of Caracalla. I might have been a starling in migration, holed up in hiding from a hawk, trilling warnings in a turret of Castel Sant'Angelo. Or a dolphin, laying down the delicate body of a boy, nearly drowned, upon Ostia's sandy shore. Or perhaps a loaf of bread, baked on chestnut coals in the ovens of Lariano and carted on the back of a mule trudging up the via Appia Antica. I might have arrived as a thousand flakes of snow, sheltered under the arches of the Colosseum. Or as a surge of water careening down the channel of an aqueduct, spilling with abandon into the basin of the Trevi Fountain.

There are so many ways to arrive.

❧

For Sigmund Freud, simply getting to Rome proved a long-standing psychological challenge. Beginning after his graduation from high school, Freud repeatedly planned trips to Rome, canceled those plans, and then began planning again. On occasion he made it partway, traveling across the Alps and more than halfway down the Italian peninsula, only to turn around when nearly there. Writing to his friend Wilhelm Fliess in 1897, shortly after one of these failed attempts, Freud called his simultaneous longing for and hesitation about Rome "deeply neurotic."

Wilhelm Fliess was a nose and throat specialist who, as Freud's interlocutor, would influence the development of psychoanalysis. In his own work, he studied the biological bases of neurosis. Resting on his now mostly but not entirely discredited naso-genital theory, which posited that the nose was connected intimately (so to speak) to the genitals, Fliess twice operated on Freud's nose in an attempt to cure the Rome neurosis that so dogged his friend. But the effort was to no avail.

What was holding Freud back? He tried to explain. His inability to arrive to Rome was, he claimed, "connected with my high school hero worship of the Semitic Hannibal." Hannibal—the legendary military general from Carthage, in modern-day Tunisia, whose entry in 218 BCE, together with his army numbering tens of thousands, into northern Italy by way of Spain and France, and then over the Alps on the backs of thirty-seven African elephants, was among the most celebrated arrivals in history. And yet, despite his unmatched military prowess, the Carthaginian general never made it, not once, to the gates of Rome. Like Hannibal, Freud yearned for Rome, desired it, stood in awe of it. At the same time, however, he feared it: where pagan Rome had been hostile to the Semitic Hannibal, Christian Rome, he knew, was in some elemental way hostile to him. And yet, like his hero, Freud was always striving to get there. Always striving but never arriving.

In the 1897 letter, written when he was in his early forties, Freud informed Fliess, "This year in fact I did not reach Rome any more than [Hannibal] did from Lake Trasimeno." Halfway between Florence and Rome, the lake had been the site of a major battle in 217 BCE. The Battle of Trasimene was one of Hannibal's most decisive victories over the Romans and one of the most shattering defeats the Roman Republic had yet endured. According to the Greek historian Polybius, more than fifteen thousand Roman soldiers lost their lives. The following year, Hannibal won another astounding victory, this time at Cannae, a supply town more than two hundred miles southeast of Rome. Although Roman troops outnumbered Hannibal's by a ratio of two to one, an astonishing number of those fighting for Rome died in the battle. Because of the totality of his triumph in the face of extremely hostile odds, Hannibal's victory at Cannae is often seen as the greatest tactical success in Western military history. But even after Cannae, with the Roman army in shambles, Hannibal knew he could not defeat Rome head-on. For nearly fifteen years, until he was recalled to Carthage, he and his army wandered the Italian peninsula, menacing Rome from afar and engaging in small battles. But neither Hannibal nor his army ever laid eyes on the capital city itself. As Freud traipsed up and down the same peninsula in his own elusive search for Rome, he carried Hannibal's experience in his mind.

In 1898, almost a year after his about-face, Freud continued to anguish about his prospects of getting to Rome: "I am not sufficiently collected . . . to do anything . . . other than possibly studying the topography of Rome, the yearning for which becomes ever more tormenting." Ten months later, at the end of summer, he was still daydreaming. "What would you think," he asked Fliess, "of ten days in Rome at Easter (the two of us, of course) if all goes well, if I can afford it . . . ? A long-standing promise!

Learning about the eternal laws of life for the first time in the Eternal City would not be a bad combination." But once again, he did not make it.

Freud's fascination with Rome was such that, before ever having set foot on a Roman street, he made a metaphor out of the city. In *The Interpretation of Dreams*, which he published in 1899, Freud likened daydreams to a Roman palazzo built out of fragments left over from the past that have been mixed, rearranged, and reconstituted into something new. Our minds, as Freud saw it, are the composite result of countless fragments. Freud could find no better city than Rome—than the seemingly whole Roman palazzo rising from the chaos of a million fragments—to represent the inner workings of our minds. The power that Freud attributed to Rome as a paradox of renascence and ruin simultaneously attracted and repelled him. On the one hand, the accretion of human history in Rome captivated him. But on the other, what countless traumas, he wondered, lay buried, dormant, in its soil?

In August 1901, when he was forty-five years old, Freud finally overcame his trepidation, and, for the first time, set foot in the Italian capital. In a letter to Fliess, he described his arrival as "overwhelming," and "a high point of my life." So taken was he with Rome's ancient ruins that "I could have worshiped the abased and mutilated remnant of the Temple of Minerva," he wrote. And he found the modern capital city to be "full of promise and likable." But medieval Rome, the spiritual center of a persecutory, anti-Semitic Catholicism, weighed heavily on him. "I found it difficult," he wrote, "to tolerate the lie concerning man's redemption, which raises its head to high heaven—for I could not cast off the thought of my own misery and all the other misery I know about." Even though elements of its history discomfited him, Rome would never again trouble Freud as it had before. He had finally arrived.

Decades later, Freud returned to the theme of Rome in *Civilization and Its Discontents*. By the time of its publication in 1930, Freud was again investigating the connection between Rome and the human psyche. Specifically, he likened the accretion of history to the topography of the mind: "Let us make the fantastic supposition that Rome were not a human dwelling-place, but a mental entity with just as long and varied a past history." By means of this thought experiment, Freud tried to sort out what happens to memories: Do they lie submerged, or, once forgotten, do they disappear entirely? How stratified are the layers of our personal histories? How interlaced are memories, how interdependent upon one another? To answer this question, Freud challenged his readers to imagine the notion of Rome as a place "in which nothing once constructed had perished, and all the earlier stages of development had survived alongside the latest." For Freud, the idea that the human mind could be described as an infinite pile of unsorted mental debris was unsettling.

Let's take, as an example, the Pantheon. To achieve what Freud asked, we must envision the building as it stands today, as the Church of Santa Maria ad Martyres, and hold that image alongside all of the building's previous iterations, going back to the structure built by Agrippa and the ancient temple, now buried, that preceded it. We must, as it were, go down into the earth and pull up every structure standing there as it has ever existed. We must see the ancient temple smoking with fires, Agrippa's building riven by earthquake, cracked by lightning. Alongside those images of destruction, we must imagine the building restored, patched, emptied of debris. We must see it gleam in bright sunlight, see it slick with rain on a winter's night, hold in our minds a shower of hail cascading through its oculus. We must see gilded bronze tiles go up, come down, the massive bronze doors close into place. We must watch the bronze letters of the original inscription fall off, one by one, then watch as centuries later they are replaced. We must imagine the pediment free of Christian symbolism, then watch it acquire a single bell tower on one side of the facade, then another bell tower on the other, listen as passersby mutter about the indignity of what they call those "asses' ears," and think how strangely bare the structure must have looked the day the towers were finally removed. We must observe the cement gradually pocking under acid rain and glimpse the black layers of automobile fumes accumulating on the outer walls. In short, we must hold all time—distant past up to the present, and every iteration in between—equally before us in space. This was Freud's challenge.

He could not do it. "The same space," he concluded, "will not hold two contents." Not two, nor two hundred, nor the infinite number needed to contain such a history. To continue the thought experiment further would be an "idle game." Ultimately, Freud concluded that the human psyche cannot be understood by means of visual representation. And so the uses of Rome for Freud's psychological theory fell short of his initial aspirations. All the same, the city served in his life's work as a potent source of creative energy, born of both fear and desire, and it deeply informed his quest to locate the connections between individual memories and dreams, and the long arc of history.

⊸⌀⌁

Sixty-some years after Freud devised his thought experiment, I watched from the taxi as the Roman countryside flew by. Early-morning sunlight was already scattered among the unruly grasses and poppies in the fields beside the highway. Atmospheric heat refracted through the glass windows, gently baking Annie and me into a stupor.

We curved around a field out of which rose a stone pedestal and some fragments of a column. Or was it a statue? I sat up straighter to see. "Annie," I said, "look." A hundred yards off, in the middle of a field, was an ancient wall, now playing host to the weeds and wildflowers that sprouted from between its bricks.

I had never seen ancient objects so wild, so free in their abandonment. All the ancient things I knew were cordoned off in museums, preserved by the cotton-gloved hands of professionals—objects labeled and lined up, like butterflies snuffed of life and pinned to boards. Where I came from, a house seventy years old was historical, had a plaque affixed to its wall. Here was something different. Here, my first glance seemed to confirm, the past could go on living alongside the present. It could even, the ancient wall seemed to say, be free.

Salty with heat and spinning with jet lag, we clambered out of the taxi in front of the Hotel de la Ville before nine o'clock. Much of the street before us was still awash in morning shadow. As we retrieved our backpacks from the taxi's trunk, I drew a deep breath. Fresh and brisk, with traces of pine and diesel exhaust. But the sun, already rising over the Spanish Steps just behind us, hit hot on my shoulders.

The fancy hotel stay was a gift from Annie's parents, who wanted their daughter's first experience of Rome to be plush and forgiving. Rotating glass doors spun us into silk brocade, gilt frames, and tasseled curtains. Our room would not be ready for a few hours. Having never traveled alone, we were unaware that we could ask the hotel to watch our bags, and no one offered. Disappointed, we settled in for the long haul on a cool, thickly upholstered couch. We lounged, first upright and then increasingly slouched and spread-eagled, our bodies sinking into the cushions, our long hair spreading messily over the back of the sofa, our heads lolling off to one side and then the other.

The clock wound its way forward in fits and starts. A half hour sailed by, followed by ten interminable minutes of sleepless haze, hotel guests much older and better dressed than we fumbling through papers at reception, murmuring about breakfast, inquiring about a taxi here or a ticket there. It was past noon when the receptionist—with a sigh that revealed his relief at our imminent departure from his lobby—finally handed us a

•

key. It had a silk tassel, little spirals of red threads, each one tidily knotted at the end.

Our room, as I remember it, was appointed with two tall windows draped from ceiling to floor in thick green silk. I remember a commanding armoire made of dark wood that had been polished so that the sinew of its grain glowed. The room felt sumptuous, but also surprisingly austere. The way a church, say, can feel at the same time both ornate and dour.

No sooner were we in the room than we looked for ways out. Facing us on the other side of the street was a sienna-colored building whose windowed facade looked so much like a mirror that I half expected our own images to be reflected back to us. I reached up and turned a brass knob on the window frame, and the pane of glass swung in. Right away the mournful wail of a scooter filled the room. Followed by that tickle in the nose, diesel exhaust. I leaned as far out as I could and craned my head to the left. Via Sistina extended straight and long and narrow, and as far as the eye could see.

Of the month Annie and I planned to spend in Italy, ten days would be spent in Rome, five at either end. Those first five days, we set out onto the city streets each morning armed with a list of Very Important Places that Annie's father, a Roman history enthusiast, had compiled for us, and which we at first took very seriously. I remember that we traipsed around the Colosseum in a blinding midday light, and that we sat for a picnic lunch in the grassy remains of the Circus Maximus. That our New Englanders' stride was too brisk for languid, early-summer Rome, and that I struggled to move at a suitably slow pace. That I made an effort to walk straight and tall, copying the young Italian women around me. That we jostled for miles along narrow sidewalks, choking on diesel exhaust, chanting "the ants go marching one by one" to relieve the tedium of our almost soldierly marches. That we obeyed the guards wearing sunglasses and spiffy suits who made us cover our shoulders before entering Saint Peter's, and that we lined up to plunge our hands into the marble mouth of the Bocca della Verità, which according to legend will bite the hands of those who lie. (It did not bite ours.) That we marveled at the oculus in the Pantheon's ceiling, and also, no less, at the legions of minuscule three-wheeler trucks, the armies of pigeons, the parade of cats, and even the solo cart-bound donkey that swayed, unimpressed and half asleep, before the Pantheon's great portico. I remember that we drank peach juice with the zeal of converts, and that we ate at a restaurant with no menu called Der Pallaro, which upended my idea of what a restaurant was, because, as I wrote in my journal, ANYTHING THEY FEEL LIKE COOKING, YOU EAT. YUM!

I remember, too, the attentions of men and boys who whistled, clucked, serenaded, hazarded their *ciao bella*s and their best guesses as to our country of provenance (*Americana? Inglese? Tedesca? May I pay you a compliment?*), and feeling in response variously perplexed, interested, unnerved, flattered, self-conscious, and annoyed. But however I actually felt, I tried to appear unperturbed, confident, and determined, like I knew where I was going and could not be blown off course. I remember studying the route to our destination before leaving the hotel or restaurant, because, as we quickly learned, there was no greater magnet for boys than foreign girls consulting a map. I remember the way some sidled up next to us in a brooding silence that implored us to acknowledge them, and the way others were more insistent, and that to the latter, Annie sometimes reacted with force. However they approached us, it felt to me like a game whose script had already been written: their obligation was to make the approach, and ours was to turn them down. They seemed to expect, in fact, that we would, and did not seem at all heartbroken over it when we did. I remember enjoying the attention when it was scarce and polite, for we met a few boys who came across as curious and kind. But I remember, too, feeling as if we were always on display, and in my self-consciousness, which was not just about men but also about my place in the greater world, I struggled with how to *be*.

I remember the great quantity of graffiti. Some poetic, some political. Some funny, if puzzling—so many ducks!—and some decidedly less so, such as swastikas. We were at first dumbfounded when we came across swastikas on walls, paving stones, and ancient columns. Sometimes we spotted them beside, and even over, proclamations of love—*Valentina ti amo*—scribbled in marker. We were surprised, too, by the casual way people strolled past them on the street. Annie soon took to chipping at the walls with rocks to remove them, while I cowered nearby, worried we would be arrested for destruction of property.

I felt that there was no end to what we could find, if only we just kept walking. That in traipsing and jostling, in striding with feigned confidence or learning to walk slowly, in speaking or withholding a *ciao*, and in bypassing or confronting graffiti, we were taking the first steps on an adventure that would come to define us in ways we could not yet know. Those early days were at times bewildering, and I struggled hourly with a hundred forms of unease—yet I was exactly where I wanted to be.

On the afternoon of our second day in Rome, Annie and I visited Villa Borghese. The park offered us respite from the heat and crowds of the city center and relieved us of the self-consciousness we felt on city streets. We were driven in those first days by the determination, rooted in a combination of self-defense and pride, to look at all times like we knew where we were going, so reluctant were we to appear naive, or lost, or vulnerable in any way. Which is, of course, exactly what we were. And so for a while we sat on a park bench, fanning ourselves with our city maps. We watched people, mostly couples, strolling by. We let go, as best we could, of the constraints of our own awkwardness. Later, while Annie was out calling her parents, I sprawled across the cool green coverlet of our bed. I wrote an entry in my journal: "I am going to live in Rome someday."

On our third day, we venture to the Tre Scalini. From across Piazza Navona, I spot the café's awnings unfurled against the midday blaze. Under them, a host of small tables, and chrome chairs crisscrossed with cane. Annie and I cross the sunlit piazza and step into what I remember as a cool marble, chrome, brass, and dark wood interior. Thinking of Mr. V, I order the *tartufo cioccolato*. A waiter intuits that we would like to sit and shows us to a table outside. We each pull up a chair, squinting in the bright shade. Just a few paces off, a fountain gurgles away. It feels peaceful, the fountain, despite the tumultuous scene—man battling octopus, horse rearing in panic—it depicts.

The *tartufo* arrives. It is simple, beautiful. A roughly hewn cylinder of chocolate as dark as earth. A white ceramic plate below, a snowy tuft of whipped cream above. Lying across its top, like a jaunty hat, is a profiterole.

"*Dal 1946*," the café signs say. Since 1946. The year my grandmother arrived in Rome. It didn't cross my mind then, but I wonder now if my grandparents ever ate here. If they, too, sat on caned café chairs, squinting against the sunlight, daydreaming of the brighter world heralded by the *tartufo cioccolato*. And whether, in the years following the Second World War, after all its legions of privations and profound devastations, to eat a chocolate truffle felt any different. When the memory of war and death and the tyranny of hunger was still in the air. When women were washing clothing in the Trevi Fountain and gaunt children hawking street finds for a penny. When the Jewish quarter, only half a mile away, was still eerily empty, over a thousand of its residents having been boxed, packaged, shipped, and murdered. Whether the pleasure of a newfangled confection then was greater. Or whether it felt indecent.

Time changes even the simple act of eating. The same chocolate truffle, produced with identical ingredients and served on the very same plate, might seem like one thing today, and something else entirely tomorrow.

Reading your essay is like—I wedge the metal spoon into the truffle's firm carapace, extract a deposit, deliver it upon my tongue—*having a tartufo cioccolato at the Tre Scalini cafe.* The chocolate hits you first as temperature. Against a warm tongue, it is very cool. Neither cold, like ice cream, nor room temperature, like cake. It is something all its own. The cocoa flavor, deep and dark, floats in next, somewhere between bitter and sweet. When you begin to chew, thick shavings of hard chocolate bump up against the insides of your cheeks. By the third bite, the whipped cream makes its entrance, leaving a waxy residue on the roof of your mouth.

In my journal that night, I sum up my experience: "It was amazing. I've been wanting that for months. I love Rome!"

So cheery, so blithe. So adept at not reporting anything real.

The truth was, I did not find it amazing, exactly.

It was tasty, to be sure. But in its richness, its unfamiliar texture, the waxiness it left on my palate and lips, the truffle was strange. But it was more complicated than that. Eating the *tartufo* was not only about the flavor. When I ate it, I had the pleased, and slightly incredulous, feeling of accomplishing a major objective. Less than a year before, I had written an essay. My teacher wrote a response. I worked, saved, embarked upon a new language, and crossed an ocean. There, I tasted something new. It was not "amazing." It was both less than amazing and much more. Wrapped up in the *tartufo* was the effort and work of the past school year, the daydreaming and the deciphering, the pushing at the outer limits of my world. In it were the discoveries of worlds past, the anticipations of worlds future, and the heady feeling of growing into someone whose contours I was just beginning to perceive. What I loved, what *was* amazing to me, was not the *tartufo* per se, but the accomplishment of attaining it.

⤶⤸

My memories of the *tartufo*, of dining at Der Pallaro, of discovering peach juice, and of sitting on the windowsill in our hotel room are specific memories, and in their specificity, they lend the impression of reliability. In my mind's eye, each of those memories is embedded in an image: the *tartufo*'s chunky chocolate gleaming in the sun; the beaded curtain that separated the outdoor patio of Der Pallaro, where we ate, from the restaurant's interior, which we never saw; the dark recesses of the small shop on via del Corso where we searched refrigerated shelves for peach juice; the luster of the green silk curtains in our hotel room. Each of these memories arrives in a single frame, like a photograph, stilling time. The frame surely *is* the memory.

But if I prod the frame a bit, sensory details begin to emerge. I feel the waxiness of the *tartufo* on the roof of my mouth; I hear the crash of a plate, dropped, as it shattered on the floor at Der Pallaro; I recall the dewy sweetness of chilled peach nectar as it slid down the throat; I feel the smooth brush of the silk curtains as we pulled them back to lean out our window and take in the city; I smell the acrid exhaust—diesel, pleasing in its novelty—as it singed our nasal cavities.

I want to trust these images and the sensory details that emerge from them, but the historian in me knows something about the perils of memory. Now, nearly three decades later, I pull out my photo album from that first trip. It is the first time in many years that I have consulted it. The sixth photo in the album is of a room I do not recognize. It shows a bed with a flowered pink coverlet, and behind it, a small white desk and chair beneath a mirror. In the corner stands an armchair, and in the center of the room, a single window framed by long, flowery curtains, also pink.

Curious, I extract the photo from its plastic sleeve and read the words scrawled on the back: "Our room in Hotel de La Ville/Roma."

I turn the photo over again and examine the room that my own handwriting insists was ours. I can believe it only reluctantly. The room looks neither "sumptuous" nor "austere." It looks fusty. And so small. Were I shown this photo under penalty of perjury, I would swear before the court that never in my life had I been in it.

Adding to the case against me: There was no green coverlet. There were no green silk curtains, nor any "commanding armoire made of dark wood that had been polished so that the sinew of its grain glowed." So what was this *other* room I thought I remembered? One in which solid green dominated what in fact had been patterned pink, in which dark wood convincingly substituted for a painted white. My mind had completely altered every aspect of it.

It should not have surprised me. The inaccuracies, the inventions of memory, are the sign of the interpreting self. They are the signal, the proof, that we have run our memories through the mill of interpretation and assigned them meaning. What meaning they hold for us might not be immediately apparent, but meaning they have, for had they lacked significance, they would have long since been relegated, like most of our lived experience, to oblivion. That I remember our room in Hotel de la Ville at all is evidence of its relevance.

And that's the rub of it. The details may have been all wrong, but the essential feeling of the memory was right. Namely: that although our hotel room was a refuge from a chaotic, bright, and unfamiliar city, Annie and I felt out of place in it.

Between the two of us, Annie and me, it was I, the incidental corecipient of her parents' gift, who belonged there less. The significant cost of their gift had not escaped my notice. The plush hotel made me self-conscious of my general state of being—young, awkward, flagrantly lacking in the worldliness I so craved. In my memory, perhaps I ramped up the room's masculine formality, introducing the gleaming wood and the silk curtains and coverlet because, as an eighteen-year-old girl who had scraped for months to make the trip happen, that was just how odd a fit I felt in it.

༺⚬༻

My journal from that trip affords scant attention to the details of that room. Aside from the room number (203), it contains merely a mention of the street outside (via Sistina, beautiful) and of two qualities related to the window: light (lovely) and noise (deafening when open). Instead, the teenage girl reflected in the journal is focused on making sense of the place and culture outside that room. She tends toward abstraction and an antiquated writing style. The result is stilted and self-conscious. She makes perplexing logical leaps. She is preoccupied with her youth, which she views as a shortcoming, and with being "naïve." She worries about how strangers perceive her. She does not want to be seen as "American," but she does not know quite what "American" means to her, or what it means, precisely, to others.

At the same time, she is enthusiastic about the task of travel. She assesses what resonates with her and what does not, and why. Some places she dismisses cursorily, for reasons never articulated, but often she is curious about the place before her, and its history. The lens through which she views the world is often odd to her adult self, but one senses an effort to challenge her own preconceived notions.

JUNE 15, 1993: [ON THE PLANE]
6:15 AM. This whole trip feels right to me.

JULY [SIC] 16: ROME
Rome seems to me a very civilized city. The people here are used to being crowded, shouted at, whistled to, and run over by cars and Vespas.
[The waiter] told me that I was not like other Americans.

JULY [SIC] 18: ROME

I had a tartuffo *[sic]* ciocolato *[sic] at the Tre Scalini Café. It was amazing. I've been wanting that for months. I love Rome!*

JULY [SIC] 19: ROME

[On meeting two Roman boys:] I had peach juice to drink, which I love, and both Luco [sic] and Marco had milk with mint, which was disgusting. They tried to hold our hands, and in the end, to kiss us, but they were too gross and I told them so.

JUNE 21: POMPEII/SORRENTO

Too many guys approach us. Annie is offended and afraid.

We swam offshore, then found out it is horribly polluted. I got 13 splinters in my right foot from little sea porcupines. Probably will die from some disease.

JUNE 26: FLORENCE

I love the Italian language. Here in Florence, our room overlooks Piazza Filippo Brunelleschi. During the hot afternoon hours, I lie in bed and I listen to the voices that pass.

I miss the enchantment of <u>Rome</u>.

JUNE 30: BOLOGNA

[Bologna] is a city full of universities, even of the first university in Europe. Therefore, there is a great diversity of people around the town. The people are . . . the most honestly congenial of any that we've seen so far. One random girl said ciao *to us.*

JULY 2: SIENA

[Following the Palio, *the historical horse race held in the city's main piazza:] Today I saw a ghost and witnessed Death.*

July 7: Orta San Giulio, Lake Orta

I have not written since the day of the Palio. *On that day, a horse died in front of my eyes. I will never again go to that race.*

In the other days on which I still abandoned my diary, I went to Venice and then left. I do not like Venice.

July 11: In transit

HOME AGAIN TO ROME AGAIN!

By the journal's end, the room at Hotel de la Ville was a distant memory to the girl. She and her friend would spend the last four nights of their trip in a budget hotel in Rome's city center, where the housekeeping staff furtively eat nearly half of the Baci chocolates she bought as gifts for her family. She writes nothing more of Rome other than how happy she is to be back, but of the substance of that feeling, or of what it is in Rome, specifically, that makes her feel that way, she has left no trace.

❧

Saint Agnes, the patron saint of girls, was buried outside Rome's walls, in a church along the via Nomentana that bears her name. At some point, her skull was detached and carried back into the city, where it now resides in a church in Piazza Navona.

Saint Birgitta of Sweden was forty-seven by the time she got to Rome. Bits of her skeleton remain in residence in her church in Piazza Farnese.

Saint Catherine of Siena left her body, minus her head and one thumb, and possibly a foot, in the Church of Santa Maria sopra Minerva.

———

Santa Cecilia was buried in the catacombs. Five or six hundred years after she died, a pope unearthed her remains and reburied them in a peaceful section of Trastevere.

Saints Digna and Emerita were martyred in Rome. The Church of San Marcello al Corso claims that both women reside in full under the main altar.

Saint Frances Xavier Cabrini, the patron saint of immigrants, was born in Lombardy and died in the United States. While most of her remains lie in New York City, her heart was returned to Lombardy, and her head was sent to Rome.

Saint Helena, mother of Constantine, left bits of herself behind in the Church of Santa Maria in Aracoeli, at the top of the Capitoline Hill, looking out over all Rome.

Saint Mary Magdalene died in Ephesus, but her left foot resides in a reliquary box, crafted by Benvenuto Cellini, in the Church of San Giovanni dei Fiorentini, nestled inside the Tiber's bend.

Saint Teresa of Ávila was born and died in Spain. During his long dictatorship, Francisco Franco kept one of her hands close by at all times, embracing it even on his deathbed. But Teresa's right foot had long hied off to Rome, finding sanctuary in the Church of Santa Maria della Scala in Trastevere.

Girls and women from far and wide, leaving bits and pieces of themselves behind in Rome. Rome, scrap heap of bodies and souls.

My memory, having been confronted with factual evidence of its own act of invention thanks to the photograph of the room at Hotel de la Ville, is now in crisis. At first, I observe as it unwittingly tries to assemble a collage, something like Freud's palazzo in *The Interpretation of Dreams:* a green coverlet, some flowered curtains, a smattering of dark wood, a small white desk. But it's no use. The pastiche cannot hold. The two images, the green and the pink, are irreconcilable.

As the fragments of Freud's palazzo pry apart, my original memory grows harder to retrieve. To visualize the room as I saw it for decades in my mind's eye, I must now make a conscious effort, and when I do, it survives only for a flash—a fraction of a second, maybe—before my mind overwrites it with the pink room documented in the photo. But the pink room holds no emotional resonance. It is flat, dead. And it is destroying the original memory.

The room with the green silk curtains has begun to warp and vanish like a photo that, licked by flames, bubbles up and curls in on itself. I don't think it will survive for long. By writing about the room, I have not preserved its memory—I have given it up. So, too, the girl who wrote the journal: the more I reach for her, the more she recedes.

The girl left Italy and returned to America. But something of her, a fragment of her being, remained behind.

11.

AMERICAN BEATRICE

The previous school year, as I sat each evening in my bedroom bent over my Italian workbook, I did so beneath a poster that a friend had gifted me in ninth grade. It was a black-and-white image by the photographer Ruth Orkin titled *American Girl in Italy* (1951). In the photo, a tall young woman strides down a city sidewalk through a gauntlet of men who regard her from all sides. The motion of her calf-length skirt makes it clear she is walking briskly. Of the fifteen men pictured in the photo, a few are laughing and apparently joking around, one whistles and grabs his crotch suggestively, and the rest look impassively on. With her back straight and her eyes downcast to avoid their collective gaze, the young woman seems to be willfully ignoring them. This image would remain on my bedroom wall for a decade, until early 2000, when my mother sold the house.

Though it wouldn't be accurate to say that Ruth Orkin's photograph led me to Rome, it was under the gaze of that American girl striding down a sidewalk in Italy that my first impressions of the country were formed. My other initial sources of information about Italy—Dante, Boccaccio, Petrarch, Salvatore Quasimodo, Italo Calvino, Giambattista Vico, Umberto Eco—were all male, but here was a woman, photographed by another woman, in whose photo I saw some of my own early dreams and aspirations. To me, she appeared courageous and independent. She stood so tall and straight, like she knew exactly where she was going. Her beauty was simple, unadorned. I was curious about the experience she was having, what it felt like to walk down a street in Italy and be noticed like that. Even her leather sandals spoke to me of adventure. They seemed like the kind of shoes that Penelope, queen of Ithaca, might have worn had she, rather than her husband, set out on a journey to the limits of the known world. Like a ship's bow parting the waters, the young woman creates the motion of the photo. She slices it across the diagonal while the men, static, stand idly by.

As it turns out, both Ruth Orkin and her subject were young women with a penchant for adventure. Back in 1939, when Orkin was seventeen, she traveled alone, in turn by bike and by accepting rides in cars, from her home in Los Angeles to attend and photograph the World's Fair in New York City. In August 1951, she found herself in Florence. She was twenty-nine years old and on her way back from Israel following a commission by *Life* magazine to document daily life in the newly founded Zionist state. At Hotel Berchielli, where she was staying for one dollar a night, she ran into a (in her words) "luminescent" six-foot-tall American woman who, having just graduated from college, was traveling solo around France, Spain, and Italy. The two connected immediately. Orkin had been incubating an idea for a project about women traveling alone, and she asked her new friend if she would mind being her subject for a day. The friend, Ninalee Allen—who at the time went by the nickname "Jinx"—was enthusiastic, and the following day, the two wandered around Florence while Orkin documented Ninalee in a variety of situations—walking, visiting monuments, reading, riding in an open-topped car, on the back of a scooter, and flirting with men in cafés. "We were literally horsing around," Ninalee would later say.

A year later, a selection of photos from that day was included in an article in *Cosmopolitan* magazine entitled "Don't Be Afraid to Travel Alone." One of these was the photo of Ninalee striding down the street in Florence. It ran with the following caption: "Public admiration . . . shouldn't fluster you. Ogling the ladies is a popular, harmless and flattering pastime you'll run into in many foreign countries. The gentlemen are usually louder and more demonstrative than American men, but they mean no harm."

After its 1952 publication in *Cosmopolitan*, Orkin's photo was largely forgotten. It wasn't until the 1980s, when interest in the documentary photography of the 1950s surged, that the image began to attract widespread attention. Suddenly *American Girl in Italy* began cropping up everywhere: on calendars, mugs, magnets, and postcards. After Robert Doisneau's *The Kiss*, *American Girl in Italy* would soon become the second-best-selling poster in the world, ending up publicly displayed on restaurant and shop walls all over Italy and North America, as well as in many private homes, such as mine.

Later still, the photo would garner renewed attention as the public conversation about what constitutes sexual harassment took shape. In 2011, the photo was displayed at a Toronto gallery as part of a sixty-year retrospective. Orkin had passed away in 1985, but when her now-eighty-three-year-old subject was asked about it by journalists, Ninalee Craig (née Allen) strongly defended the photo. "It's not a symbol of harassment," she said. "It's a symbol of a woman having an absolutely wonderful time!" At another exhibition a few years earlier, Craig explained, "I clutched my shawl to me because that sheaths the body. It was my protection, my shield. I was walking through a sea of men. I was enjoying every minute of it." At the retrospective, she smiled broadly in front of the photograph—wearing the same bright-orange shawl that she had worn on that August day in Florence sixty years earlier.

Many who view *American Girl in Italy* today cannot see it with Craig's joyful innocence. In 2017, a Philadelphia restaurant removed it from display after receiving dozens of complaints from customers. Where viewers,

myself included, once saw an independent adventurous woman, many now see a woman under siege, protectively clutching at her shawl while a group of men ogles her.

Until her death in 2018, Craig remained resolute in her stance that there was nothing wrong with the behavior of the men in the photo—and Orkin and Craig both vocally resisted the idea that the photo was staged. The photo contact sheet, however, tells a more complicated story. The first shot on the contact sheet shows Craig crossing the street just beyond the familiar corner. Many fewer men are discernible, and the photo captures little sense of Craig's brisk movement. The next image is the iconic one that hung on my bedroom wall. In this second photo, Craig is a few steps behind where she was in the first image; she must have retraced her steps to walk the same route again.

When interviewed in 1979, Orkin revealed the reason for this, telling *The New York Times* that the first time Craig walked down the sidewalk, she "clutched at herself and looked terribly frightened." So Orkin asked her to try it again. "I told her to walk by the second time, 'as if it's killing you but you're going to make it,'" she said. By some accounts, she also apparently instructed the man on the Lambretta to tell the others not to look directly at her camera. Despite her protestations, it's clear that Orkin was less interested in capturing Craig's lived experience, whatever that might have been, than in rendering an image already present in her mind's eye. "The idea for this picture had been in my mind for years," she explained, "ever since I had been old enough to go through the experience myself." One presumes that Orkin was referring to being catcalled on the street, but given that she had been in Italy only a short time, it seems safe to say that her previous experience with it had occurred elsewhere. By capturing the moment in Florence, however, Orkin's photo drew some of its power by playing on the popular image of Italian men and the way they behaved with women.

We might find this questionable—like designing a study to obtain the specific result you hope for. "Art is always difficult," the photographer, art historian, and writer Teju Cole has written, "but it is especially difficult when it comes to telling other people's stories. And it is ferociously difficult when those others are tangled up in your history and you are tangled up in theirs." Orkin was telling that most ancient and universal of stories, that of a beautiful young woman navigating her crowd of suitors. In this vein, Craig is Penelope, she is Helen, just as she is Cleopatra and Eurydice and Nefertiti. But a second story, that of the attractive foreigner in Italy, underlies this photo. It is not happenstance that Craig is fair-skinned and tall and slender, the archetype of white female beauty. And that she is surrounded by men who are, largely, darker and shorter than she. As much as I admire Orkin's work, when I look at *American Girl in Italy* now, I see a photographer using an available "script"—foreign woman, Italian men—as much to narrate her own story as to chronicle her subject's lived experience.

When our time as American girls in Italy came, of the two of us, it was Annie who felt more threatened. She attracted more attention than I did—she has always been tall and athletic, blue-eyed, blond, and beautiful. The whistling and pickup lines thrown at us by boys and men genuinely flustered her, to the point that several times she reacted aggressively, either pushing them away from her or, if they were particularly persistent, spitting at them. My cheeks would burn at the public spectacle, and yet I was too meek to take any sort of stand with the ferocity that Annie could summon at the drop of a single *ciao bella*. As the child of two strong-willed parents, the oldest sibling, and the only girl, I was most comfortable in the role of mediator. My instinct was to play mediator there, too. I wished to explain to the Italian boys that my friend didn't like their attention, and explain to Annie that we were not at home, that the rules were different but that we would be all right. Of course, I didn't, and couldn't.

Only many years later did Annie confess how hard our trip had been for her. Those episodes in the street with boys had given her panic attacks. They came on at night, and she suffered them quietly. The two of us had shared a hotel room, spent twenty-four hours a day together for a month, but I had been blithely unaware of the depth of my friend's distress. It is hard now to think about her struggling to breathe, wiping away tears, while I read quietly away in the next bed, dreaming of the adventures the next day would bring.

Ognuno sta solo. Each of us stands alone on the heart of the earth. I was too young then to perceive, or believe, the brevity of life, the sudden arrival of its evening that Quasimodo's poem captures so well. But setting out in Italy had transfixed me, opened me up to what felt like bright sunlight. *The chirping of birds, the click-clack of shoes on cobblestone.* I buzzed with curiosity and good spirits, was hungry for adventure. But I was also *trafitto da un raggio di sole*, pinned down by this light, pierced by it, and from that transfixing I would never recover or be quite the same. And in its thrall, I remained isolated, *sola*, oblivious to the suffering of the person at my side.

When Ruth Orkin created her now-famous photograph, she was trying to capture an image or experience from elsewhere that she already held in her mind's eye. But she was not the only one doing this. Ninalee Craig also carried a scene in her mind. Striding through the group of men, Craig, who had recently studied Dante at Sarah Lawrence College, said that she imagined herself as Beatrice, Dante's unattainable love object and muse. "Beatrice in *The Divine Comedy*, that is who my inspiration was," Craig explained. "Walking about Florence, I felt I was Beatrice, with great dignity to uphold."

I marvel at this fact. Like Freud carrying Hannibal in his mind, Craig was carrying Beatrice, a woman who lived seven hundred years earlier and who is known exclusively through the prism of the man who memorialized her.

In *Inferno*, Beatrice is mentioned but does not appear. Virgil explains early in the first canto that Beatrice sent him to help Dante (the traveler), who has just awoken, lost and afraid, in the dark wood. When I set off for Italy for the first time, I knew that Beatrice was an essential element of the universe of *The Divine Comedy* and an allegory for Divine Love. But I would have been hard-pressed to elaborate on what that meant. Aside from knowing her status as muse, I had little sense of who Beatrice was in Dante's text. In this perception, or really lack thereof, I was certainly not alone, for Beatrice, as I now know, does not appear "in person" until the end of *Purgatorio*, where she supplants Virgil as Dante's guide through *Paradiso*. As I would later discover, Beatrice was no shrinking violet. But like many readers, I had initially dropped off at the end of *Inferno*, long before reaching her in *Purgatorio*'s earthly paradise.

So who was Beatrice? Many scholars, following an attribution by Boccaccio, believe her to have been Beatrice "Bice" di Folco Portinari, daughter and wife of Florentine bankers. Bice and Dante were one year apart in age, and although they grew up in the same city, it appears they met only twice—once at a garden party when he was nine, and she eight, and the second time as young adults when she passed him on the street. She died in the last decade of the thirteenth century at the unripe age of twenty-

five, and Dante would spend the rest of his life writing of—and perhaps
for—her.

The Hotel Berchielli, where Orkin and Craig met that August day in
1951, still exists. Curious about whether the hotel was claiming *American
Girl in Italy* as part of its history, I checked it out online. I found nothing
about the photo. I was, however, surprised to find that an earlier painting
of Dante and Beatrice had been incorporated into a piece of Hotel Berchielli marketing.

Painted in the early 1880s by the British artist Henry Holiday when he
was visiting Italy, it depicts the second presumed meeting of Dante and
Beatrice, that fleeting scene in which they were said to have passed each
other on the street. In Holiday's rendering, Dante leans with studied ease
on the stone wall of the Santa Trinità Bridge in Florence while Beatrice—
tall and straight—strides by with her friend and a maidservant. Beatrice
does not look her admirer in the eye but instead keeps her gaze fixed on
the street before her as she approaches an intersection. Her long white
dress is in motion from the briskness of her walk; her left arm—the one
closest to Dante—crosses her chest, protectively holding a rose. The com-

positional similarities between Holiday's nineteenth-century painting and Orkin's twentieth-century photograph are nothing short of striking.

The hotel's promotional image is not dated, but it has a vintage luster that lends credence to the notion that Orkin and Craig could very well have seen it in passing. And in fact, a few years before her death, Craig acknowledged that she was still carrying around a "tacky" postcard she had bought in Italy the year Orkin photographed her. On that postcard was Henry Holiday's painting of Dante and Beatrice.

∽✍つ

Craig described in an interview with an Italian paper how singular she had felt as a woman traveling alone in the 1950s: "Italy was spread out before me. There were still hardly any tourists back then. I was alone at the top of the Tower of Pisa. Even the Sistine Chapel was practically empty. I have no idea how long I sat there looking at the ceiling." Craig was living out a modern woman's adventure story. And yet she identified with Beatrice—a woman who had lived more than half a millennium before her, whose life was in all likelihood restricted in countless ways, and about whom next to nothing is known.

It is astonishing to think that the past can be carried this way. That a past so remote that it has nearly been lost to time can still manifest in the body language of a woman striding down a city street. That it can reverberate—clamor, even—in our minds and our footsteps with such precision. That it can mold the very way we see ourselves and the places we inhabit. Ninalee Craig or Jinx Allen, Beatrice or Bice, call her what you will. She is not real. She is one image refracted off another off another. And yet I cannot deny that she exists, for I, too, have carried her in my mind.

12.

KEYS TO A WALLED CITY

Back in Boston, leaves hang motionless in the humid midsummer heat while cicadas keep up their monotonous drone. Even the trolley seems static—the same old train going the same old places. I long for motion, jostling pedestrians, honking traffic, howling Vespas, lungs full of diesel exhaust.

One afternoon my parents convene my brothers and me in the computer room and announce their separation. The news catches me by surprise. My father will be moving out. He looks down, shaking his head the way he does at lamentable news. A tear slips down my mother's cheek. And my youngest brother's. This was not the kind of motion I wanted. This is the rug being pulled out from under. Still, I tell myself it's for the best. A story that, for a decade, becomes a mantra.

That night we go to the movies. We sit side by side, glad for the excuse to focus on anything that is not each other. My parents' choice: *Sleepless in Seattle*. It is only much later that I notice the bitter irony of my family watching a romantic comedy on the very evening that the romance that bound it together officially came undone.

―――――

Of the month that follows my parents' announcement until the day I leave for college, I will remember nothing. On the heels of that sunlit month in Italy, abundant with memories, comes a month that has slipped into the void.

When the day comes for me to leave for Vassar, the five of us pile into the station wagon. In my memory of that three-hour drive west to the Hudson Valley, everyone looks off in different directions out the car windows.

We pass through the Vassar gate in a long, slow procession of vehicles. For a while everyone collaborates. My father holds the door for my mother. My brother Ben laughs over my new student ID card, in whose photo I appear sweaty and wild-haired from the effort of carrying suitcases up five flights of stairs in late-August heat. I meet my new roommate. Flirtatious and upbeat, she has brought with her every manner of appliance known to humankind. But after my half of the room is set up, my parents and brothers and I having fulfilled our calling, unease about what comes next casts a pall over us. Unlike my brothers, I am poised at the threshold of freedom, my future opening before me. What I feel, though, is a looming sense of undoing. That we are on the cusp of a dismantling, the proportions of which we can hardly grasp.

As I understand it, there is little to be said but *It's all for the best*. When I try to explain—to others or, more frequently, myself—what is happening, this lexicon of stock phrases is all I have at my disposal. I don't yet know that language can go deeper, that it can be used to uncover rather than to obscure.

At the end of the afternoon, I watch our station wagon turn down the long drive and exit the college gate. It will be half a decade before the five of us are together again. And four times that before a semblance of peace— uneasy, bound at any moment to take flight and return to its distant perch—settles upon the land.

~~∂~~

That first semester, Italian 101 is where I am most at home. I am delighted to find that the professor, who is also my first-year adviser, is a Dante scholar. He is a middle-aged American man with kind eyes and a manicured beard. We sit in a circle in his classroom as he spins and turns on his leather-soled brogues, stitching simple sentences together again and again as, slowly, the class catches on. I am impatient. I already know this material, from my cassettes, from my adult-ed night class. I want to learn the conditional, the imperative, the subjunctive. I want to read novels and poetry in Italian, not sentences in a textbook. I am already dreaming of a junior year abroad in Rome, and I want to be ready. But I am not bored by this elegant man in his wool suits, whose caring goodness is apparent. Who chuckles with pleasure as he teaches.

One morning he begins class at the chalkboard, writing in white chalk:

Nel mezz . . .

and at the sight of those letters my heart skips a beat while slowly he completes the line, and then the tercet.

Nel mezzo del cammin di nostra vita . . .

The professor turns cheerfully and prompts us to recite after him. In flawed unison, we maul the first line's eleven syllables, so that they no longer undulate *mezzo staccato* but are unevenly drawled like a flimsy carriage lurching down a potholed lane. I hold myself back from completing the whole tercet, and the one after that, and the one after that.

As our professor summarizes *The Divine Comedy*, my classmates shift in their seats. To them, I think, today's lesson is not so different from yesterday's, the words they have spoken aloud just like any other new words. And so, while reciting the opening tercet together is exciting, it also feels a little like sharing a precious possession with someone who, you realize too late, does not recognize its value. "Possession" because I can't erase the feeling that the words on the chalkboard are somehow mine. In this language that is not mine, the words *Nel mezzo del cammin di nostra vita* feel like they belong to me—but not to me alone, I begin to perceive. They belong to my professor, and to Mr. V, and to others who know and care for them. In this way, even though I am enrolled in the most basic Italian course on offer, I experience an incipient sense of belonging—though to where or what, I cannot precisely articulate.

Introduction to Greek Tragedy meets on Mondays and Wednesdays. We gather in a large room backed by a row of windows: our own amphitheater of sorts. Our professor is tall, slender, and broad-shouldered, and maybe because I sense in her a dedication, a conviction, that reminds me of Mr. V's, she quickly commands my unwavering attention. We read Sophocles's *Antigone* and *Oedipus Rex* as well as tragedies by Aeschylus and Euripides. These plays introduce me to a world even more distant, even more opaque, than Dante's, and I pour myself into the challenge of making sense of them.

In class, the professor draws diagrams on the board: Oedipus, Jocasta, and Laius, bound by a triangle. Then, circumscribed by circles, Jason, Medea, and their children. Stories of families broken. Stories of love gone tragically wrong. I think the Greek tragedies speak to me because they have nothing to do with the world I live in. And because they have everything to do with it. To read them is to reach through time and find yourself, and everyone you know, on the other side. A little altered, maybe, a little strange, like a You that you don't quite know yet but that you suspect might be more You than yet you are. And then, too, there is that wild kindling of the mind, the sparking and crackling when the pieces come together, when what was once distant and opaque transforms, as if by alchemy, into a thing recognizable.

On the weekends, I go beyond the requirements of the class. I visit Vassar's impressive Gothic library, only a two-minute walk from my dorm, and run my hands along the shelves in the stacks, amazed by the multitude of books on all the world lying cheek by jowl. I like the smell in the library—all that paper, perhaps; I feel more at home there than in my dorm, where my classmates have been engaging in rituals like bludgeoning appliances to bits with metal bats and greasing their bodies to see how far they can slide down the hallways. I don't fully know how to use the library catalog yet, and am still learning what it means to study, but, akin to the seriousness once imparted by my tweed blazer, the library's stained glass and iron balustrades and dark wood and reading lamps seem to promise that my time there will not be wasted. At the very least I can nestle myself into a labyrinth of volumes and, in the space of a few hours, travel far beyond the stone wall enclosing our campus.

At Vassar I feel enclosed both by the wall itself and by the very nature of undergraduate life: the drunken dorm-room parties, the socializing day and night, the pervasive feeling that everyone, and perhaps no one more than me, is trying to figure out who they are. The friends I make are a motley crew. We are bound by circumstance, by the fact of having been assigned to the same floor of the same dorm. We get along, get each other's jokes, and occasionally get high. But I don't think we really, in any deeper sense, *get* each other. As friends, I already know we will not last.

Greek tragedy expands where friendships fall short. The course brings me back to Dante, on account not of theme but of the familiar and welcome exhilaration I derive from the process of discovery. In each successive class meeting, the professor hands us the key to a city ours for the taking. And there is as yet nothing I love more than being given the keys to a walled city. The same fervor arises in me, the same almost excessive dedication. Once again, my teacher assumes colossal proportions. My pulse quickens when I see her. One day in class, she leans forward on her knuckles over the table where she keeps her notes; her body swaying, she reads to us in ancient Greek. It is rapture, those primordial words tumbling from her mouth. I cannot understand a single one, but her recitation is endowed with a beauty and power beyond explanation and dispute. It is a secret, this language; it belongs, it appears, to her alone. At the end, she announces that class will be canceled on the day before Thanksgiving. I wonder if I am the only one crushed. Those rhapsodic Greek words are still lingering in the ether. Over our heads, just out of reach, they hover in wispy filament. In a moment I know they will dissipate and be gone forever.

By the end of the semester, I have checked out a small library of books on ancient Greece and the Mediterranean. I have piled them on my desk and next to my bed, and on weekends I thumb through them and take assiduous notes. In the weeks before final exams, I trudge through the rain across campus to meet the professor during her office hours. I have questions for her that lie outside the content of our course, questions that stem from the reading I have been doing on weekends. Really what I think I want is to be in her presence, in the indigo early-evening winter light, and to fan the flames of curiosity and desire that she has stirred in me. Though I still want for a tight-knit band of friends, I see the potential for a calling. But this professor doesn't encourage me, not exactly. She answers my questions politely, but her responses are followed by silences that speak perhaps of impatience, or indifference, and I don't know if my questions are not good ones, or whether, keys in hand, I am standing before the wrong walled city.

13.

A Sparrow Flies
into a Hall

Feeling socially unmoored and unconnected, I left Vassar to embark on a
gap year. My original idea was to sign up for a hiking trip in Kazakhstan.
Too risky, my parents cautioned. I researched outdoor programs in the
Rocky Mountains. Too pricey, it turned out. An uncle found me a for-
estry job that would have had me living alone in a cabin in the Pacific
Northwest and wielding a chain saw. "Over my dead body," my mother
declared. Then a pamphlet arrived in the mail announcing a yearlong program in Jerusalem. It combined physical labor on a kibbutz with Hebrew
language study. Although I had little interest in Israel, the combination of
work and study appealed. And I liked the idea of experiencing life in Jerusalem, a city with so much history, and of learning the modern version of
the biblical language I had been forced to study in Sunday school. Add
Hebrew to Italian and Greek drama and, bit by bit, I could fill in the out-
line of the Mediterranean.

At the tail end of the year on the kibbutz, I ended up with a boyfriend,
a brilliant, contrarian, sensitive boy from Galilee who mostly dreamed of
escaping the oppressive politics of his native land. When we first met, he
was reclining in the upper branches of a tree on the border of the Sinai
desert, daydreaming. I was sure I was lost and, late to meet my hiking

group, was yelping frantically for help. He watched with detached amusement as others deciphered my questions and pointed the way. It turned out that the tree he was inhabiting was more or less where I needed to wait. And so we began to talk. It was an inauspicious beginning but one that foreshadows with surprising accuracy what was to come in the seven years we would spend together.

This boy (I was nineteen and he twenty) did not like the modern city of Rome as I did—nor Italy, really, nor anything that reminded him vaguely or explicitly of the Mediterranean culture in which he was raised. Instead he admired England and Germany, for their literature and music, for their sense of order, their superior weather (as he saw it), the quality of their chocolate, and their verdant landscapes. Because he was studying mathematics in Israel, the first years of our relationship took place largely through the medium of letters and email. During this time, I followed him out of Italy, allowing him to lead me instead to Thomas Mann and Goethe, to Bach and Bruckner and Mahler, to Romanticism and its hallowed universe of Sublime Feeling. When I subsequently visited him in Israel during my winter and summer breaks, he introduced me as well to logic, set theory (a valiant effort on his part, especially given that the course was in Hebrew), and the piano, which he practiced three hours a day. While he played and replayed the *Goldberg Variations*, I lounged nearby in bed, reading *The Magic Mountain* or *Faust*, or scribbling in my diary about how I was reading *The Magic Mountain* or *Faust*, down to the detail of sketching the bed itself in which I was passing so many hours. Privately, I felt a measure of disquiet about my lack of direction while he stuck firmly to the passions—predominantly math and music—that for him had been long fixed in place.

My mother disliked this boyfriend and was little impressed by the lofty sphere the two of us liked to think we inhabited. She handily dismissed the *Don Giovanni* libretto he had made by hand for me, the volumes of cassettes of Schubert *lieder,* the Ladysmith Black Mambazo and Pete Atkin

CDs, and of course the countless love letters we sent each other, whose anguished pining and lamenting the young Werther might have mistaken for his own. No: what my mother saw was the guy who didn't help out around the house when he visited, the nincompoop who read the newspaper while her daughter prepared breakfast. In an effort to nudge him into the role she wished he would inhabit, she offered once to pay him to paint our porch. And he—what nerve—declined. Work, money, and physical activity—these were possibly the three things that interested him least in life, and my mother had offered him all three wrapped up in one tidy package. My mother was beside herself. This guy was staying in our home, a guest, for weeks on end, and he couldn't even be bothered to paint the porch.

"In every relationship," my mother warned me, "one person kisses, and the other offers their cheek to be kissed." It was one of her favorite maxims, one she had learned in Munich during her junior year abroad. She often spoke it in German, which lent the maxim additional authority to me back then. Although I now question its usefulness as a tool for navigating love, my mother had seen enough: I was kissing this boy, and he was letting himself be kissed. And this pained her greatly.

Having decided to transfer while on the kibbutz, I began my sophomore year at Barnard, the sister school of Columbia University on New York City's Upper West Side. All year I waffled over which major to declare. I enrolled in several environmental science courses, an upper-level Greek historiography seminar, and, at the suggestion of my boyfriend, Philosophy of Language, which was taught at the graduate level—an intimidating exercise since I had no background in philosophy. Of the eight or so of us in that seminar room, which smelled eternally of pipe smoke, I was the only undergraduate, the only woman, the youngest by at least ten years, and the only person who never once spoke. But although the content of-ten eluded me, I consulted textbooks to bolster my feeble knowledge base and completed every reading down to the last sentence, only once asking for help from the professor—a philosopher with a faraway gaze and a mop of tousled hair.

No one spoke to me in that class, nor even, as I remember, looked at me. And yet, having taken Mr. V's notion to heart that challenging situations offer you *the chance to discover what it is that you can do*, there I was, evening after evening, week after week, as fall chilled to winter, writing everything down in my notebook with the conviction that one day, with enough hard work, the subject would open itself to me.

The reason for my puzzling commitment to Philosophy of Language, I now suspect, was in part atmospheric. Much like that Harvard seminar room where my mother and I had sat in on a conversation among Dante scholars, this philosopher's classroom represented a world I wanted to be-lieve I belonged to. It had all the markers: sober-faced scholars, austere architecture, actual pipe smoke, and many long silences during which a great deal of thinking (presumably) went on. That the class was all men at least ten years my senior surely enhanced this for me even more—the more out of place I was, the greater my accomplishment would be.

As further evidence of my misguided ambition, a third of the courses in which I enrolled as a sophomore were graduate level. This included a lec-ture course on Dante that, like Philosophy of Language, was taught at Columbia. I was excited to return to *The Divine Comedy*, my familiar companion.

The professor was a Dante scholar who approached her subject with verve. Her clipped gray hair barely visible above her lectern, she gesticu-lated energetically, spun to the left and right, and scratched out key terms using lines and arrows and circles on the chalkboard. As we immersed ourselves in *Inferno*, I relished being back in Dante's universe, and my understanding of the text deepened significantly with the wealth of detail this professor offered. The problem was that she lavished so much attention on *Inferno* that by the time we began *Purgatorio*, we were well beyond halfway through the semester. In fact, we were nearly at the point at which the syllabus indicated we should be starting *Paradiso*. Nonetheless, the professor was reluctant to pare down her material, cramming the same wealth of information about *Purgatorio* into about half the number of weeks she had dedicated to *Inferno*. This was my first time reading beyond *The Divine Comedy*'s first canticle, and given the speed at which we now had to read, and the complexity of the information delivered in class, it became hard not to feel like I was drowning. Even when Beatrice appeared on the scene at *Purgatorio*'s end, I was reading so frantically that I barely registered her as a character.

By the time we reached *Paradiso*, the material that the professor had planned to deliver over at least a month was instead dispatched in one nonstop, rapid-fire two-hour session. As we raced through its thirty-three cantos, devoting no more than a scant three or four minutes to each one, I picked up on some of *Paradiso*'s general principles—the importance of numerology, the heavenly spheres, and something about a many-petaled rose—but understood little about how they fit together. Although the professor was deeply knowledgeable about her subject, my experience in her class was dispiriting, a real disappointment after the heights I had encountered in Mr. V's class.

For a long while, my desire to read Dante was diminished. And over the next three years as a college student, I never again set foot in an Italian literature class. Instead, I followed paths that led elsewhere. One of those was toward a history major. All along, history had been the connective tissue between my various intellectual interests. As a discipline, furthermore, history felt important and relatively secure, at least compared with my other interests, like writing. And, I privately reasoned, what better trove for the stories I might one day write than the long human story itself?

Over the next three years, I dedicated myself to studying history. And this path brought me back, in a roundabout way, to Rome. Although the geographic range of courses I took was wide, from Europe to the Middle East to China, it was the ancient Roman world that I first studied in any depth, in a survey course during the spring of my sophomore year. Roman history was a subject that interested my boyfriend, too, and when he visited at the start of my junior year, before his own semester had yet begun, he accompanied me to lectures.

On our way from Tel Aviv to the U.S. that summer, he and I had stopped over in Rome for a night before heading north to hike in Alto Adige, in the Italian Alps. It was his first time visiting many of the ancient sites, and he was disappointed to discover that important ancient buildings were not constructed of solid marble but instead of tuff or brick or Roman concrete, with marble facades. He did not much like the Roman cuisine— too many cheeses and vegetables—or the river, yellow with mud. I suspected Rome's disorderliness was too much like home for him—too much dust and traffic.

But I was back in Rome for the first time in two years. (*Home again to Rome again!*) I unearthed my rusty Italian from the sediment of my brain, where it had settled atop French and just under Hebrew, and procured for us, with satisfaction, directions and dairy-free meals. The city felt familiar, and yet I did not feel the intense emotional attachment I had experienced on my first trip. I was older, I had turned to other things, and with these things, my world had grown. But I was also armed with more knowledge of the city's history, and this lent me new confidence. As we wandered the Colosseum, I pointed out the cracks cleaved by earthquakes in the Middle Ages. We imagined its basin brimming with water during mock naval battles and fell silent as we imagined the innumerable beings— human and animal—who had drawn their final breaths within the circumference of those arches. I took him to the Baths of Caracalla, where we saw the ancient mosaics, still so meticulous in their arrangement, without knowing that the site, half a century earlier, had been a favorite destination of my grandparents, who heard *Aida* there, and *Rigoletto* and *Pagliacci*.

⤳

In the fall semester of my junior year, alongside my Roman history course, I took an introduction to medieval history. I thought I already knew what the period known as the "Middle Ages" was, but I quickly learned that the concept of a middle age had a long and complex history of its own.

Depending on where you look and how precisely you define it, the medieval period lasted from roughly 450 to 1450 CE. The Western concept of a "middle age," an intervening period between classical antiquity and the modern world, I learned, did not yet exist when Dante died in 1321. The term *media tempestas*, or "middle season," would emerge only more than a century later, in the mid-1400s. And another century and a half would unfurl before *medium aevum*, or a "middle age," from which our English word *medieval* derives, was coined.

The way Dante and his contemporaries saw things, they were living in the sixth, and penultimate, age of history. This age had begun with the birth of Christ under the Roman emperor Augustus and would end, they believed, with the Last Judgment, which would usher in the final, seventh age. The idea of six ages of history had originated in the late fourth century with Saint Augustine, who used the framework of Christianity to organize human history all the way back to biblical times. In this schema, history was essentially static—the only "event" of consequence being waiting for Christ's Second Coming—and in this long period of waiting, classical, pagan Rome was sometimes regarded with suspicion.

Around the time of Dante's death, however, some literary types began looking in new ways at pre-Christian Latin texts, as well as at the Greek and Arabic sources that over the previous few centuries had been translated into Latin. Increasingly influenced by those works and driven by the desire to incorporate them into their educational and literary program, these scholars—who eventually came to be known as "humanists," because they studied grammar, rhetoric, history, poetry, and moral philosophy, subjects collectively known as the *studia humanitatis*—began to redefine their relationship to the past. The humanists used ancient Latin and Greek texts as models for reviving classical rhetoric, and as the basis of a new textual criticism. As a result, Rome's pre-Christian history was quite suddenly revived as a valid subject of inquiry.

Petrarch, who was well versed in the letters of Cicero, the renowned Roman statesman, lawyer, and philosopher who died in 43 BCE, was among those taking special interest. "For what is all of history," he asked, "but the praise of Rome?" And by "Rome" he meant, above all, pagan Rome—the Rome of the republic and early empire. For he felt that by the second century CE, the influence of emperors from Spain and North Africa—"barbarians," he called them—had altered the Roman enterprise beyond repair.

By this logic, Petrarch considered the long period that followed the fall of the Roman Empire—with its fragmented political systems and its rejection of classical pagan learning—a period of *tenebrae*, of "darkness." No longer divided into six ages or into four world empires, as others of his day had postulated, history as Petrarch conceived it consisted of two periods: the *antiqua* (old) and the *nova* (new). When he called the early Christian era "dark," he also reversed the prevailing medieval trope that the ancient world, which had never known Christ, lived in the gloom of error, while the period following Christ's birth had been illuminated by his teachings. Although Petrarch was deeply Christian, for him it was ancient culture that shone. And he centered Rome as the very pivot on which history turned.

The humanists who succeeded Petrarch, and the Enlightenment philosophers who came after them, adopted Petrarch's demarcation of the fall of the Roman Empire as a watershed event. In their desire to restore the "light" of classical learning, many of Petrarch's successors dismissed an entire millennium of human history as the "Dark Ages."

In the 1440s, about seventy years after Petrarch's death, a Florentine historian by the name of Leonardo Bruni took these ideas to their natural conclusion, writing a history of Florence that divided the past into three parts: ancient, medieval, and modern. This powerful but problematic framework, in which the categorization of history into discrete periods was defined by the fall of one city, would stick: it has remained the defining paradigm of Western history for nearly six hundred years.

The notion that the Middle Ages were "dark" has long been rejected in modern scholarship but has nevertheless persisted in the popular imagination. Consider, for example, the way the period is often portrayed in film: a thousand years of brutal cavalry warfare in early-morning fog. In this way, popular culture frequently uses the Middle Ages as a kind of funhouse mirror to convince ourselves in the West of how very evolved we are and how far we have come.

Unlike those who would gloss over it as irrelevant, I was immediately captivated by the alien quality of the medieval world, by its myriad systems and symbols and ways of thinking that were so different from what I knew. In the first class meeting that fall, the history professor, who would become my adviser, asked us to ponder the chasm between an age when a single seed of wheat might yield only three or four seeds at season's end, as was the average wheat yield in the Middle Ages, and today, when a single seed planted could yield forty. "Just try to fathom that!" he said. I had never thought about crop yields, nor considered how much grain might be stored in any given year. But these questions now struck me as tangible and relevant, as if, in taking us back to such basic issues, they illuminated something essential about the long human struggle to persevere. And they impressed on me another realization, too—that the world I took for granted, the one around me, was only one of many possible worlds. Things could change, in grave and unexpected ways.

After a semester abroad at the Hebrew University in Jerusalem, where I studied Roman history from the other side—from the East, looking west—and lived near my boyfriend for the first time in our two-year relationship, I returned to Barnard and began work on my senior thesis. I had chosen the obscure topic of fifth-century Frankish law, not because I had a passion for legal codes or for the Franks, the Gallic tribe that settled largely in what is now the south of France, but because of a primary source: Gregory of Tours's *History of the Franks*. Gregory's *History* describes a world in which people were negotiating various, and often competing, sets of laws and customs. The book raised questions that piqued my curiosity, and to which I could find no thorough answers in the existing literature.

I found this period alluring because it was comparatively little studied and I hoped I might develop my own argument about it. This, in itself, marked an intellectual turning point. By my senior year of college, I was pursuing a historical question for its potential value for the field rather than for my personal connection to it. Like any scholar worth her salt, I was training my head to lead my heart.

⌖

During our final semester, four or five fellow history majors and I petitioned our adviser, the historian Joel Kaye, to lead an independent study on historiography. We were, by then, deep into the yearlong process of writing our senior theses. But while we each burrowed into our specialized topics, we also wished to grasp the larger picture of how Western historians, over the course of recorded history, had understood the march of human life: what sense they made of the past, what role it played, why they thought it was important. These questions felt especially relevant because the neoconservative American political scientist Francis Fukuyama had recently argued that humanity had reached "the end of history": that following the end of the Cold War, Western liberal democracy constituted the final culmination of humanity's long series of ideological experiments with models of government. All over campus, debates about this theory were in the ether.

Professor Kaye was reluctant. He explained to us that normally such a class would be taught only in graduate school. But we did not expect him to teach. Our idea was to create the reading list and lead the meetings ourselves. We wanted him there as guide—our Virgil, if you like. Professor Kaye hesitated but, after giving it some thought, agreed. His stipulations: Our class would meet one evening a week. We would devise reading and writing assignments for ourselves, and he would assign no grades other than pass/fail. We were off and running.

We began with Herodotus, the fifth-century BCE Greek historian, geographer, and storyteller whose *Histories* detail the long conflict between the Greeks and Persians. Even though Herodotus is often criticized for incorporating storytelling, some of it fantastical, into his historical account, Cicero would later dub him the "father of history." Ever since I had first read the *Histories* in the Greek historiography seminar two years earlier, I had found Herodotus engrossing. Particularly so his perceptions, sometimes firsthand, other times relayed to him by others, about the ways different people live and think. I liked the eyes-wide-open curiosity with which he observed and made conclusions about his world. I liked, too, his way of telling: his frequent digressions, the way one story led to another— history a chain of linked stories punctuated by occasional analysis.

From Herodotus we moved to Thucydides, who aimed for a more analytical kind of history, and then to Polybius, who was the first to emphasize the importance of facts and written sources. From there we sped on to

Tacitus, hovered a moment on Livy, then leaped out of the ancient world and into the early medieval Christian milieu of Gregory of Tours, with which I was already familiar. We read Isidore of Seville and Bede, and others I have since forgotten, then catapulted to Machiavelli and on to Hegel. Each progression a leap over centuries.

Professor Kaye, initially so hesitant, relaxed. As a creative exercise toward the end of the term, we tried sketching our subjects' concepts of how history "moved" on the classroom chalkboards. For Herodotus we did not succeed, I don't think, at discerning any particular shape, while for Thucydides we ended up with a spiral, and for Polybius, a circle. The medieval historians were challenging, since for them the human experience was essentially ahistorical, a flat line, maybe, awaiting only the Last Judgment, which would end all history in a single flash. Machiavelli stumped us (a line with circles? or a circle with lines?), while Hegel was simpler: a line optimistically ascending toward human freedom. And at the top of that ascent, in Fukuyama's view, was a full stop: the end of history, beyond which, he claimed, no higher ascent was attainable.

"Mark up your books!" Professor Kaye would exhort us, week after week. He believed you couldn't fully interact with a text, or read it deeply, without underlining, circling, voicing your reactions and thoughts, your moments of confusion, in the margins. As if reading were not a solitary activity but a vigorous conversation across space and time. This was a difficult lesson for me to absorb. Not because I shied away from engaging but because I had long been forbidden from writing in schoolbooks, which were rarely my own. The only books I had marked up were Dante's *Inferno* and Italo Calvino's *The Uses of Literature*—notations I made with no small amount of guilt. In school we were expected to protect our books as if they were precious artifacts, instructed not to scuff them or damage their corners. Once they were distributed and taken home, we carried on that timeworn tradition—spreading the book atop paper grocery bags, marking one inch beyond each edge, then cutting out the rectangle. A fold for each edge, Scotch tape applied diagonally across the corner—never touching the book itself!—and a clip of the scissors on either side of the spine. When the time came to return the book, we lined up and handed them to the teacher for review. The teacher would flip through the pages, scanning for underlining, comments, or doodles. On that day, there was always a stash of new erasers on hand. If your book was sullied, you were sent back to your desk with a fat eraser—a pink badge of shame.

But here was Professor Kaye, insisting that we circle and underline, draw arrows and question marks and even entire questions and comments. His own copies of the books we were reading—worn and dog-eared, crisscrossed with commentary—displayed his commitment to his method. I can see it in my notes from the time, my deepening engagement with the texts apparent in the margins. Even though I liked Herodotus, the pages of my copy of *The Histories* are largely blank. A cautious underlining here, a lightly circled word there. As if after making the mark, I was awaiting retribution. But by the time we reached Polybius, I was scribbling with (sometimes pompous) abandon. In the context of the Cretan constitution, for example: "Why no mention of Thucydides or a multitude of others? XENOPHON? Come on, really?" With the zeal of the convert, I threw my public-school taboos to the wind. I was all in.

∽⁂∾

In that final semester, as my work on my thesis was reaching fever pitch, I had also enrolled in a senior seminar for history majors with the renowned medievalist Caroline Walker Bynum, who taught across the street at Columbia. Soft-spoken and petite, Professor Bynum sat at the head of the classroom's single expansive wood table. We numbered about a dozen students, and we arranged ourselves around her like the apostles at the Last Supper. With some surprise, I noted to myself that this was my first time in a small seminar with a female professor. I had had a handful of female professors before—such as the professor of the lecture class I'd taken on *The Divine Comedy*, and another who taught architectural history, with great charisma, to a packed auditorium—but I had never studied intimately with a woman professor.

I didn't question why that was so. I assumed (as many of us did in the 1990s) that equality between the sexes had more or less been achieved, and that the opportunities available to me would be the same as those available to my male classmates. But the majority of my influence had come from male teachers, and I saw little reason to specifically seek out the tutelage of women. I sat around a table for three months with Professor Bynum and never once asked her for advice on how to navigate the field that I increasingly saw as my future. By the time I reached her classroom, Professor Bynum had already navigated this world with aplomb. She had written several widely influential books, and one year later, in 1999, she would be Columbia's first female faculty member ever to be appointed University Professor.

In her seminar on medieval religious thought, we read in spectacular detail about saints' bodies and theological depictions of the afterlife. We read lengthy texts on the intricacies of the body in Christian thought— what early medieval thinkers said, for example, about prospects for resurrection if a body was not whole, if it had suffered from amputations or if, following death, parts of the skeleton were scattered. Would Saint Agnes, who had been martyred in Rome, come back whole, or would she have to pass her infinite days in the afterlife without her head? I came away from the seminar with a capacity for detailed reading and a conceptual framework for the development of medieval religious ideas. But perhaps the most important skill my classmates and I derived from that class was how to write.

No one has ever, before or since, treated the nuts and bolts of my academic writing with as much care and attention as did Professor Bynum. The first paper she assigned was on the thirteenth-century writer Gerald of Wales, whose *Topography of Ireland* was a defining text in the Middle Ages about Ireland's history, people (saintly and non-), flora, fauna, and customs. Gerald's text was more accessible than some others we had read, and I wrote and submitted my four-page paper with confidence. When she handed our papers back to us a few days later, I was stupefied. Every margin—top, bottom, left, and right—on every page was filled with Professor Bynum's small red print: "This sentence lacks a subject." "Correct verb?" "What is the main idea of this paragraph?" and so on. I had thought myself a decent writer. And I considered this paper on Gerald of Wales typical of my standard of writing. It looked very much, in fact, like the writing I was doing for my thesis. A lot came crashing to the ground for me, and for my classmates, too, in the moment she returned our papers.

In her gentle but firm southern accent, Professor Bynum gave us a talking-to that day. "I'm freezing the syllabus where we are," she said, "until each of you learns how to write." Our next assignment would be— the same assignment all over again. We would pay attention to each word in our sentences, each sentence in our paragraphs, each paragraph in the structure of our arguments. We would learn to write.

I returned to my room and wrote the whole paper all over again. This time I was diligent, attentive. I refrained from generalized, unsubstantiated claims. I used the source text more sparingly. At the next class meeting we handed in our papers, and a few days later, Professor Bynum slid them back to us. Once again, red ink filled the margins. "Better," she said to us, "but still not particularly good." We were to write the paper a third time.

Back in my room, I returned to my desk and pulled up the document on my computer. I compared her comments with the words on the page. I began to perceive what she had labored to point out: the inconsistencies in tone and the nonlinear progression of thoughts, my choice of weak verbs and my tendency to overstate arguments. But I could see, this third time around, that I was making progress. When I handed it in, it was with a new kind of confidence—less cavalier, more hard-won. The confidence of knowing you have worked for something, that no matter where you stand on the spectrum of achievement, you have progressed. It was a lesson in the value of commitment. It made clear that art and skill are acquired not blithely but by slogging repeatedly through the mud and finding your way slowly out, slowly upward.

It was not enough. My third revision earned yet more red marks. They were dwindling in size and number, for sure, but red still dominated the page. Nearly a month after we had submitted our first renditions, our entire class was still stuck on the same four-page paper. It became my objective to write it well. And to apply what I was learning to my senior thesis, which, over these same weeks, was taking definitive shape. I found my central argument and clarified it. I broke long circular passages down into smaller, logically organized segments. I went sentence by sentence, as if with a microscope, working out the kinks. There was, my classmates and I could see, no other way out of this labyrinth. We might lose our fingers writing this piece; we might, crouched over our keyboards, destroy our bodies. We were not medieval saints, but we, or at least I, had the sense that we would come out of this effort somehow bettered.

By now deeply humbled, we submitted our papers for the fourth time. Many of us considered it eminently possible that we would spend the entire semester writing and rewriting these same four pages. When, a few days later, Professor Bynum passed them back, we caught sight of red marks here and there. But she was sitting up pertly in her seat, smiling. "When you know how to write, as you all are starting to, you begin to learn how to think," she said. She let elapse a long pause. "Very well done," she said.

Together, we opened our books and moved on to the next chapter.

༄

Near the end of my final semester at Barnard, I visited Professor Kaye during his office hours to talk about my prospects for graduate school. My boyfriend had already been accepted to a few PhD programs in mathematics, and we had visited several campuses before deciding jointly on Cornell. That summer, we would move to Ithaca. I would find a job and work while he studied. Even as I felt so alive to history, and could see myself as a professional historian, I remember feeling as though the future stretched out long before me, and that what mattered to me most were experiences that would change and broaden me. If asked, I would have said that I cared less about career and more about living. In my innermost thoughts, which I would never have expressed out loud, I perceived that my formation was destined to be a long one. And that "living" would complement history as a source of stories I might one day tell. Still, near the end of my time at Barnard I went to talk to Professor Kaye about the history I saw in my future, while admitting that I was in little rush to find it.

Professor Kaye echoed my thinking. The biggest danger, he warned, was to enter a PhD program too young, when you haven't yet had a chance to experience the world. "Get a job," he said, "and see where it takes you." I nodded in agreement. If, in a few years, I was still thinking about graduate studies in history, we could talk. But he felt he should let me know, without beating around the bush, that the job prospects for PhD candidates were poor and likely only to get worse. His own family, he told me, had worried that his decision to leave carpentry in midlife and embark on doctoral studies was irresponsible. After all, he had a child to support.

I registered Professor Kaye's admonition—I had even been predisposed to welcoming it. But then something strange happened. As I was packing up to leave, Professor Kaye added what seemed like a contemplative afterthought: "But if you ask me, there is little better than the life of a scholar." He was looking off into the distance, as he sometimes tended to do. "Sometimes I can't believe I actually get paid to talk about ideas." He turned to me. "You get to talk, and listen, and contribute to a conversation about what the human experience means. It's a good life, a meaningful life."

I had never heard a simpler, more compelling case for any vocation under the sun.

⤳

Where do we come from and where are we going? In the eighth century, a Benedictine monk known as the Venerable Bede wrote an ecclesiastical history of the English people that attempted to answer this question. He imagined a conversation from the early 600s in which the advisers of King Edwin of Northumbria deliberated adopting Christianity, a religion new to them.

Life, says one adviser, has always felt like the flight of a sparrow through a banquet hall on a winter's eve. There you sit, with your ministers and counselors, warmed by a comforting fire, while outside, rain and snow beat against the roof. A sparrow flies into the hall through one door, which has blown open with the wind. The sparrow streaks across the room and flies out the other side. For the fleeting, bright moment that the sparrow is under the banquet hall roof, she is sheltered and safe. She is, ever briefly, warmed by the fire. But a moment later she vanishes back into the wintry darkness, never to return.

We are the sparrow, the adviser says, and the banquet hall is life.

14.

ITHACA

On the afternoon that I met Professor Hyams, whom I would come to call Paul, for an informational interview, snow was accumulating fast. I looked out the window of the small, poorly heated apartment my boy-friend and I were sharing and made an estimate: about four inches. By the time I left and headed toward the Cornell Arts Quad, it had already risen up past my ankles and was approaching the bottoms of my calves, skim-ming the hem of my long skirt.

In the Temple of Zeus café, I recognized the professor immediately from his photo on the department web page. He sat under the glare of fluorescent lights at a table near the window overlooking the now-white expanse of the Arts Quad. On the other side was McGraw Hall, home to the history department. With somber fieldstone walls, a tower, and a man-sard roof, McGraw Hall reminded me of the orphanage in the children's book *Madeline*. It felt imposing and yet also, strangely, like a home.

Steam rose from Paul's cup, swirling into his reddish-brown-gray beard. I bought a tea and sat across from him. Snow was banking against the outside of the window frame, climbing the glass. Paul was personable, asking me about my new life in Ithaca. I told him of my two part-time jobs—at the science library and the horse farm—and of the boyfriend who was studying math. He asked, too, about my undergraduate work and my reasons for wanting to pursue graduate study. I told him about my senior thesis on early medieval law and explained how, living in Ithaca since August, I was immersed in—and yet on the outside of—the academic life. I did not mention Professor Kaye's warning about letting some years elapse before going to graduate school or ask Paul to weigh in on his gloomy predictions for the future of the profession. All I knew was that in the eight months since graduating from college, I had missed the academic life and wanted back in.

Paul had a paternal air about him. As I would see in coming years, he liked to invite students to his home, or to dinner with his wife, and he was easy to chat with. He displayed a wide-ranging curiosity and was well read across many fields. But Paul puzzled me, too, often speaking in locutions I could not understand, and I frequently found myself unsure of what exactly had been said. I felt that day as I would chronically come to feel: that a good bit of what he was trying to express was never actually articulated, and it was up to me to sift through the oblique associations and the implications of his words to find his meaning. It took a long while to discover that I was not alone in this, but at twenty-three I thought the deficiency was mine alone and considered it my responsibility to sort it out.

An hour later, the snow had taken on a late-afternoon blue. The fluorescent lights above us hummed. We were gathering our hats and gloves, readying ourselves to head out into the gloaming, when Paul cheerfully informed me that he would push my application through. The following semester, I could be his student. My heart soared as I briefly visualized my future as a graduate student: searching for books in the library stacks, walking to and from classes, meeting others just like me, who dreamed of contributing to meaningful conversations about the human condition.

Then Paul asked: Was I was sure I wished to be a pedant?

"A pedant?" The word caught me off guard.

Yes, he affirmed, a pedant. A pedant, he explained, was what I would be were I to become a historian. Particularly a medieval historian, he said, which is a period no one in the U.S. knows or cares about. Except maybe as it pertains to Tolkien, of course. Was I ready to be a pedant?

The question jarred. To answer it I had to race through the corridors of my mind: Becoming a pedant was obviously not my goal, but would graduate school necessarily make me one? Couldn't I just be a historian without the "pedant" part? And what about my teachers in high school and college—were *they* pedants? I had never thought of them as such. I saw my professors as knowledgeable, cultured people—people who took part in that conversation about the value and meaning of life. In my eyes, they were anything but pedants. Why was he asking me this now—was it some kind of warning?

In the end, I didn't so much answer his question as laugh it off. After all, obscurity didn't frighten me: I had just spent a year writing a thesis on one of the least-known periods of European history. And yet, still, I felt jolted. Maybe it was the suddenness with which Paul had tossed it into the conversation, the sudden negative turn, and the fact that I hadn't asked him to clarify what he meant.

As I walked home, my enthusiasm gradually gained purchase over my doubt and confusion at Paul's comment—question, joke, whatever it was. The hem of my skirt was dusted with snow, which had by now completely covered the bridge over the gorge, transforming it into a mass of pillowy forms and indigo shadows. I did not want to be a pedant. But if being one was the cost of going back to the world of the mind, maybe it was a cost I was willing to pay.

❧

You can't be a historian of medieval Europe if you don't know any Latin. Latin, after all, was the language of ancient Rome, and it continued to be the default language for written communications in Europe for the entirety of the Middle Ages. College had taught me to read and interpret texts, to build arguments and to express them logically in written form. It had given me the conceptual apparatus to be a historian. But it did not give me all the actual tools. Shortly after meeting with Paul at the Zeus café, I was formally accepted into Cornell's graduate program in history. But to go any further in my studies, I would need Latin.

Paul recognized this gap in my studies and urged me to fix it. In the summer, before most of my new cohort arrived, Cornell ran an introductory course in medieval Latin. The professor who taught it was one of the best medieval Latinists in the country. I signed up for her class right away, bought the books, and cracked them open. The first was a textbook: *Wheelock's Latin*, fifth edition. First published in the 1950s, *Wheelock's* Latin primer has probably taught the ancient language to more American students than any other Latin grammar book has or likely ever will.

Wheelock's reminded me a bit of the Italian cassette pack and its accompanying booklet I had borrowed from the public library years earlier. Set out before me on the page was a new language: conjugations, verbs characterized by their endings, nouns with genders. Thumbing through it, I found vocabulary lists and numbered exercises. Even though I had never studied Latin, this way of presenting a language on the page was familiar.

In the hand, *Wheelock's* felt soft and floppy—a little like puppy-dog ears, or a worn-out phone book. And much like phone books used to, *Wheelock's* gave you the hopeful sense that what it contained—in this case, the Latin language—was knowable. Its pages were light beige and wispy, like newspaper, with white space between sections and a simple, predictable typeface. Its examples, furthermore, were drawn from ancient authors, and so it gave the overall impression that the language was largely fixed and unchanging. I saw the textbook as a chest full of keys to locks I hadn't encountered yet. But I knew what the locks looked like, and how to use the keys once I acquired them. Despite the impressive erudition behind it, *Wheelock's Latin* was a book you could be friends with.

The other book I bought for my new language project was a primer called *Reading Medieval Latin*. You could tell right away that it was a more specialized work. It was smaller than *Wheelock's*, denser, with stiff white paper, high-quality ink, and a compact, sophisticated font. Its spine was rigidly bound and its pages resisted opening. You are going to have to work, it seemed to say. Despite its small stature, it weighed more than the textbook. It had heft, backbone, carried itself with dignity. Maybe, it occurred to me, a little too seriously?

When I opened *Reading Medieval Latin*, I felt like a chiropractor cracking a patient's spine. A tormented sound escaped the book. Whether it was the paper or the glue, the semirigid covers or the spine, it clearly did not want to budge. Scanning its pages, I found numerous excerpts of texts arranged chronologically from the fifth century to the fifteenth. Many words on every page were highlighted in bold to signify deviations from classical usage, or because they were new terms that had emerged over centuries as European culture Christianized, expanding its lexicon, and as it absorbed words and lexical patterns from Hebrew, Greek, and Arabic, and even came to be influenced by its own offshoots, the Romance languages. The Latin visible on these pages was a language in evolution, a language whose conventions differed to some degree depending on time and geography. Looking at the primer's detailed footnotes, its dizzying chronology and source list, I felt a gnawing sense of uncertainty about the endeavor before me.

In search of guidance, I headed for the introduction and landed on the following sentence, close to the book's beginning: "Ludwig Traube once said: 'There is no such thing as Medieval Latin. Consequently there will never be a dictionary or a grammar of Medieval Latin.'"

No such thing as medieval Latin? *Uh-oh.*

So it was one of *those* books—the kind that contradicts itself, stumbles over its own feet (purposely, to show how complicated it is) in its very first sentences. Like the savant who can't find the car keys, or who accidentally heads to work in slippers. And who, for that matter, is Ludwig Traube? I flipped back and read the previous few pages but found no mention of him. It was clear: the reader was supposed to know.

The fact that I had no idea was unsettling. But I quickly realized that my lack of familiarity with Ludwig Traube was not the first intellectual shortcoming that *Reading Medieval Latin* had pointed out to me in the forty-five seconds we had been acquainted. No, the first deficiency—and perhaps the gravest—was not knowing Latin at all. Coming face-to-face with this deficiency had already taken a little luster off what I had previously thought to be my quality education. In the Preface to *Reading Medieval Latin*, in fact, the editor—surely a kind and erudite person—handily summed up the deteriorating educational landscape of which I was a part: "Fewer and fewer students arrive at the university with as much as a year or two of Latin under their belt and many can now graduate, even in medieval history, without having to acquire a working knowledge of the language. This has led to the need for crash courses as late as the MA level." How humiliating—he was describing *me!* The most incriminating word in those two sentences was a very small one: *even.* "*Even* in medieval history . . ." It was the *even* that made my stomach twist. Could the editor somehow see me reading his book, the flush of rising panic on my face? He was right. I had *even* written a senior thesis on Frankish law, had *even* graduated in medieval history, had *even* found my way into a PhD program, all without a lick of Latin. If anyone needed to get cracking, it was me.

But wait, not before fully considering the shortcomings of my education. Second in line after not knowing Latin was the fact that I had zero familiarity with medieval Latin specifically. Forgivable, I suppose, since I was here to learn. But of course the book had already informed me that, well, there was no such thing as "Medieval Latin," even though those two words, in that order, occupied two thirds of the real estate in the book's title.

So even if it was aesthetically pleasing to behold, I can't say that *Reading*

Medieval Latin was an inviting book. And should you be the courageous type who persists and ventures in anyway, the type willing to crack spines and force entry, you then discover that the book immediately plunges you into a cold sea, reminding you in no uncertain terms of all that you don't know while also unraveling the little you think you do. If you can get past all that without succumbing to despair, then and only then have you earned the right to contemplate that nagging question: *Now who is this Mr. Traube?*

It is only now, nearly two decades after first opening *Reading Medieval Latin*, that I have taken the time to think about this question. I put it to Google. In a comfortingly straightforward fashion, it reveals that Ludwig Traube (the son, not the father by the same name) was a German Jewish paleographer who, around 1900, held the first chair of Medieval Latin (yes, "Medieval Latin") in Germany. What Traube meant when he said "there is no such thing as Medieval Latin" was that Latin is Latin, no matter the period in which it is written or spoken.

Traube, I learn, was not only a good Latinist. He was one of those philologists ready to put his love for language and literature in service of his country. He worked in the central management of the Monumenta Germaniae Historica, a formidable project begun in the early nineteenth century whose aim was to compile a complete archive of all the primary sources relating to the history of the German nation. Originally focused exclusively on medieval texts, the MGH, as it is commonly abbreviated, now fills three hundred volumes. In the coming years, I would frequently bump up against it while searching for sources for a research paper or simply because, given the sheer quantity of its huge tomes on the library shelf, chances were you'd eventually, literally, bump into it.

A compendium as vast as the MGH does not much invite you to think about authorship. It is the creation, it wants you to believe, of a nation. But in fact, as is often the case with institutions, the MGH grew into what it was in part because of the dedication and perseverance of individuals.

When Traube passed away in 1907, he donated his library to the German state on the condition that it be added to the MGH. His library contained a wide assortment of paleographic studies and medieval manuscripts, many of which he had acquired from secularized monasteries. Like many archives, the MGH depended on bequests from individuals. Traube, a Jew, donated his medieval Latin texts, many of them deeply Christian in nature, and by doing so, helped to cement the historical foundation of German nationalism. It would be an inadvertent and deeply unsettling outcome of his lifelong passion.

Latin was everything to Ludwig Traube. He made a career, a life, and an institutional legacy of it. But what was Latin to me?

~⁊∾

I no longer recall how I found out about the storied Latin course taught by the American friar every summer in Rome. Word of it must have been in the ether, and yet, in the spring of my second year, I was the sole Cornell graduate student who applied. To get in, I had only to fill out a simple form and take a Latin assessment test. I remember folding the papers into an envelope and walking it to the post office. Within weeks, I received an acceptance letter. It came with detailed instructions about dates (most of June and July), the specific Latin dictionary we needed to bring with us (known as "Lewis and Short"), a few rather vague suggestions for finding housing (try the newspaper *Porta Portese*, or monasteries/convents), and detailed directions to the classroom (near Porta San Pancrazio). I reread the letter, the words rising off the page. I would be returning to Rome.

~⁊∾

Porta San Pancrazio. What is it about an ancient city gate, and the wall in which it finds itself, that so captures the imagination? A wall has never been anything but a tragedy waiting to happen—the moment of breach not an *if* but a *when*. A wall is a blunt instrument, but a gate is a precision tool: it keeps you out in the blinding sun until suddenly it lets you in; it holds you in until, *poof,* you're out. That fleeting moment in the shadow, that chill that raises the hair on the nape of your neck—that's the gate.

Where I come from, cities know no walls. It would be inconceivable for Boston or New York. Even Ithaca could not in any practical manner be enclosed by stone. My cities, big, small, medium, like to stretch their legs. They yawn with self-complacency. Who needs a wall, anyway?

How diminishing to stand at the foot of an ancient city wall. Diminishing in the most sublime way. For the wall has been doing its work for hundreds or even thousands of years, even though its task, as we all know, has been lessened by time. Rome—the ancient *urbs*—called on its wall only at the very beginning and the very end of its long life. The wall a testament to its moments of weakness rather than strength. But how striking to come up against one of these walls, crick back your neck and take in its towering height, and say, *Hello, I have come to find you and here you are.* And then to lean into its cracks with your body, with your face, and to breathe in the scent of rock and soil, of fiber and sinew, the organic ferment of centuries gone by. And to know that when evening falls upon you, so suddenly after your brief flitting about, the wall will go on standing sentry, moldering, immortal.

15

LIVING LATIN

Reginald Foster, his blue denim shirt awash in the tangerine splash of late-afternoon Roman sun, stands as unmoving as an obelisk in the center of a broad expanse of asphalt. His gaze is riveted to the hazy spot in the distance where the road meets the horizon. I am busy cowering with other students in the meager shade of a desiccated hedge. Even here near breezy Formia, a small coastal city about halfway between Rome and Naples, the day is relentlessly hot. Our bodies are languid, sweating, as we chat and stare off into space.

We are here for Reginald's eight-week-long immersion course known as Living Latin. Now in his early sixties, Reggie has been teaching this class since 1985, and by the time I arrive in Rome, in June 2001, it has achieved cult status in the Latinosphere. In the class with me are about seventy others, predominantly in their twenties and thirties. Most are American and Canadian, with a few from England, France, and Australia and one woman from Korea.

Today is an excursion day. Earlier in the afternoon, we stopped outside Cicero's former villa. It was not open for visiting, but nonetheless, Reggie's pedagogical principles state that, when in the presence of an important site of *Latinitas*, a toast is always in order. He had been carrying the two boxes of wine all day, all the way from Rome, one large handle gripped in each fist. Tipping the boxes at long last, Reggie poured seventy or so cups of red, one for each of us. We raised them above our heads as traffic whizzed by, and together we toasted the Roman orator: *Dum vivimus vivamus!* "May we live while we are alive!" And while meditating on the gift of life, we went on, wending our way through the brush to the presumed site of Cicero's brutal beheading at the hands of Roman soldiers, where an ancient stone monument over seventy feet tall stands in his honor. Standing in the shade cast by this undeniably phallic protrusion of rock and brick, we read some lines about the beauty of friendship from Cicero's letters and recited another toast. From there we walked the mile or two to Formia, where we relished a cathartic meal at a restaurant near the beach. By the end of the day our bodies and minds are tired. We have walked under the hot sun for much of the day. We have read a lot of Latin. We have drunk quite a bit of red wine, much of it on an empty stomach. We are still feeling, by virtue of the experience, the taut connection between Rome the city and the Roman countryside, the way the pulsing city can vibrate so strongly out here, even in this bucolic landscape. We are waiting for the bus that will take us to the train that will take us back to the city center, and Reginald, our tireless Latin teacher, remains our stalwart sentinel.

～♉～

Living out in the commuter town of Ciampino for the summer, I am seasoned in the art of waiting for public transport. Upon my arrival in Rome a few weeks before, I headed to the *pensione*, where I had booked a three-day stay, harboring the quaint illusion that I would find a room to rent for the rest of the summer using the local newspaper, *Porta Portese*, recommended in my acceptance letter. When three days of pounding hot city pavement led only to dead ends, I called my boyfriend and my parents in desperation. They seemed so far away, so safe and comfortable. It was after midday on my last day at the *pensione*, and I had no idea where I was going to sleep. I cautiously asked the owners if I might continue my stay at their establishment. They regretted to tell me that the *pensione* was booked, but they owned an empty—or nearly empty—house out in Ciampino, if I wouldn't mind the commute. They could drive me and my suitcase out that evening. Faced with the choice of the streets or Ciampino, I chose, without hesitation, Ciampino. This meant a daily train ride into Termini Station, and then a ride across the city by bus to Porta San Pancrazio. Each trip, late morning and early evening, would take an hour and a half.

I am the only student living so far away. Most of the others have found rooms in convents or monasteries, which with hindsight might have been the better option. But I like having a house to myself. Or almost to myself. There is an Italian girl living upstairs, I have been told, but we have only ever met once, in passing. She is so quiet that I only know she is home when I glimpse, on the second-floor terrace, her white underwear drying in the breeze. Though it comes at the price of time, I take pleasure in having what sometimes feels like a home. I relish the simple fact that when I turn the key to the gate near the sidewalk, it swings open for me. In the mornings I savor quick trips to the fruit and vegetable market in the piazza, where I buy the cheeses and cherry tomatoes that soon constitute the majority of my diet. And on Friday evenings, if I am home early enough, I walk to Piazza della Pace and sit on a bench to watch the parents ordering *pizza bianca* for their children, who devour its salty goodness in great gulps while other families stroll casually about on their evening *passeggiata*.

On the whole, I even enjoy the experience of commuting. I am young enough that it is novel, and while I wait for the train, I observe the people around me and imagine their lives, while pretending that I, too, live here and that today and tomorrow, and every day this summer, are just like any other day. Sometimes when I return home in the evening, the train is full of sleepy, subdued soldiers just starting out on the long night ride to Lecce, where there is a military air base. As the train rolls along its tracks and a warm wind blows through the cabins, I feel I am sharing in some elemental collective experience—of youth, maybe, and the somnolence of summer nights. My life as a Ciampino commuter is a pretend life, in some ways, but the satisfactions I find in it are real.

❧

A son and grandson of Milwaukee plumbers, Reginald Foster's future as modern-day Latin prophet was hardly assured. But he knew early on that he wanted to be a priest and entered seminary when he was only thirteen. He became a Carmelite monk, and then an expert in Latin. By the time I set foot in his class, Reggie has already served for thirty years in a position rather unlikely for someone born to a working-class midwestern family: secretary of Latin letters for the pope. He is working for his third pope, John Paul II, when I meet him in 2001, and he will stay on for a fourth, Pope Benedict XVI, before retiring in 2009.

The antiquated title for Reggie's post was *Secretarius Brevium ad Principes*, or Secretary for Briefs to Princes, which in the late 1960s became the Vatican's Latin Language Department. His job description: to draft official papal correspondence, speeches, and encyclicals, and to translate official documents into Latin. Not only is Reginald the first American to hold this office, but he can trace his professional lineage in pretty much a straight line back to the first secretary of Latin, Saint Jerome, who by translating the Bible into vulgate Latin in the late fourth and early fifth centuries became one of history's most important Latinists. In subsequent centuries, the post would be filled by Poggio Bracciolini, Pietro Bembo, and other renowned Renaissance humanists who sought, studied, and imitated the

Latin literature of Roman antiquity. One Vatican Latinist called Reginald Foster "one of the greatest masters of the Latin language since the Renaissance."

Under Reggie's passionate instruction, Living Latin requires stamina—both mental and physical. We meet for four hours each afternoon, six days a week, in a classroom atop the Janiculum Hill—the hill just south of the Vatican—to speak, read, and listen to Latin. On the seventh day, Sunday, we leave the classroom behind and use Rome and its environs as our textbook, visiting historical sites on excursions that typically demand many miles of walking and easily last twelve to fourteen hours, often more. All seven days, we must each lug around Lewis and Short's Latin dictionary. At six pounds, it weighs more than a brick, or almost as much as three liters of water, and in terms of volume it occupies most of my backpack. All summer long, Lewis and Short is my constant, and cumbrous, companion.

To teach Living Latin, Reggie rents our classroom space—at his personal expense, we later learn—from a Filipino religious school. The accommodations are spare. We must fold our limbs into desks sized for children. There is often a powerful odor of sweaty feet. For all seventy of us, there is one bathroom, with one toilet. Paper towels would constitute an extravagance, and the mere suggestion of air-conditioning would make anyone here laugh. During these classes, I have never seen Reggie sit down, take a bathroom break, or eat a bite of food. In this classroom, we develop and practice our own brand of scholastic asceticism.

The four-hour daily class is only the beginning. For the motivated, Reggie offers an additional two hours of informal Latin conversation six evenings per week *sub arboribus*—under the trees—in the nearby garden of his Carmelite monastery. These I am unable to attend. Ciampino lies more than ten miles away, and the *sub arboribus* classes run until nine in the evening, by which hour the last train for Ciampino has already departed Termini Station, on the other side of the city. For the same reason, over the course of the summer I am never able to eat dinner with friends, for the trains peter out, inexplicably, at the same time that the Roman dinner hour begins. Instead, I go home early in the evening and begin work on the dense homework packets that Reggie calls *ludi domestici* (games to be played at home), which are due the next day and which take me, on average, three to five hours to complete.

With only one medieval Latin class under my belt, I am about as beginner as they come in Reggie's class. The rest of my study has been informal and mostly self-directed. I have often allowed my Latin study to give way, furthermore, to more pressing classwork, and my progress over the first two harried years of graduate school has been halting. Even so, Living Latin is not really aimed at me. Latin teachers are Reggie's target audience, whom he hopes to inspire with his unorthodox pedagogy. And yet after only three days of class, Reggie has learned my name, along with everyone else's. He calls on us regularly. When I fumble, or someone else does, he sometimes turns impatient, his face flushing red, and it's evident that he's gathering his composure to explain the concept again. A moment later, though, he chortles spontaneously over a word or a phrase or a passage he remembers with delight from the encyclopedia of Latin literature that is his mind. In Reggie's classroom, we are all in the same boat, charting a dizzying, zigzag course through 2,300 years of Latin.

Everything in Latin is fair game, whether it's Cicero's speeches and letters, about which Reginald is unparalleled in his expertise, or Seneca or Saint Augustine or Saint Teresa of Ávila or Spinoza. Whether it comes from the second century BCE or the twentieth-century office of the pope. Whether the text be Christian or Jewish, pagan or secular, or translated from Greek or Arabic into Latin. Whether it was written on stone or parchment or paper and kept in a library or scrawled furtively on a bathroom wall. Whether it is pious and chaste or ribald and risqué, it is fair to say that Reggie wants to live, and share, all of it. For this he charges no money, accepting only voluntary contributions. Living Latin is an enterprise of love.

A love so dedicated and unwavering, it is contagious. Under Reggie's instruction, I begin to glimpse the beauty and contours of the language. And I begin to notice, to really see, that Latin appears all over the modern city of Rome: on surviving ancient buildings and inscriptions, obviously, but also on modern signage. We are even stepping on Latin every day, on the city's manhole covers, and, right beside a depiction of *la lupa*, there is Latin on my monthly bus pass. At first, the gap between Latin and Italian feels like a yawning chasm: Latin was then, Italian is now. But as Reggie points out, as two delivery men clatter about on the small patio outside the classroom doors, Romanesco—the variant of Italian spoken in Rome—contains many lingering remnants of Latin. "'*Mo vengo*,' did you hear that?" he says with delight. "*Immo venio*—'I'm coming!'—these Roman guys are speaking Latin!"

❧

Reggie's class was in session when the announcement was made: a little after five p.m. on a mid-June afternoon, the AS Roma football team won the Champions League title. Explosions of cheering from neighborhood homes and bars reached us in the classroom, but we didn't get out until almost an hour later. A few friends were going out to celebrate. I vacillated, wanting to join them, but knowing that such a delay might mean I'd miss the last train back to Ciampino, I had to decline. Disappointed, I climbed onto the 75 bus. We sailed down the winding streets of the Janiculum on our way to Termini Station. An infectious exuberance was in the air. When we passed small groups of celebrants in the streets, the bus riders cheered, leaning against the windows and hurrahing to those outside. As I would learn from the headlines the following day, this victory was just AS Roma's third, after more than seventy seasons of playing in the league. The last title had been won in 1983, and before that, 1942. I had never been a soccer fan per se, nor a die-hard fan of any sport, but I was happy for the team, happy for Rome, happy to encounter the unexpected.

Once we crossed the Tiber, our bus sailed straight into the tidal celebration that was taking the city by storm. On via Marmorata, celebrants from Testaccio pressed into the street from all sides. Our bus had only traveled a short distance before we were moored among the frothing sea of bodies. We could move neither forward nor backward. Outside the windows streamed men waving yellow-and-red-checked flags, women in face paint, children in AS Roma uniforms held aloft. Our bus began to rock, jostled by the crowd. A small boy with a red-and-yellow scarf draped around his neck passed by at my window's height, riding on his father's shoulders. "*Forza Romaaaaa!*" the father bellowed.

Like the other passengers, I soon gave up on the idea of reaching Termini by bus. There was nothing to do but step carefully down onto the asphalt and out into the tide. With no idea where to go or what to do, I sensed that personal volition was not part of the equation of the moment. The crowd was pushing this way and that, its only clear goal a celebratory togetherness. Teenage boys shouted in elation, grasping their friends around the waist or shoulders. One lifted another into the air. A man holding a giant pair of cardboard scissors covered in aluminum foil pumped it up and down, mimicking the motion of slicing up the uniform of SS Lazio, the opposing team and AS Roma's principal foe. Two teenage girls in red-and-yellow bras and face paint stood with their backs to a storefront, dispensing kisses on the cheek to boys passing by.

One hour later, I had moved little more than a block. Two hours later, hardly more than that. I had stopped even trying to get out. Our abandoned bus sat darkly among the crowd, like the hull of a sunken ship exposed by low tide. All of Rome, it seemed, had flooded onto via Marmorata. I noticed another bus stranded in the fray, or maybe it was a parade float. Atop it were three men silhouetted against the darkening sky. Their shirt-less arms were bare and muscular, and around their chests they had strapped vests that lent them the fur and teats of *la lupa*—that ubiquitous symbol of Rome. The men's faces were hidden behind wolf masks, long of ear and tooth. Each man wielded a thick black whip. In slow, dramatic motion, they whipped the air, paused, and posed while the crowd whooped in revelry.

There is no one true Rome. And yet this fragment of history, in which I was caught like a fish in a net, spoke to me of some essential quality of the city. Some vital electric current that has vibrated in its ether for as long as anyone can remember. The sanctified crowd, the feral corporality, the surrender. As palpable as the asphalt beneath my feet.

⚘

On a weekly, if not daily basis, Reggie, or Reginaldus, as he calls himself in Latin, rails against the brittle formulas, the dry and dusty tables, to which Latin teaching has, for at least the past hundred years, been reduced. "Don't think, talk!" he shouts in his booming voice. Latin, he insists, must be taught as a living language, spoken rather than haltingly absorbed through word charts that students must choke down like powder from a spoon. He is helping to ferry the ancient language into the twenty-first century, drafting encyclicals and other communications that are beyond the ken of most other Latin experts.

"How do you say 'computer' in Latin?" he demands, though with a mischievous smile. *"Instrumentum computatorium!"* he answers his own question, pronouncing each of the ten syllables with relish. In his class we talk about the whole world, modern and ancient alike. We talk about the price of gas—*Non omnes periti quos auscultamus a societate Conchae conducun-tur* ("Not all the experts we listen to are employed by Shell")—about the

Renaissance humanist Pietro Bembo, and about what Reggie sees as the dismal state of contemporary Latin pedagogy. He loves it all, and his motto, were he the type to have one, could well be *Nihil est quod Latinae dici non posset* ("There is nothing that cannot be said in Latin").

But some terms, usually modern concepts, *are* difficult, Reginald concedes. Like *globalization*, which is one that he has apparently been struggling with. "You can't translate it," he explains to us, "because no one will be happy with anything we say." He puts forward one possibility: "You can explain the idea first with *conformatio totius orbis*—conforming of the entire world—and then use *globalisatio* after that. Do whatever you want with that awful word, I don't care."

He throws up his hands.

"But *globalisatio*—that's spaghetti Latin."

His eyes brighten suddenly and he giggles.

"But that's the marvel of Latin! You see? You can't get away with anything! You don't know what globalization is? Then you can't even talk about it. Latin is so specific, and so concrete, that it forces you to define whatever it is you want to talk about."

I had noticed a similar specificity in Hebrew. Since it was an ancient language when it was revived late in the nineteenth century, it lacked words for modern concepts. One of the first new Hebrew words created by Eliezer Ben-Yehuda, the father of modern Hebrew, was *milon* (מילון), which means "dictionary." An English speaker with a limited vocabulary might look at or hear the word *dictionary* and have no idea what it means. But in Hebrew, the connection between word and meaning is often very close: *milon* contains the root for *word*. You could translate it as "wordery." As Anne Carson has said of ancient Greek, these very old languages bring you "down in the roots of where words work, whereas in English we're at the top of the tree, in the branches, bouncing around." Latin, we learn, requires the speaker to refer directly to the concrete world at hand.

Though Reginald has earned his place in the rarefied ranks of Latin scholars, there is not an elitist bone in his body. His is an erudition completely disassociated from snobbery. This begins with his clothing—a blue polyester workman's uniform that he sources from JCPenney—and ends with his accent, which is straight-up Midwest. The Swiss guards at the Vatican reportedly refer to him derisively as *il benzinaio*, the gas station attendant. His plebeian clothing aptly reflects his complete indifference to the material fluff of the modern world. A student in the class sneezes and asks if anyone has a tissue. Reggie's eyes light up with opportunity.

"How do you say 'wipe your nose' in Latin? Did Cicero use Kleenex? Of course he didn't!"

We get to work figuring out the locutions. Kleenex, paper, toilet paper, nose . . . In the end, he guides us to the answer: *Quam saepe tuum patrem braccio suo emungentem!* "How often did I see your father wiping his nose with his arm!"

This man, I decide, is perhaps the most classically learned person I have ever encountered and, at the same time, with his wide-open love for Latin in all its shapes and forms, the furthest thing I can imagine from a pedant.

After class ends for the day, and before some head over to the evening *sub arboribus* session, a small group of friends and I go out together. We have taken to buying olives and crackers and a bottle or two of wine and carting them to the Doria Pamphilj park across the street. We sit on the dry grass under the tall pines as the late-afternoon sun sinks toward the hills on the horizon, emblazoning us in gold. We emulate Reggie, raising toasts to the trees, to the setting sun, to the pine nuts that, scattered in the soil, have gotten caught between our toes. What we are also toasting is the suspension of time that happens when you are young and immersed in the pursuit of something, and surrounded by others who share in that same endeavor, so that this pursuit becomes your common language, what ties you to each other—but also, most importantly, to yourself, because it is there, in the sheer effort and care that you have invested in your pursuit, that you have found yourself most alive. And then you realize, with a start, that the sun is nearly down and your train, your train. And, tossing on your heavy backpack and shouting a panicked farewell, you run as fast as your legs will carry you.

~~~

One Sunday we travel to Ostia Antica, ancient Rome's port city, now preserved as an archaeological site. We visit the Baths of the Seven Sages, which is the lyrical name of one of the bathrooms in an ancient apartment complex. The bathroom features an elongated stone slab punctuated every few feet by a hole.

Reggie begins to giggle, a mischievous delight rising in him.

"Toilets!" Reggie proclaims. "Who needs privacy in the bathroom when you can have company? The Romans knew everything!"

On the frescoed walls above, we make out the images of seated men. The words are difficult to decipher, so he points us to our handouts.

Ut bene cacaret ventrem palpavit Solon.

"To have a good bowel movement," Reggie translates, "Solon pressed on his stomach." He laughs. "Can you imagine this on the wall of a public bathroom in Iowa City? Of course you can't! The Romans were so far ahead of us! They didn't need silly grape leaves to cover themselves with!"

We try to decipher the rest on our own.

There is *Bene caca et declina medicos*, the equivalent of "A good shit a day keeps the doctor away." One of the most advanced students, though, murmurs that what is actually written is *Bene caca et irrima medicos*—"Shit well and blow the doctors"—a reading that none of us has the intention of clarifying.

"Don't miss that one over there!" Reggie says, pointing. *"Agita te celerius pervenies.* Who can translate?" He calls on one of the youngest in the group, a twenty-two-year-old British girl, who blushes enormously. "Push hard, you'll get done faster?"

"Yes! Exactly!" Reggie replies, positively exulting in the wisdom of these seven sages.

Our next stop in Ostia Antica is a courtyard. This is the location, purportedly, where Saint Augustine and his mother, Monica, held their final conversation. They had just come from Milan and were on their way back to North Africa when Monica fell ill. Gesturing up to a window overlooking the courtyard, Reggie challenges us to imagine Monica, just on the other side of it, living out her final moments on earth. Augustine is at her side, and they are engaged in a conversation both hopeful and intimate.

We retrieve our handouts and read together from the *Confessions.* "We advanced step by step through all bodily things," Reggie reads in Latin, "up to the sky itself, from which the sun and moon and stars shine out over the earth, and we ascended still farther in our interior cogitation, conversation and admiration of Thy works and came to our own minds." At the conclusion of their shared vision, Reggie narrates, "mother and son come back to earth, back to human language, and Monica looks around and asks, 'Why am I still here?' And then she dies."

A tear slips down Reggie's ruddy cheek, and he wipes it away without a trace of sentimental affect.

"My friends, these are the most beautiful words you will ever read."

In Reggie I find a person who has followed unerringly what he loves most. All of his knowledge and passion he gives freely; offer him a gift, this man of few possessions warns you, and he will give it away. He has followed his passion even though its outcome was uncertain, and even though it likely made little sense, at least initially, to those who knew him best. In this, he is like a ship steaming toward a horizon only he can see. At twenty-six, my own path bears little likeness to his. It has already meandered, and will soon meander more. I do not think I could ever be like

Reggie, so stalwart and single-minded. And yet he has helped me perceive what it means to dedicate oneself to the pursuit of something for the love of it, to follow its animating desire. I can see the shape of that dedication, and I know what it sounds like, what it feels like. I know that it can weigh six pounds, or as much as three liters of water, and that you must carry it with you everywhere. That it is what keeps you walking for twelve or fourteen or even sixteen hours, and at the end of it, you earn your right to raise a glass and offer a toast to life.

"We just barely touched Wisdom with the whole effort of our hearts," wrote Augustine about his last earthly conversation with his mother. After Living Latin, I recalibrate my inner compass. I begin to pay attention to its quivering needle, deciphering in its movements where it is I want to go. I may not have found Wisdom that summer in Rome, but I learned what it means to give the whole effort of the heart.

～⌒⌒

We know from experience that a language is not a fixed entity. That it changes, dramatically, with time. How different English from fifty years ago can sound to the modern ear. The vocabulary, the intonation, even the syntax. Go back a century, and those differences grow even more pronounced. What happens when we go back five or seven hundred years? Or a thousand? What we think of as "our language" slips slowly from our grasp. At some point, it ceases to belong to us. Neither ear nor eye can any longer quite parse it. What we do not understand suddenly outweighs what we do. Middle English is a significant stretch for the untrained modern reader (and listener), Old English a nearly impossible leap. And yet they are both "English."

With Latin, though, we trace this process in the opposite direction, watching it progress—some would say decline—from antiquity onward.

What fascinates me is the transformation: those points at which we see the first tendrils of a new language unfurl. From Latin, French peeled off first, then Italian and Spanish, Portuguese, Catalan, and Romanian. But where exactly did each of these languages begin?

Like the first groupings of cells that make up new life, the first stirrings of a new language are nearly undetectable. They are as ephemeral as a morning fog, more likely to burn off than to hang around. Those who speak new words have no way of assessing their weight or longevity. Often what they are speaking is "incorrect," their words and phrases unsanctioned by the keepers of language and grammar.

For the earliest unfurlings of Italian, before Dante's Tuscan, we have to go to Rome. We don't really know exactly where Italian was spoken first; all we know is where it was first written down. Or, more accurately, where the earliest record of writing in the Italian vernacular has been found. That place is the Basilica of San Clemente, a stone's throw from the Colosseum.

I visited San Clemente for the first time toward the end of my Living Latin summer. I spent hours wandering through its depths. San Clemente consists of at least three structures built on top of one another. In this way, it is a building holding on to its own history, an embodiment, perhaps, of Freud's palazzo. At the surface is the "modern" basilica—in this case, early twelfth century. With cosmatesque mosaic floors and a gold-mosaicked apse, the feel of the upper basilica recalls that of Santa Maria in Trastevere, another Romanesque basilica built in the same period. Even up here at street level, the basilica offered welcome respite from the July heat.

Descending its humid stone stairways, we move ever further back in time. Down here, we come upon an older basilica, built in the fourth century and home to one of Europe's largest collections of surviving medieval wall paintings. This basilica was damaged in the late eleventh century, either in 1084 when the Normans sacked Rome, or by Pope Paschal II, who wished to obliterate the memory of his rival Clement III, whose remains he exhumed and tossed unceremoniously into the Tiber. Whatever the cause of its destruction, however, the remains of this early basilica were filled in with soil, providing a foundation for the twelfth-century basilica above. Inadvertently, the soil provided an insulating layer for the medieval wall frescoes, which, like the structure itself, have been remarkably preserved.

This level betrays a neatness uncommon for such old remains. Its brick and stone walls have been restored and show little sign of decay. The floor is swept and tidy. With its lightly arched ceiling, it has the practical feel of an old wine cellar. And it is down here, deep underground, that the first evidence of the Italian language can be found—in an eleventh-century fresco painted on one of the interior walls. The fresco depicts an episode from the life of Saint Clement, who lived in the first century CE. According to the legend, Clement miraculously healed a Roman patrician named Sisinnius of blindness and deafness. But Sisinnius, a pagan, was angered by his wife's interest in Christianity, and he ordered his servants to kidnap Clement and do away with him. In the fresco, the servants are pictured carrying off—by divine miracle, one supposes—a stone column rather than the body of the saint. Next to the image, much like in a comic book or graphic novel, written text narrates the words spoken by the irate and jealous husband Sisinnius:

Falite dereto colo palo, Carvoncelle, Gosmari, Albertel, he shouts. "Get behind him with that stick, Carvoncelle." *Traite, fili de le pute, traite!* "Pull, sons of bitches, pull!"

This colorful sentence is the earliest known instance of the Italian vernacular, captured in the moment of its metamorphosis from Latin. The syntax has already left Latin behind, for instance in the way it makes use of a preposition ("*colo palo*," *with* that stick) rather than relying on the ablative case, or when it uses possessives ("*fili de le pute*," sons *of* bitches) instead of the genitive. The fresco captures a moment in which one linguistic epoch was ceding to the next. It reveals, in exquisite fashion, an act of unfurling, a moment of passage. As in all metamorphoses, something was lost, and something else gained.

Standing before this fresco, I regretted that Reggie was not there to share my delight. I imagined him pointing his robust index finger at the words and chuckling with pleasure. *Fili de le pute, traite!*

San Clemente does not end at the fourth-century basilica. Descending farther, the stairways grow narrower and darker, the walls moister. At the bottom, if a bottom indeed exists, we walk among the ruins of a first-century home that once belonged to a patrician Roman family. Its patterned brick floors, its arches and hallways, are still miraculously in place. Adjoining this home, we chance into a second-century temple to the Indo-Iranian deity Mithras, whose cult attracted male followers, many of whom were soldiers, from across the Roman empire. In this long, narrow room lie two broad benches on which the celebrants reclined, and between them, an altar carved with the image of a bull. The ceiling is vaulted, with stucco stars and eleven slits that once let in light from above.

My summer with Reginald Foster is coming to an end. I want to hold on to this place where, over the past eight weeks, I have recovered a connective thread to a past self. On this lowest level of San Clemente, I am struck by the sound of gurgling water. Following it, I enter a small room, in the corner of which is a stone basin, near the floor, flowing with water from an underground stream. As the water drains, it continues on its way down, behind the walls, deeper still into the soil. This channel is thought to have been a part of the hydraulic system that brought water to the underground lake in Nero's *Domus Aurea*, his Golden House, nearby. To me the sound of that water, running through this very channel for seventy generations, or more, is primal. In its presence I feel I am standing at a sacred spring, a font of life. I want to touch it, capture it, be a part of it, and so I kneel down and let it run into my cupped palms. But of course it won't be caught. It spills through my hands and races along on its way, following its own predetermined course, and I am left alone with my futile desire to hold on to all that is fleeting, miraculous, and alive.

16.

REVERSING COURSE

Back in Ithaca, I held my interest in medieval law up to the light. I had so far studied at Cornell with two legal historians: Paul and a young scholar just beginning her career. But by the beginning of my third year, the young scholar departed, and I was left with Paul, who was also my adviser. This had been determined mostly by the process of graduate school admissions, which in my experience was nearly feudal in its arrangements. I had written a college thesis on medieval law, a subject in which Paul was an expert. When I became interested in applying to a doctoral program, it was Paul I contacted. It was he who encouraged me to apply. When the program offered me a spot, it was Paul who called me to confer the news. I accepted as fact that I would be his student, that he was my lord and I his liege. As in any feudal relationship, I felt indebted to him for my acceptance to the program. In return, I owed him fealty. Going to work with another professor, it seemed to me, would constitute the surest act of disloyalty.

My choice to study at Cornell was predicated on the idea of writing a dissertation with Paul on medieval legal history. But now I tried to summon what that interest felt like: the image that came to mind was an empty hull. Though I feared it would be a betrayal, I plunged the oar into the river of my studies to reverse course.

I rowed back in the direction I had first started out: toward Italian literature and history. A year of coursework at Cornell would be followed by a year in Italy for dissertation research. In our department, pursuing medieval or early modern Italian history meant studying with John, a historian of Renaissance Florence. I had visited his office one afternoon before the semester began, and we chatted about his upcoming course offerings. He was enthusiastic about my returning to Italian. Shelves filled with books I wanted to read lined the length of his office. I was elated: I would be turning back to Italy, to Italian, to the path I had long thought I would walk, and yet from which I had strayed. But had I strayed? Or was my path, in essence, a winding one? Whatever the answer, I floated out of John's office, knowing that in choosing Italian history, I was returning not just to a subject that invigorated me but, in some fundamental way, to myself.

John studied Florence, but I decided almost immediately that under his tutelage, I would go back to Rome. I was aware of how understudied Rome's late medieval period was. My professors knew little about it, most history books either devoted a few scant pages to it or jumped over it entirely, and, though a number of Roman scholars were at work on it, there were only three or four recent studies in English about it. For medieval historians studying or working at American universities, Florence and Venice were infinitely more popular choices.

It quickly became apparent that I would be largely alone in this endeavor. John's contacts, and the archives with which he was deeply familiar, were in Florence. Paul, who had little direct experience of Italy, could be of even less help. And, in retrospect, I believe he took some umbrage that I would not be following more closely in his footsteps. Although he never openly criticized my decision, I perceived that, from that point on, he was less invested in me. Here and there, he made oblique comments that subtly dismissed the value of my endeavor. "Wouldn't we all like to spend time in the sun," he twice said over the phone. In Rome, I certainly hoped for a lot more than a tan.

~~~

For my second-year coursework, I took John's lecture course on Machiavelli and his graduate seminar on the Medici principate. I dove into Machiavelli, marking up my books with all the fervor Professor Kaye could have dreamed of. I reveled in the connections I found between texts, and in constructing another interconnected literary universe. I was not alone. In the Medici principate seminar, held evenings in an Olin Library seminar room, I met three friends who shared my passion for Italian history. Seated around the seminar table at first, and then around dining tables at night, we became so tight a group that John soon took to calling us "the Gang."

Niall was the oldest among us, in his midthirties, simultaneously innocent and worldly, and because he had a homey apartment off campus, it was at his place that we often gathered. Sophus was the youngest of us, a precocious undergrad who enrolled in many of our seminars. He came from an affluent Scandinavian family, their home consisting not only of a house, as the lore went, but also of a separate structure outfitted with mobile shelving—his father's library. Sophus was always falling deeply in love and just as often pulling his hair out about it. Bob was the tower among us. He was a formidably learned former law student who was now just as devoted to studying history—the best student the program had seen in more than a decade, as Paul liked to say. Bob was witty and cheerful, and you could count on him for encyclopedic recall of almost anything. He was also beset with sadnesses he could not bring himself to share, at least not with me, which he balanced out with a kindness of spirit that he shared with all. Over the next few years, the four of us came to need each other in some elemental way. I felt protected and loved by this group of friends, just as I felt protective of and loved them, feelings that continue to bubble up even now, so many years later.

We spent countless long nights together, cooking, drinking wine, talking about history until one or all of us fell asleep on the couch, or on the floor. Time was plentiful then. Nights stretched so long before us that, even after dinner, the end was nowhere in sight. Around the table we read *The Italian's Trophy Mistress*, a romance novel, out loud for laughs, debating, in this day before any of us had cell phones at hand, whether "to lave" was a real verb, and what, if anything, was specifically *Italian* about the protagonist's handsome lover. With the Gang, my lexicon for romance sparked, grew more robust and braver. We got excited about arcane books, went to the movies and watched two, sometimes three films in a row. We waited in line in the early morning for the public library's annual book sale and, when the doors opened, made a beeline for the history aisle to unearth rare gems. We did these things for the pleasure of being in each other's company, and without irony. We sat in restaurants—talking, angsting, laughing, sighing—until they closed, only then trudging out, bracing our bodies against the frigid Ithaca night. My boyfriend did not like these gatherings and often did not come. Which was better anyway, because those of us in the Gang were always falling in and out of friend-love with each other and it was nicer to be alone.

It was one of those times in life when it seemed everyone wanted to kiss each other. I wished Niall would kiss me, but I didn't know how to broach it. Sophus tried out a kiss late one night while we waited to cross a street. It was pleasant, but not the kind of kiss that was going anywhere. Bob seemed shy for kissing, though I suspect that the heat of an embrace might have been what he most needed, melting a small hole in the fortress with which he guarded his innermost self. Niall, at a party, was ambush-kissed by my roommate, and one guy, soon after kissing me, confessed that he would have liked to kiss Niall too. Not long after that, I would leave my boyfriend, who went off and kissed someone else. From what I heard, she eagerly kissed him back.

Just after the New Year, Ithaca was at its grayest and coldest. The door to our car's gas tank had frozen shut after a hard sleet. Icicles eighteen inches long hung from the edge of our roof. While the outer world was immobilized by the cold, inside I was in flux. I reassessed my relationship with my boyfriend. We had been together since I was nineteen. I was now twenty-six. That biblical number, seven years—more than a quarter of my lifetime. I didn't know adult life without him. But I began to perceive that, for me at least, we were at the end of our line. I had no idea how to end it. It was like ending life itself. Who knew what lay on the other side?

It was my dentist who'd first noticed the signs. "Look," she said, holding a mirror up, pointing to the way that my top and bottom teeth aligned like expertly dovetailed joints. "You've been grinding your teeth." I was incredulous. Me? Come on. I was too calm and collected for weaknesses of that sort. I considered myself skilled at minimizing life's stressors, or ignoring them entirely—a strategy I learned from my mother, who has a certain kind of resilience on account of it. She had a lifelong friend, a high-profile interior decorator, who suffered from severe depression. My mother was often impatient with her. "You get out, you meet people!" she liked to say. It frustrated her that her friend gave in to staying home all day in her bathrobe. "Of course she's depressed!"

My dentist sent me to the pharmacy with instructions to buy a mouth guard to wear in my sleep. On one side, the packaging depicted a man in football gear, on the other, a teenage boy with a lacrosse stick. The rest of the world needed this product for dangerous, high-contact sports, and I needed it for bed? At home I dipped the gummy, waxen half-moon into boiling water, then clamped down with my teeth. In the mirror, my reflection sailed back to me, my lips distorted. My teeth, the hardest, the most durable aspect of our physical being, the last part of our bodies to disintegrate after we die, had been the first to alert me to the vulnerabilities, the soft edges, of my psyche.

My boyfriend was sullen, increasingly prone to depressive fits that he hoped I would bail him out of. But—*you get out, you meet people*—the tools I had were inadequate. He, too, stayed home in the proverbial bathrobe. Eventually, my will was inadequate, too. He wanted to come to terms, hash things out. But the more he talked, the more certain I was that we were through. Why belabor it? My parents had been together one day and separated the next, with little warning. The rug had been pulled out, so to speak. Why should this be any different? It felt awful to pull it, but it had to be done. Pulling it, suddenly and forcefully, was the only method I knew.

Although it had been my choice, the breakup was still hard. Daytime was all right. I rented a room in a house owned by a charismatic Lebanese American woman a few years older than me. She was a scientist with a penchant for lacy lingerie and lavish brunches, and we got along well. But when night fell and I was alone in my unfamiliar, sparsely furnished room, I was sometimes seized with panic. Paul took me out for a walk, during which we meandered down one of Ithaca's spectacular gorges. He encouraged me to channel my sense of loss into my work, and I knew he was right.

The upside was that I was finally free to ask myself what I wanted from life. I had for years resisted buying books because my boyfriend had considered it wasteful given our access to libraries. But I always liked owning books, seeing them lined up on my shelves, and remembering where and when I had read them, on what occasion, and with whom. I enjoyed their companionship, and the record they held, like an archive of a personal past. I went to the used bookstore downtown and, with relish, bought a whole stack of them to cart home, new companions for my new life.

John, I noticed, was an excellent close reader. I admired the way, in his classes, he teased meaning out of small segments of text. And he could remember passages from books he had read long ago and recite them nearly verbatim. When he took me and the Gang out for fajitas and margaritas, he grew relaxed and funny. We talked about Italy, and research, and university life, and all of it felt alive and meaningful and hopeful, and even, I would say, charmed. I felt fortunate to be at that table, with those people, experiencing the life that Professor Kaye had once described to me: talking about ideas and contributing to a conversation about the human experience. One winter evening I seized upon an idea. It seemed logical at the time, though as many acts of love or infatuation do, it looks absurd with a bit of perspective. I took a pretty tin of tea from the kitchen cabinet and walked the short distance to John's house. I knocked on his door, offered up the tin, and he, with a look of surprise, accepted it and invited me in. John was single, but he was much older than me: fifty-eight to my twenty-six. A lamp on the mantel over the fireplace cast a soft glow over the room. His house felt welcoming and warm, and comforting in its stability. We drank a cup of tea and talked. Within a week, we were an item.

〰〜〜

"What do you make of the word *consequences*?" my therapist asked. At the suggestion of my father's partner, herself a therapist, I was trying therapy. The process, the whole way of thinking, was new to me. I was perplexed. Relationships between professors and students happened all the time. One professor we knew had recently left his wife for a graduate student, and another had been living with his former student for years. There were some raised eyebrows, sure, but that was about it. Another professor had multiple complaints from female former graduate students, and yet I could perceive no real consequences for him. I'd even played a role in mitigating those repercussions: every year I was asked to attest in writing that he had acted professionally with me, and despite his occasional suggestive comment, every year I fulfilled that request without blinking. I was being asked to evaluate "professionalism" without really knowing what it meant, while beginning my career in an environment in which the term seemed to have no clear definition. So what was all this fuss about "consequences"? Why did the therapist insist on using such an unpleasant word?

As I began ruminating on the concept of consequences, John absorbed me into his rather unbending routine. Each day we ate precisely the same lunch: half a can of soup, two slices of turkey, and six pretzels, followed by one small scoop of frozen yogurt. This we ate in front of the television, watching sports or sitcoms that made John laugh out loud. All this, even the laughter—the sound of which I loved—was a novelty, and I joined him in it as both participant and observer. In my current state, his routine was grounding—even though, when faced with his meager diet, I was always hungry. I was younger and more active than him. I wanted twelve pretzels, or twenty. I wanted the entire can of soup. Or three.

There was no part of the routine that was mine. The things John ate, and the order in which he ate them, remained precisely the same as the day before I knocked on his door. I brought no recipes of my own. Not that I didn't have any, but it was easier just to slip into his life. I had managed to buy books, find a room of my own, and declare a new direction for my studies, but I balked at applying such self-determination to the entirety of my life. I think John would have liked me to bring more of myself into our relationship, but at the same time, not too much. He wanted someone to fit into his already very solidly defined life. Who could blame him? He was fifty-eight.

"Maybe you should have a fling," my therapist said one day. A fling? I was astonished at her recommendation, but she was completely matter-of-fact about it.

"But," I sputtered, "I have no clue how to have a fling!"

"It might be good for you," she said, unflustered. "And the recipe is simple. Meet someone you like. Have a fling."

The more I was absorbed into John's life, the tighter he wanted to draw the cord around me. He didn't trust me when I went out at night with my friends, seeing every male friend of mine as a rival. I protested: *It's not true! He's an old friend!* John insisted I stay home with him. I chafed: *You're so old-fashioned!* He resented: *Of course they want to kiss you!* For a short while, we went on like this.

Without John, the emptiness of my little life scared me. I had never before felt its dark corners—there had always been another person to fill the space. With John, I quickly sped back to what I knew. The comfort of a routine. A furnished home. A person who made me laugh and who liked to talk about the things I did. In addition to that, he was someone who saw promise in me, who took the edge off the stream of negative feedback that was, at least then, inherent to the life of a graduate student. Yet I watched what I said. As the weeks passed, I perceived the shadows of "consequences" lurking at the edges of our interactions. I raised the issue with him once, told him I was nervous about what might happen. He reassured me—the risks, he said, were all on his end. I must have really wanted to be reassured, because I believed him.

John quickly began to dream about our future. We sat on his back patio drinking tea, listening to the flocks of geese flapping and honking their way back to their spring nests. He could retire soon, he suggested, and the two of us could move to Italy. We could buy and run an olive oil farm. Retirement? Olive oil? His fantasy for our future sent a shock wave through me. During these weeks I had not thought much about the thirty-two years between us, the generational chasm that even he tried to impress on me as huge. But thinking about retirement while I was still training for my career unmoored me. He didn't seem to notice. He went on. After he died, he said, I could move back to the States and continue my academic career with my second husband. Second what? Words like these jolted me right out of being twenty-six. Suddenly I felt I could be forty or fifty, even sixty. Retirement, transcontinental moves, widowhood, and a second marriage were not hypothetical events in some distant future but possibilities to be imminently considered. It was too much.

That night when I came to bed, John was already asleep. A ray of moonlight had fallen across his head, illuminating his gray hair with a radiant white glow. The luminosity of that white, a visual reminder of the gulf between our ages and expectations, halted me in my tracks. We had been together nine weeks, and I was fond of him. But I wanted back to youth. Not to mention parity and freedom.

The consequences would come later.

17.

THE PAST IS A GREAT DIN

When you begin studying history, you think there is just one voice. The textbooks sound like this—unanimous, confident, declarative. Then, when you look more closely, when you read other books, you begin to distinguish the many voices in the room. At first they appear to be speaking in unison. But then you notice the dissonance: that one over there is not happy with this one over here. *No*, says one, *this is how it was. I'm sorry*, maintains the other, *but you've got it all wrong*.

You begin, too, to notice the voices that you think should be in the room but are not, as well as the quiet corners, the spaces between the words. Then you read the articles and the book reviews and you hear, singly and in stereo sound, each of the countless conversations that are happening upon the floor. This person talking to that one—now you can hear it!— and this one to that. You wonder, were those two enemies? Lovers? Rivals? Each voice, you begin to understand, is a person—a real person with a stake in the game, and reasons for thinking about the world, the past, themselves, the way they do.

So many are these conversations, printed in ink and suspended in time, that you must move swiftly from one to the next to perceive how a field has been built, over years, decades, centuries—and in some fields, like history, even millennia. But if you move too quickly, you will begin to spin, and the cacophony will overwhelm you and you will need to cover your ears. The past, when you listen, is a great din.

❧

Beginning in the late spring of 2002, I spent nearly four straight months in my office in the basement of the history department building, watching one red sunset after another from the shoulder-high window. I shared the office with three other graduate students, but they were away for the summer and I had the place all to myself. In this office I had my own desk and bookshelf, and even a couch, where occasionally I slept. My grandmother, the one who had lived in Rome, lay sick, and probably dying. My friends, even the Gang, had all left campus for the summer. Instead of crying over my losses—the lost boyfriend and the lost professor and the grandmother who was soon to go—I threw myself into my studies with the fervor of a desert mystic.

After three years at Cornell, my coursework was behind me, and before me lay my qualifying exams. I would face one exam in each of three subjects—medieval, Renaissance, and early modern history—each individually administered by the professor whose subspecialty I was being tested on. For the Renaissance and early modern exams, I was to write about fifteen pages each in response to two questions, as well as prepare an extensive annotated bibliography of all the reading I had done (and would do over the summer) in each field. These assessments were scheduled for August. But for my medieval history exam with Paul, we decided that legal history would not be part of it. Instead, he generously agreed that I could instead compile a syllabus for a future course I might teach on medieval Rome. To do this, I would read all the literature I could find on it, decide upon an organizing principle for the imaginary course, and lay out the period's most important themes and questions. This exercise would also provide me with a foundation on which to write a dissertation on medieval Rome, as well as a sample syllabus to take to the eventual job market. In September, I would face the cumulative oral exam, during which I would defend what I had written in the presence of my three examiners.

In preparation, I read and wrote and wrote and read. I walked to my office in the basement of McGraw Hall on quiet summer mornings, and I returned home at ten or eleven at night, or later. On the bookshelf next to my desk, I arranged by call number the hundred or so library books I had checked out. On the floor lay the expanding file case, already bulging, in which I stored xeroxed copies of articles. My desk became an archipelago of books and journals and the many scraps of paper on which I had written my notes. On the wall above my desk, I taped a sheet of paper on which I had written *"l'amor che move il sole e l'altre stelle"* ("the Love that moves the sun and the other stars"), the final line of *The Divine Comedy*, and one of its most famous. Reminding me of Dante's frequent affirmation that love and desire underpin any endeavor worth undertaking, I resolved to dedicate every ounce of myself to my pursuit. Underneath was the feeling that my studies, my writing, and my direction in life depended on it. Because I felt that summer as if I were standing before a gate, and I would need all my faculties and resources to make it to the other side. What would get me through that gate was love—not love for a person or even a specific love of my material, but love as a moving force within me. Any time I was dispirited, or reached a state of exhaustion, I summoned this line for its power to motivate me. What animated the line—and what I hoped would animate me—was not the prospect of external reward but rather the intrinsic reward of harnessing the life force within oneself.

During June and July, I read and wrote as I never had before. And I dove so deep into the history of medieval Rome that there were many days when I never quite found my way out. Peering out my office window, I saw the Roman countryside rolling out before me. Nights, I dreamed I was there. I woke up in a haze of communal governments and the recovery of Latin texts and the relationship between the city center and its rural periphery. My body may have been in Ithaca, but my mind, my imagination, was in Rome. Not the Rome of today, of course, with buzzing scooters and diesel clouds and crowded buses, but the Rome of the 1300s, with its center huddled in the bend of the Tiber, its millworks floating on the river's surface, its vineyards sprawling out to the Aurelian walls, its clamor of hooves, the commotion of rivalries playing out in its squares.

I wrote the syllabus: an introductory course on the history of Rome from the twelfth through the fifteenth centuries. It was geared toward the student with little or no knowledge of the Middle Ages, nor indeed of Italy, and it was divided into twelve sections on topics such as "the myth of empire," "the idea of the commune," and "Rome as widow." For each section I laid out the historical background, the principal interpretations of historians on the topics, and the open questions of the field. When I finally came up for air, it was more than one hundred pages long. And it was as comprehensive as any recent work published in English on the topic. I felt I had done something significant, forged a path for myself. John, perpetually cool following our breakup, said that in the context of the qualifying exams he had never seen anything quite like it. I did not know how to take his comment. I worried he meant that I worked too hard but that I had still, somehow, come up short.

What I put down on paper that summer was one thing. What happened in my mind was something else. In an effort to save money, I had moved out of the home of my Lebanese friend and sublet a room from a Cypriot friend who had returned home for the summer. The room was in a damp, semisubterranean apartment whose only other inhabitant, besides the multitude of giant millipedes, was another subletter—a Romanian computer science student who eyed me suspiciously on those evenings when we would accidentally cross paths on the way to or from the shower, one or the other of us wrapped in a definitely-not-big-enough towel.

His habits of consumption unnerved me. First there was the curdled milk, which to some unknown end he fermented in smelly vats on top of the fridge. Then there was the fruit, the only other category of food he seemed to eat. Fruits of all types, meticulously sliced and dried at a glacial pace on expansive sheets that colonized every surface in the kitchen, inviting entire weather systems of fruit flies that could not believe the extent of their good fortune. And the one fresh fruit he appeared to allow himself, a nightly watermelon, which he devoured, balancing it on his knees in front of the television, his jaws dripping with its pink juice. His only utensil: a foot-long machete.

I briefly entertained the notion that a grown man who consumes only fruit and milk must perforce be a gentle creature. But on the other hand, there was the fact that he neither smiled nor spoke. That he barely looked me in the eyes. The history of the Middle Ages brims with idealists endorsing strict and austere diets, but their histories show that there is no inherent contradiction between idealism and acts of savagery. And, of course, there was the machete.

My office on campus was a refuge from the millipedes and the Fruit Man. My studies, a haven from the breakups. One evening, I stayed up working under my piles of dog-eared books and color-coded index cards and reams of photocopied materials so late that the whole building was empty. I had just summarized the umpteenth article in my bibliography of late medieval history when I closed my eyes. And in that moment, like any desert mystic worth her salt, I received my vision: the shape of history.

What it looked like: a giant sphere, larger in circumference than was possible to perceive all at once. Like a crystalline planet, with points of light and great expanses of darkness. From the surface of the sphere emerged a host of tall spires, each as delicate as a space needle, pointing off in every direction. High-energy filaments, each as thin and strong as silk thread, pulsing with information traveling forward and back across centuries and millennia.

For a few months after the oral exam, I felt capable of perceiving, and retrieving on command, many of the long sequences of ideas that constituted the development of my field. I could revolve the sphere this way or that, tell you who was responding to whom, or how a particular idea about history evolved from one decade to the next. Each individual idea a gossamer thread, each subfield a spire, the field itself the energized sphere, the great din. All the historians and theorists I had read were there, their thoughts connected, interdependent, divergent, while those I hadn't read, did not yet know, remained dark. Whole sections of the sphere still off limits on account of my unknowing. But what was there, what was illuminated, was a reverberating conversation.

I tried to hang on to my vision beyond the exam itself, which had gone well, but the more I tried to retain it, the more it slipped through my fingers. I was aware that at any moment it could vanish. That, inevitably, it *would* vanish. That it was a privilege to have perceived it, to have felt its weightlessness, to have glimpsed its spindles, its spires, its dark lunar expanses, the delicate bones of its immense architecture.

18

WINTER WILL MELT AWAY

During my last year in Ithaca, I found a house to rent with a fellow graduate student. It was a once-beautiful run-down house, built in the German style with white stucco walls and brown timber framing. It had charming details like leaded windows, a large fireplace, and a kitchen with a breakfast nook. Within a short time, pictures hung on the walls of my room and, what's more, in frames. My kitchen boasted two new ceramic bowls and mugs—white with cheerful red-and-blue midcentury-modern designs—that a friend had gifted me, the prettiest I had ever owned. My mother came to visit, and she bought and hemmed two pieces of white cotton fabric with eyelets and white embroidered flowers, and voilà, the breakfast nook had curtains. The living space was drafty but sweet and homey.

My exams behind me, I began trying to conceive of a dissertation. Where to start? Writing the syllabus for Paul had been a crash course in the history of late medieval Rome. Covering almost four centuries, it was broad rather than deep. The time had come to dive in.

Some deep-seated instinct pushed me toward the 1300s. This is the period commonly described as the nadir of Roman history, the decades when the city, in many senses, hit rock bottom. But the 1300s were also where I had begun, ten years earlier as a high school senior, when I had been transfixed—*trafitta*—by a text considered by many a pinnacle of Italian literature. It was strange now to think of that paradox, nadir and pinnacle, while also realizing that in some ways I would be coming full circle.

It was a dramatic period for Rome, which was suffering from two major injuries. One was fresh, and the other, a long-standing wound that refused to heal. Dante expressed the pain of this latter wound in *Purgatory*, which he composed mostly in the 1310s:

> *Come, see your Rome who, widowed and alone,*
> *weeps bitterly; both day and night, she moans:*
> *"My Caesar, why are you not at my side?"*

The emperor ("Caesar") was Henry VII, the elected figurehead of the Holy Roman Empire, that strangely titled, sprawling conglomeration of semiautonomous territories that in this period extended as far north as Hamburg, east to Vienna, and to Marseilles and Pisa in the southeast and south. Although the empire's capital was theoretically Rome, the Holy Roman emperor had never actually resided there. Instead, the empire relied on the *idea* of Rome as the foundation of its authority, and on the physical city as the site for its infrequent but highly symbolic coronation ceremonies.

Henry VII, for whom Dante imagined Rome crying out, had been elected emperor while in Germany in 1309, pending a coronation ceremony at Saint Peter's Basilica in Rome. Before him, the throne had sat empty for six decades, which helps explain the high hopes people like Dante placed in him. Throughout the sixth canto of *Purgatory*, Dante implores Henry to come to Italy and witness the disastrous effects of the empire's long abandonment. In these impassioned passages, Dante refers to Italy as "a ship without a helmsman in harsh seas" and laments that "the saddle is empty." He begins four tercets in a row with the same relentless entreaty: *Vieni* ("Come"), that the emperor might see the strife in the deserted "garden of the empire" and unify the fragmented Italian peninsula under a single monarch. As did the many who shared his worldview, Dante looked to the arrival of Henry VII in Italy with almost messianic hope.

There was also Rome's more recent injury. This was the departure of the pope and the papal curia from the city around 1304. Like a peacock whose lush plumage trails so long and voluminous that it nearly dwarfs the bird's body, so too did the curia take with it an unimaginably wide swath of Roman society. With the pope went myriad representatives of the church hierarchy, among whom were the cardinals and archbishops and the abbots general of the mendicant and monastic orders, jurists and judges, as well as all those who administered the papacy's jurisdictions and attended to the papal household, such as merchants and bankers, notaries and scribes, accountants, theologians, diplomats, painters and sculptors, personal servants to the pope, and a host of aides and attachés. In 1309, the papacy and its sizable retinue settled in Avignon, where it could assert a stronger presence in the disputes between the French and English monarchs. It would not return to Italy until 1379. The papal court had wandered before, but never so far or for so long.

For Rome as a city, this was unfathomable. And for me, the almost cinematic drama of the period lit my imagination. The "plucking" of all that plumage meant that the city was effectively, and suddenly, depopulated. With the notaries gone, there were few left to record the basic transactions of everyday life. Visitors to the papal curia—those petitioning its courts or conducting any number of practical affairs with church prelates or administrators—now journeyed to Avignon, not Rome, to conduct their business. The demographic crisis sparked an economic one. The city's coffers drained. And on top of this there floated a nebulous crisis of identity. The papacy and Rome had for centuries been tied at the hip.

There was even a Latin expression for it: *Ubi papa ibi Roma* ("Where the pope is, there is Rome"). But where was Rome now? If the pope had carted the "real Rome" off with him to Avignon, what was the city that had been left behind? No one in Rome quite knew what to do, or how to define themselves or their city. And in a period in Italy's history when one's city defined one's identity as much as or more than the nation-state defines the identity of its citizens today, what did it even mean to be Roman after the papacy had departed?

These were the questions that began to consume me. I wanted to understand what happened when a powerful city, origin point of a sprawling civilization, retracted, when it lost its claims to power and the veneer of prestige. I knew what it felt like, for me, to walk through the beautiful ancient ruins of *Roma capitale*, the capital of a unified Italian state, or to glimpse them, as a teenager, from a speeding taxi. But I wanted to perceive, as viscerally as I could, what it felt like to fourteenth-century Romans to live knowing that their small, impoverished city had been stripped of its medals, was capital of nothing, lay abandoned by its major institutions, and that its greatest asset lay not in the hard currency of laws or military might but in the more diaphanous tender of memories and dreams. And I wondered whether, out of the chaos and struggle, Romans emerged with understanding, something gleaned, a tiny gem hewn with effort from the rough stuff of life. In fourteenth-century Rome— and perhaps in my own life, too, although back then I never noticed the parallel—I was looking for the cloud's silver lining, the hope within the gloom, the opportunity for transformation that comes hand in hand with any worthy crisis.

In November, two historians, a husband-and-wife team, came to Cornell from Toronto to give a joint talk on early modern Rome, the period running from approximately 1450 to the French Revolution. The next day they took me to breakfast. Over bagels, Tom—an inventive and generous scholar who would later join my dissertation committee—and Libby, herself an accomplished Roman historian, spoke about their many decades of exploits in Rome, where I'd be returning the following September to begin my dissertation research. With Tom and Libby, I hesitantly floated the idea of studying Rome's fourteenth century. The primary source material for the period was famously sparse, and, I admitted, I did not yet have a sense of how to approach the research. But it was undeniably fascinating. To my surprise, they did not urge me to reconsider. On the contrary. They gave me a long list of books to read and the names of Roman scholars to be on the lookout for once I arrived. They were enthusiastic and supportive, and for the first time in a long while, I did not feel alone.

⤛⟋⟍

Thirteen hundred years before Dante, during the reign of Emperor Augustus, Rome had been bursting at its seams. Each day, up to one million people drank from its fountains, drew water from its river, or wended their way over its paving stones. Although the precise numbers are contested, it is agreed that no other city in the ancient world reached Rome's magnitude. The closest had perhaps been Carthage, in modern-day Tunisia, which at its largest—before the Romans burned it to the ground in 146 BCE—numbered perhaps 500,000. It would take another thousand years for any other city to reach the million-person threshold: Baghdad around 900 CE, and Kaifeng a few hundred years later, around 1200. Not until the nineteenth century would any other city break well over the million-person mark. The size of ancient Rome was a spectacle in itself.

After the empire fractured, Rome's population shrank dramatically. By the 1310s, residents numbered only eighteen to thirty thousand—which reduced the city to about one third the size of Florence. In the early fourteenth century, had the entire population of Rome gathered in the Colosseum, only about half of the amphitheater's seats would have been filled. Or to put it another way: for every hundred or so people who had lived in ancient Rome, by the later Middle Ages there remained a mere two or three.

As a drying puddle leaves behind concentric rings of dark soil, so the shrinking city left behind open spaces, which transformed over time into fields and pastures for roaming livestock. The old Servian Wall was already crumbling, and the Aurelian Wall, so expansive in its ambition, lay far from the city's small center. The densely inhabited portion of the city, cradled in the Tiber's bend, became known as the *abitato*, the inhabited land. And the rest, the farms and vineyards and fields dotted with churches and monasteries that now extended out to the Aurelian Wall, the *disabitato*.

The ruins we know today—the Colosseum, the Forum, the Mausoleums of Hadrian and Augustus—were then already ruins. For centuries, people had been living in and under them, carving humble shelters from the monuments' shaded nooks and crannies. When tensions bubbled up, rival noble families used the monuments as their personal strongholds. In the expanse of the Colosseum's interior grew hay and trees, and its walls and archways hung green with countless rare and nonnative species of vines and flowers, whose provenance is conjectured to have been the paws, fur, and stomachs of the animals transported from faraway lands to fight in the amphitheater's spectacles. The Forum was a pasture for cows and sheep and was littered with fallen stones. The million bodies of ancient times had long since been burned or buried, and so had their children, and their children's children, too. To imagine fourteenth-century Rome, I would have to immerse myself in the idea of a withered city, a city that had lost almost everything that had previously defined it. Everything but its name, and the memory of what it had once been.

Three months before my lease is up, the gray Ithaca winter stretches as far as the eye can see. Autumn is a distant memory, and spring an impossible dream. The roads are permanently iced, the waterfalls stand still. At night, windswept traffic lights sway over empty intersections.

A friend of a friend holds a party. In small groups, we dance off the cold. Halfway through the evening, I retreat to a corner to check on a friend, a German woman entangled in an unhappy marriage to a country doctor, when I happen to lock eyes with a man across the room. Years ago, he and I were in a class together. A few minutes later he walks over and reintroduces himself. My dispirited friend steals away to pour herself more wine. The fellow and I start talking. About what? Who knows.

What I do know: He has dark brown eyes that are curious and lively and kind, and the kind of eyelashes that provoke in some women a desperate kind of envy. His left earlobe has a tiny hoop earring in it—the tiniest earring you have ever seen. He waves his hand as he's saying something, and: Is that a wedding ring? In a bout of wishful thinking, I tell myself maybe Spanish men wear rings on their ring fingers that are not wedding rings.

What's going on here? I don't even know this guy. And anyway, in six months, I'll be off to Rome. And all of this will dissolve into thin air. The Ithaca winter will melt away. I'll forget this house, this party, this man and his eyes and his ring that is or is not a wedding ring. Surely, I'll forget that he said he would invite me for a hike, that he will bring his dog, and then how, together, we will make our way through the woods, winding our way up the side of a waterfall so frozen that no water falls. And how during this walk my body will alight and life will careen forward like water, once retained, now suddenly set free through a sluice.

❧

Turns out, he *was* married.

It's complicated, Javier told me over coffee at the Zeus café the day after our hike. We were seated at the same table where Paul and I had met four years earlier, where I had first pondered whether I wanted to become a professional pedant. Complicated? His wife was enrolled in a graduate program and living far away. She was seeing someone else and had encouraged him to do the same. Were they separating, I asked? He shook his head. They loved each other. They were just making adjustments.

I had never had a fling. But a fling with a married man: Isn't that the universal, number one, no good, very bad idea?

The difficulty: he was lovely. In his bearing, there was goodness, an honesty, an emotional balance I perceived, even if I could not put my finger on it with precision. He had been forthcoming about his marriage and his commitment to it. Yet all the same, within minutes of meeting him at that party, I had, to my own astonishment, glimpsed a future with him. That counted for something, didn't it?

I told him I'd think about it.

❧

How to Have a Fling:

Show up for dinner a little after the appointed time. Show little concern about the scant food in the fridge. Think how lucky you are that this man is preparing a meal for you at all. Consolation: tomorrow morning you can go to State Street Diner and eat a truck driver's breakfast. Keep your hands in your pockets and smile.

Regard the photos of him and his wife on the fridge—making funny faces, kissing, posing handsomely with their dog—with detached interest. Find the one of him rock climbing with a friend and ask about that one.

Watch as he slices a baguette, as he spreads cheese on the small rounds. Watch as he removes the roasted peppers from the jar and lays them carefully over the cheese. Notice how your mouth has begun to water.

Accept the glass of Spanish white. Ask him how to say "spinach" in Spanish. Say it: *espinacas*. Do the word justice. Place the accent correctly. Watch him as he slices onions paper thin. Enjoy how the knife rests so naturally in his hand. Regard his hands—capable with a knife, capable with a pen, capable, you imagine, with your body. Savor the flavor of not really knowing.

Notice how at home you feel in his space. Sit on the sofa next to the dog. Let the dog nuzzle his head into your lap. Stroke his warm velvet ears. Marvel at how quickly this dog brings you into the fold. You could stay here forever.

Return to the kitchen to help with the fish. Pour the olive oil as he instructs. Watch as he adds a bit more. Notice how he shakes the pan. Sprinkles the herbs. Dices the red peppers and adds them. Keeps an eye on the garlic to make sure it does not burn. Notice the skilled efficiency of his movements.

Realize: with a mere eight ingredients, this man is cooking you a feast. Realize: you could marry this man. Realize: you do not know how to have a fling.

⌒

My lease to the tired but cheerful German-style home was expiring at the end of June. By the end of May, the Gang had dispersed: Sophus back to Norway, Bob to Chicago, and Niall to Toronto. Javier and I were spending more and more time together: hiking, climbing in Cornell's indoor rock gym, sharing meals. In a few weeks, he was moving to Providence to start a teaching job. We decided that I would stay with him for the summer and leave from there for Rome. I didn't know if I would ever return to Ithaca, and—for the first time when it came to Rome—I was dragging my feet. I had begun to feel at home in Ithaca, and now, within a few weeks, I would have no home at all. The person with whom I had glimpsed a possible future was moving to a city I hardly knew—and, lest I forget, was still married to someone else. I felt I was moving across a thin surface, beneath which lay giant plates that might at any moment shift one way, or another.

On a visit to Ithaca, Javier's wife raised the word *separation*. But he was not ready. I could see it was good that I was going—good for both of us. We needed time.

In typical Ithaca fashion, it rained. A warm, soppy start to June. Like swimming in tepid soup. Occasionally you'd get chilly just from the moisture. Then you'd put on a sweater and begin to sweat. It thundered and lightninged. You had to keep the lights on all day. In the kitchen, fruit flies begat fruit flies begat fruit flies. Ten years after his separation from my mother, my father was marrying again. As a gift, I bought a plain wood coffee table and painted it. In the center of it, a rooster—crowing, colorful. The paint struggled to dry.

On the floor of my room, a battalion of cardboard boxes stood at the ready. As the days wore on, these dampened boxes filled steadily with books, with papers, with thousands of pages of printed-out emails between me and the Gang. For the past year, Sophus had been sending us an "Art of the Day" email. Each day he sent an image of a piece of art, accompanied by some wild, often hysterical interpretation of it. Followed by our responses, our endless chatter. Into the box the emails went. I pulled my framed pictures from the wall and wrapped them carefully in tissue paper. Into the box they went.

Before Bob had left for Chicago, he had looked morosely around our shared office, which had also been packed up into boxes. "This is the end of the Gang," he said.

"Not really," I said, as usual trying to cheer Bob up. "Just the end of how it is now."

We were both right. It was the end of what we knew. And yet it was also a beginning.

Part III

19.

SANT'IVO ALLA SAPIENZA

Without a word, the taxi driver stopped in front of a block of apartments in the northern residential quarter of Rome known as Trieste. He pulled my suitcase from the trunk and set it down heavily on the sidewalk, then folded back into his seat and sped off. Lugging the suitcase, I walked around the building in search of the right bell. When I found it, I rang up, then pressed my fingers to my eyelids, which were hot and swollen.

It had pained me to leave Providence. Javier's new apartment there had a sunny kitchen. Its windows faced east, and in the morning we ate across from each other at his little table, sunshine falling across his bare shoulders. Afternoons we went on long bike rides, the Narragansett Bay slipping by us, a shifting canvas of blues, grays, and greens. On rainy days we went to the climbing gym. But the apartment in Providence was Javier's new home, not mine. It was filled with the furniture, cookware, and ornaments of his married life. Even though Javier had said that he was committed to our relationship, the objects of his former married life preoccupied me. In my more vulnerable moments, these objects—a table his wife had made, a blanket she had crocheted, a photo of the two of them smiling radiantly at a summer music festival—made me feel that I had camped out in *their* life. That summer I lived in a landscape of domestic sentiment to which I had no map. This landscape felt enormous, of Jurassic proportions. And still, I had not been ready to leave it.

But not going to Rome was not an option. I could never have explained forgoing such an opportunity, even to myself. *Above all* to myself. And of course, I wanted to go. It was just hard to locate the feeling amid all the others getting in the way.

On the first of September, Javier dropped me off at Logan Airport. I cried when the plane's wheels lost contact with the ground, and I cried as Boston fell away into the green vortex of New England, and I went on crying as all earth blanched into an opaque white haze. The cruelty of the airplane is that it propels you with complete indifference into your future while disregarding any plea, no matter how impassioned, to look back.

The landlord, a tall, gangly woman with disheveled hair, led me into her office. It occupied one of the apartment's three rooms—by far the biggest one—and she sat me down among a host of scruffy potted plants. I signed some papers while quelling a new wave of sobs. Peering over her glasses, she reiterated that the lease was for one month only: September, emphasizing, *of this year, 2003.* When she was sure I understood, she rose and led me on a short tour. The other room, she explained, was rented to a German girl who would be staying until winter—I would probably meet her in the kitchen one evening when she was cooking up one of her monstrous meals, I should just *see* how much butter she eats, god knows how she is still alive. Then, peering at me over her glasses as we stood on the threshold of the kitchen, she ventured to ask whether I, too, cooked like a German, or did I, *magari,* cook like an Italian, with olive oil and, god forbid, a vegetable or two, or—and this seemed just to occur to her—did I cook like an American, meaning not at all? Relieved to hear that I cooked, she demonstrated how to light the flame on the stove using a long plastic starter. Then she led me down the hall to a narrow bedroom—mine—that had a pleasing simplicity and a large window at the far end. The bathroom was shared, she informed me, before rather abruptly gathering her belongings and locking the main door behind her.

I was back in the city I had so longed to return to. And yet landing in Rome had not felt like a beginning. It was the tail end of summer. When I went out that afternoon to take a walk, the city's energy felt low, hushed. Dry leaves banked the edges of mostly empty sidewalks. Schools were not yet in session for the year, and the children I saw that first day appeared melancholy, as if summer's delights had long since expired. When night finally fell and it was time to sleep, I stood at the window and looked out over the hushed city. In every direction, countless buildings, dark boxes but for the glowing windows in which small, unknown figures moved about. Millions of people in Rome, and yet I knew not a soul.

✒

The next morning, I headed out for the Istituto Storico Italiano per il Medioevo, the Italian historical institute where I would spend the next two weeks charting my course. The bus, jammed with morning commuters, wound through Salaria, a residential neighborhood, then down the via Veneto and around the edge of Piazza Barberini. Instead of riding all the way to Piazza Venezia, I got off early to walk the final stretch. Passing cafés, I was reminded of the morning melody, ubiquitous throughout Rome, of clinking ceramic cups and plates. I admired, with undiminished awe, the great portico of the Pantheon and its legion of Corinthian columns. I wound my way through still-sleepy Piazza Navona and experienced a renewed sense of pleasure from this place that, despite all my contradictory longings, still struck me deep.

I had come to Rome with the idea that I would examine notarial registers—books containing the handwritten public records of transactions ranging from sales of real estate and livestock to marriage contracts, business partnerships, and last wills and testaments. Notarial registers of this period are rich with the details of daily life, making them ideal sources for social and economic history. These formal documents were the foundation on which central and northern Italy's urban and commercial life were built. The notarial profession was consequently very strictly regulated, and for many notaries in the fourteenth century, it offered pathways for promotion into the administrative and legal life of Italian city-states. At the *istituto* I would not find the original registers, but I could access published editions of those that had already been transcribed. Using those, I would set out to familiarize myself with the territory.

A few days in, when reading through these registers—in Latin, mostly concerning property transfers—came to feel particularly onerous, I picked up a book that was shelved just beside my desk. This was when I happened upon the story of Petrarch and Stefano Colonna walking down the via Lata; the elder nobleman, Colonna, sharing his premonition that he might outlive his sons; the poet, a decade later, consoling him on the losses Colonna had foreseen, his loyalties divided between the family of his patron and the man who had caused his pain, the man whose aspiration he shared to restore Rome to its former glory: Cola di Rienzo. *Good story*, I wrote in my journal, and moved on.

After two weeks in the *istituto*, I was ready to head to the Archivio di Stato, Rome's historical state archives, to begin my research using the notarial registers. A stone's throw from Piazza Navona, the complex that houses the archives is easy to miss. The imposing wood doors that face busy Corso di Rinascimento must be almost twenty feet tall, and even when they are open, they seem to create a barrier to entry. I have noticed over the years that many people stop here on the threshold to peer in. Sometimes they bend at the waist, feet remaining outside, as if to enter the courtyard would be trespassing. Many must conclude that it is private property, given the colossal doors and the palpable serenity that lies beyond them.

In fact, inside the doors lies one of Rome's most remarkable public spaces: the intricately designed courtyard, church, and palazzo that together make up Sant'Ivo alla Sapienza. This was the seat of Rome's first university. Originally called the *studium*, it was founded in 1303 by Pope Boniface VIII, a contemporary of Dante. The *studium* taught ecclesiastical studies and for the first six centuries of its existence remained closely tied to the papacy. In the seventeenth century, it became known as La Sapienza, the name it still goes by today. Although *sapienza* means "knowledge" or "wisdom" in Italian, in the seventeenth century, the term also commonly connoted "university." La Sapienza would remain on this spot until 1935, when Mussolini commissioned a new university site in the northeast of the city. The palazzo at Sant'Ivo then became home to the Archivio di Stato, Rome's municipal archive, which serves as a repository of documents dating from the ninth to the nineteenth centuries.

Stepping off Corso di Rinascimento and through the great doors, there stretches a long, rectangular courtyard paved with a geometric pattern of black and white cobblestones. On the left and right are two long galleries punctuated by columns and arches. And to the far left, an open-air stairway leads up to a balustraded second-story corridor that rings the courtyard on three sides. A striking feature of the courtyard lies at its far end: the receding facade of the church of Sant'Ivo, an architectural wonder designed in the 1600s by Francesco Borromini.

Before this mid-September day, I had only read about Sant'Ivo. But standing in the courtyard's embrace, I immediately felt its geometry of triangles and ovals, of alternating edges and curves, of massive stability—the weight of all that stone—giving rise to a wispy immateriality. It felt like standing in a fugue, a triple helix of courtyard, palazzo, and facade. The sky above, an impossible September blue. I ascended the stairs to the second floor, to that archive strung so improbably between azure and earth, where my dissertation research began.

༄

When you get close to a medieval manuscript, the first thing you notice is the acrid smell. This comes from the ink's tannic acids, iron sulfate, and perhaps wine, centuries old but still potent. Sometimes you can almost smell the ink burning the paper or parchment. And in some cases, especially with paper, the ink actually does burn through, leaving small holes that make the page look like it has been eaten by worms. At such close range, the letters on the page loom large. Their edges are predictably less smooth, more jagged than they appear from afar. And if you look carefully, you can make out dark spots in each word where the scribe's hand paused, or where the pen retraced its path, leaving ink that pooled before it dried.

I had been sitting for two hours in the archive with my nose in a notary's book. It was thick and small, like a voluminous diary—the kind of object a person could comfortably carry around. I hoped to make out who was trading what, who was connected to whom, and how far their business and social contacts extended. With these details, I could potentially construct a chart of urban networks that I hoped might form the base of a broader argument about the period. But for one problem: I still had not managed to read a single word.

Here I was, with the lock in my hands, and the key would not turn. Not even with the help of the Cappelli paleography lexicon that Bob had gifted me before I left Ithaca—a small, thick, indispensable book that lists and identifies, by century, the common but innumerable abbreviations and styles of lettering found in medieval Latin and Italian manuscripts. Every so often, when another researcher in the room flipped a page, I felt a searing envy. At Cornell the year before, I had taken a yearlong paleography course. We had learned to read one medieval script after another: uncial,

Carolingian, notarial, chancellery, Gothic . . . the list went on. But even supposedly defined scripts can vary, and the one on my desk was, to me, entirely illegible.

As if indifferent to my paleographic anxieties, the archive had a relaxed way about it, a casual air that seemed part of its DNA. Its doors and windows were open, letting in the sounds and smells of the outside world—pine trees, diesel fumes, baked goods—that wafted in on the occasional breeze. This was not the kind of archive that demanded you wear gloves, or that asked you to leave your bag in a locker. Materials were housed in the stacks, but once you ordered them up, they could remain overnight on "work-in-progress" shelves in the center of the consultation room. Each work was visibly bookmarked with the name of the scholar working on it, so there was little privacy about who was looking at what.

This nonchalance extended to the archival materials themselves. Scholars were regularly photographing their documents, the clicking and flashing of their cameras a background constant—this despite the signage prohibiting flash photography. At first I waited expectantly for an archivist's reprimands to fly, but they never came. The place just hummed on.

Focusing once again on the letters, my effort suddenly paid off: I made out an *s*, then a mysterious scribble, then an *i*, followed by what were beyond any doubt two *m*s. A minute later, though, I began to doubt: the *mm* had morphed into *nin*. First one reading convinced me, then the other. I found no progress, only uncertain undulation. A humid breeze wound its way through the wide doorway, ruffling the pages of the manuscript. In its wake, a six-hundred-year-old smell, acrid and bitter, rose from the page. I traced the letters with my finger, as if such a motion might help, as if the letters might suddenly and magically turn to braille. For a moment I wished the words *had been* in braille, for that would certainly be easier to interpret, I reasoned, than this notary's script.

With renewed determination, I went back to the *s* and *i* and the two *m*s—when suddenly, to my astonishment, the words leaped from the page.

Finally! Like a revelation, they stood out in relief against the recalcitrant page: "swimming pool"—*swimming pool!*

But, oh.

The realization hit like a lead pipe. The document was in Latin, of course, not English. From the fourteenth century. I slumped over the document and drew its bitter vapor deep into my lungs.

For days I watched the archivist, seated at her large desk, rummaging through piles of documents and thick tomes, confidently recording notes in an endless ledger. Every morning she carried a stack of manuscripts over to the group of graduate students who had taken up residence in the corner of the room. They wore roughly identical uniforms of Converse sneakers, jeans, and T-shirts in neutral colors, and they spent the workday giggling, comparing notes, and entering and exiting the room for reasons I could not decipher. I was certain of one thing, though—any of them would have been capable of reading my documents in a single glance.

My frustration swelling, I approached the archivist's desk and waited to be noticed. Seated behind a bound manuscript over half a foot thick, she peered at me at long last over her tortoiseshell glasses. I asked her timidly, in my bookish Italian, where I might find a paleographic guide to help me decipher the notarial document I had been looking at all week. For a long moment, she said nothing.

"Have your studies not prepared you?" she finally asked.

I mumbled that the paleography I had studied hadn't been specifically Italian, and that perhaps we had skipped this particular script. I thought of Tom and Libby in Toronto, wondering if they might be able to help. Every summer they visited the Archivio di Stato to conduct their research, and surely they could advise me on how to proceed. But because I felt they were not strictly responsible for me, and maybe, too, because I felt no small measure of embarrassment at having so quickly reached such an impasse, I concluded it was my problem to sort out.

The archivist sighed. "I don't know what to tell you. Go visit the university and see if they have a course you can take. We don't do instruction here."

"But I'm not asking for inst—" It was no use. She had stood up behind her desk and was already leaning over her notes. I had been dismissed.

"I'm sorry, *signora*," she said, penciling in a check mark on her page. "There's really nothing I can do for you."

She folded a manuscript into her thin arms and walked back to the group of students. One of them turned to look at me over his shoulder. Red-faced, I made a beeline for the exit, abandoning my notebook on the desk and my bag dangling from the back of my chair.

I left the archive and walked down the gallery corridor that overlooked the courtyard below. Into the giant gray box that dominated the end of the hall I put forty-five *centesimi*. The machine, taller than me and twice my width, spit out a tiny, feeble plastic cup, then shook and screeched as it expelled espresso. I held the hot plastic gingerly between two fingers, then stirred in the small pile of sugar that the machine dropped onto its surface with the thin plastic strip, also dispensed from above, that passed for a spoon. The machine was so huge and overwrought, like those 1960s computers that commanded half a room, while the product it dispensed was so flimsy. The contrast made me chuckle. When I was a teenager, my brother Nick had stashed a bulky television he had found in a neighbor's trash in our family's garage. He dubbed it "the Admiral" on account of its massive size and its antiquated authority. I had no one to share the joke with, but I named the hulking espresso machine "the Admiral" in honor of my brother, and when I approached, if no one was around, I clicked my heels together and saluted it.

Espresso in hand, I was standing over the arcade's stone balustrade when I glimpsed a man and a boy—presumably father and son—playing in the courtyard below. The rectangular floor of the courtyard is cobblestoned with the typical Roman *sampietrini*, or "little Saint Peters," as they are called, since they were first used to pave Saint Peter's Square. But interspersed in the field of black stones is a geometrical pattern of white ones: two solid circles with stone stars at their center, from each of which radiate eight white lines. These lines form squares or triangles or stars, depending how you look at them.

The boy was very young. Although coordinated, he was pudgy in the arms and calves, his frame still small for his head. I guessed him to be about four. He and his father trotted around the courtyard, following the white lines of stones, tracing patterns and shapes with their bodies. They ran together, side by side, following a single line. Then when they reached the end, they broke off, one turning left and the other right. Now on opposite sides of the square, they kept apace with one another, mirroring one another symmetrically until the paths brought them together once again.

The sun glinted off the boy's hair, which bobbed as he ran. The father's long arms swung at his sides. Throughout their entire game, as they glided under the billows and recesses of Borromini's facade, they exchanged only a few words. They dashed from sun to shade and back once again into the sun. The courtyard around them was quiet but for the occasional chirping bird and the passing of a gentle breeze. No one else ventured in. From above, I watched in still silence, unobserved. I did not wish to intrude. I felt I was witnessing something private, an intimate moment, as the father and son etched their forms into the history, the architecture, the sunlight and the shadows, the perfect geometry of this courtyard.

20.

VIA DELLA SCALA

It is not easy to find a place to live in Rome. As I learned the summer of Living Latin, the way you find an apartment in Rome in the early years of the current millennium is by buying *Porta Portese*, the local paper that lists apartments for rent. If you, like me, do not have a cell phone, you must go to the closest *tabacchi* to buy a phone card. Then you locate a public phone, most of which are near bus stops. They are freestanding, with no booth, no insulation between you and the world. Which means that you will struggle to hear the person on the line because buses will continually be screeching into or roaring out of the bus stop during your call. While searching for an apartment, you will inhale an untold volume of diesel exhaust. People will shove past you in their race to reach the bus doors that will inevitably close them out. They will then hang about with an air of defeat. But their momentary defeat is nothing next to how you feel when the third landlord in a row hears your foreign accent, says, *Stranieri, no,* and then hangs up on you. During the first weeks, the cutting phrase "no foreigners" will reverberate in your ears.

The phone calls will be unforgiving exercises in language study. Sometimes, when things go awry and words fail you, you will simply hang up, knowing that you can never call back and redeem yourself. On the upside, you will quickly master vocabulary pertaining to apartment rentals: *affittare, disponibile, camera, donna single, a breve termine*—to rent, available, room, single woman, short-term. When your time frame has dwindled down to one week, you begin biting your nails. You need a room *subito*, immediately.

Increasing your odds, you notice that some phrases resonate better than others, cause the voice on the line to tick upward, as if what you have just told them were a pleasant surprise. "Twenty-eight-year-old single student," for example, does not do very well, but "twenty-eight-year-old married doctoral researcher"—you find this works a little better.

When you finally find a room whose owner is willing to show you the place, you cannot believe your luck. The apartment is in Trastevere, very central. Then the worry returns. You have one day left before you must leave your current room in the northern neighborhood. You have begun envying children, and all those who know where they will be sleeping that night. Your nails are bitten to the quick.

On your way to visit the apartment, you pass through the outdoor market in the square known as Campo de' Fiori. There you spot a pair of silverish rings for six euros. From now on, wherever you go, you are as good as married. You nurture a small nugget of pride at how well you are upping your game.

On a central pedestrian street in Trastevere called via della Scala, you press what you hope is the right bell and after a long second, the arched green door clicks open. A stone staircase softened by centuries takes you to the second floor. On the way up you pass an opening—a window with no pane—that looks into an inner courtyard populated by a scramble of potted plants. At the landing, an almost-but-not-quite-old woman peers out from behind an irregular wooden door. She regards you suspiciously. In French-accented Italian, she asks if you are alone, if you remembered to close the door behind you until it clicked. Yes, you say, showing her how responsible you are, how reliable. You mention your "husband" who lives in the United States. She eyes the ring on your finger. Worn for only half an hour, does it shine too brightly? An elderly brown-and-white-mottled dog stands by her side, its hind legs quivering. Every now and again the dog lays its ears flat and barks at you, as if it, too, can sense your falsehood.

When the woman, who introduces herself as Sabrina, beckons you inside, you realize you don't even care what the room looks like. You follow her sedate figure down the hallway. At the end of the hall is a room, with a ceiling and a bed, which is really all you're asking for. It is light blue. Blue everything. Blue walls, blue rug, blue curtains, blue coverlet on the bed, blue pillows. Even the ceiling is blue. Although the late September sun is high in the sky, scarce light enters from the room's single window, which overlooks the plant-filled patio. In this room a perpetual winter solstice twilight reigns. You learn that the room used to belong to the daughter, who has gone to live in Paris. *I can be your daughter,* you think.

Please please please, you plead in your mind. It will cost you 650 euros a month—not cheap, in fact a sizable portion of your research fellowship, but substantially less than the 1,200 euros you nearly coughed up a week earlier for that spiffy studio apartment, only to be dismissed at the last moment by the real estate agent who decided to hold out for "a politician who'd be happy to pay that, and more, to rent the place for his mistress." At which you experienced a fleeting envy—for which you immediately reprimanded yourself—of the mistress, so secure in her lodging.

With Sabrina you will share a tiny, tenebrous kitchen and, for reasons unrelated to light or its lack, you will not be able to find a bowl the proper size for granola or yogurt, and so for the first month you will eat these things from a tiny teacup you repeatedly refill. Your territory in this apartment will be small and circumscribed: your room, your bath, the hallway, on occasion, when necessary, the kitchen. You will only ever glimpse the living room from the end of the hall, because every afternoon when Sabrina returns from the dusty shop where she sells antiques from her native Algeria, she will turn on the television in the half-light and slide back into her body's imprint in the lumpy sofa. There she will remain, in a game-show-induced trance, until sometime in the wee hours of the night, when she will presumably drag herself to bed, drawing the beige curtain across the nook that houses her crumpled mattress. Every so often she will ask you please not to throw coffee grains down the sink drain, and every time she will regard you with suspicion when you remind her that you have never prepared coffee at home. You will resent the accusation, while reminding yourself that this melancholy woman is the only person in all of Rome who opened her door to you when you needed it.

But let's not get ahead of ourselves; here you are on this auspicious morning, the day of your great Roman real estate triumph, and when Sabrina asks when you can move in, you say *domani*, tomorrow, as cheerfully as you can. You try to show off an open American smile, your trustworthy American teeth. Your swiftly moving in would be advantageous for *her*— more income sooner! And when Sabrina verifies, for the third or fourth time, *No men?*, you shake your head vigorously at the ostensible scandal of her suggestion. Only my husband, you say, who will come for a short visit. You won't mention, of course, that he is not your husband, that in fact he is still married to someone else. Today is not a day for extraneous details. You finger this man's new ring in your pocket, warm to the touch now from the heat of your distress.

21

THE HOLY ROMAN
ALPINE CLUB

In the beginning, I had the *istituto*, whose empty rooms echoed with distant footsteps. And then the Archivio di Stato, with its shelves of manuscripts worn velvety and ragtag with age. And, before the move to Trastevere, my quiet room in the northern quarter. After a few weeks, I also had a routine. I rode the bus to the archive in the morning, pored over this or that notarial document with varying degrees of success, and returned home by late afternoon to go for a run. I had chosen a running route that took me past the Catacomb of Priscilla, burial site of numerous popes and saints from as early as the second century CE, and then into the groves and sloping fields of Villa Ada, Rome's second-largest public park. I ran in a swirl of dust and pebbles and fallen leaves as brittle as parchment, for it had rained—and would rain—only once that September. And yet the arid early-autumnal air was laden with the scents of pine and laurel, both of which grew in Villa Ada in defiant abundance. I followed small, winding paths that led to long stairways ascending to wide boulevards that cut through orderly groves, and footpaths descending to the park's small lake. Unlike in the archives, in Villa Ada I relished losing my way. Might this narrow path circle me back to the lake? Or better yet, might I end up somewhere I had not yet been? What secret corner might I chance upon?

What piece of statuary, or sculpture? What remarkable tree? Getting lost here was a pleasure, an adventure, a way of pressing at the boundaries of the city I was coming to know. As I ran, I observed children splashing in a pond, lovers caressing on the grass, readers bent in solitude over their books. The motions of the living world.

It was only when reentering my room after these runs that the weight of my solitude returned. I had no group here, as I had had in the Living Latin course, no built-in community, no travel companion, not even another lost soul in the archive with whom I might share a sympathetic understanding. Javier had suggested that I find a hiking or rock-climbing class. It had the shine of a good idea. I could *get out, meet people.* But: Taking up a newish sport with new people in a new place in a language I was still working to improve? It was intimidating, too.

One morning, I gathered my courage. I retrieved the phone book from the walnut desk in the hallway, brought it to my room, and laid it on the bed. And there it was, just waiting to be discovered: Club Alpino Italiano. Via Galvani, 10. By the time I moved to Trastevere on the first of October, I was enrolled in a ten-week-long, intensive rock-climbing course.

The club's headquarters are scruffy and appealing. Each week we have one evening "theory" class there, one meetup at a climbing gym near the Tiber, and on Sundays, from dawn to dusk, excursions to the countryside around Rome.

On the evening of the first meeting, the instructors inform us that we are joining a legendary class. The next ten weeks, one says, might change your life. I look around at the seventy or so people around me, from teenagers to sixtysomethings. I am bashful at being a nonnative speaker of Italian. I hate that my name sticks out so conspicuously among the other names on the list, the Rossis, Bianchis, and Riccis. When I have to spell my name out loud, slowly and laboriously, for the attendance list, I blush and want to die. I never bothered to memorize the phonetic pronunciations of the Italian alphabet, but the man sitting next to me helps me out. I write down the letters I don't know, and he speaks them for me. He helps again when, in my nervousness, I incorrectly record the emergency phone numbers. I worry who in this room will choose to be suspended from a rope belayed by such a person as me, when I cannot even manage to correctly record a phone number or spell my own name. But the man, who introduces himself as Paolo, only smiles, as if to say: You found us.

~

On the morning of the first outing, I climb into Paolo's red Volkswagen van along with a handful of others and we head west and then north up the coast. This landscape, hilly and fertile, was the land of the Etruscans, the forebears of the Romans. We park under an oak tree in a field of dry grass, hoist our backpacks, and follow a lightly worn trail uphill through pastoral Mediterranean scrub in the direction of a rocky outcropping. The persistent drone of humming and buzzing suggests a vast world of insects going about their daily tasks. A small herd of sheep slowly chews its way across a distant field. We have reached Ripa Maiala, a mound of rust-colored volcanic rock jutting out improbably from this otherwise generous and verdant landscape.

From the field, our walk to the base of the climbing routes is short. A rain has fallen and the damp soil is sticky, I assume with clay. As we walk it gathers around the soles of my shoes like rubber bumpers or some sort of clownish snowshoe. We divide into small groups while the instructors set up the routes with ropes. We have each brought our own equipment. I lay mine out on a rock before me: my climbing shoes, my *imbragatura* (harness), two *moschettoni* (carabiners), a *discensore* (belay device), and a few *fettucce* (lengths of webbing). These I bought at a sporting goods store near Piazza dei Re di Roma, just outside the Aurelian Wall. My equipment is stiff and new, and carting it around the city, the shoes tied by their laces to the outside of my backpack, makes me feel proud: *my* equipment, *my* climbing life.

When it's my turn, I climb the first route with ease. My fingers find the pockets in the volcanic rock, my toes the ledges. Javier's advice echoes in my head: *legs, not arms* and *hips close to the wall.* I practice trusting my feet, using the angled point at the front of the climbing shoe to perch on small features in the rock. My instructor compliments me on my form. Others do too. I see that good form is not a given. One middle-aged man, strong and fit, shakes and wobbles his way up. A teenage kid freezes halfway, trembling violently. A woman panics, shouts, "*Cala, cala!*" Lower me down! Others, like me, find their stride quickly on the wall.

By late morning, the October sun is high in the sky. Birds chirp all around us. When I turn around at the top of the route, I spot Paolo's red van parked among the other cars and the green fields that slope westward and under which lies a vast Etruscan necropolis, chamber after elegant chamber of the dead. Just beyond, the Tyrrhenian Sea glimmers silver in the distance. A windsurfer, silent as a satellite, glides along its surface.

In my group is a young woman, like me in her mid-to-late twenties. She has a self-deprecating sense of humor, and she laughs when she finds herself in strange positions on the wall. I show off my knees, already bruised, as barter. We eat lunch side by side. Giulia is a teacher living in Monteverde, a residential neighborhood adjacent to where I live in Trastevere. She shares almonds with me, and in return I offer her some of my Clif Bar, which I've brought from home. But she waves it off, wary of processed food. Dried apricots are more her style, and she readily accepts a few from my lunch bag. One instructor, who clearly has not heard me speak, asks if we are sisters. But my imperfect Italian is no impediment to enjoying the day. No one balks, as I had feared they might, at the prospect of belaying me, or at my belaying them, as I hold the rope, quite literally, from which they dangle. It is a relief to find myself in a group, to be among people who do not ask me to recite my research plans or scrutinize my trustworthiness, but who instead accept, and even welcome, my presence.

While Giulia and I are eating, a middle-aged woman offers us the climbing guidebook that has been making the rounds. Climbing guides tend to be practical texts, containing illustrations or photos of the rock wall with superimposed lines that show the various climbing routes. But this guide is peppered with essays. Giulia and I flip to the pages for Ripa and discover that the routes we have just climbed are rated 5a and 5b—beginner routes. We also find that the routes have names such as *La Cia ci spia* ("The CIA is spying on us") and *Pista Ho Chi Minh* ("Ho Chi Minh Trail")—names that, the guide says, "appear to have been written by an agent of the Comintern."

As I munch on what is rapidly becoming an imprudent number of dried apricots, Giulia points out a sentence that makes us both giggle: the rock climber, it says, represents a "worrisome regression of the human species, which once believed itself ordained for luminous achievements in service of inevitable and relentless progress, but which instead has sunk once again into the obscurity of fetishistic cults and aberrant practices." You can recognize the climber, it says, by their "hooked and deformed hands" and their "locust-long legs and enormous forearms that come at the expense of a cramped cranium." Rock is the climber's "object of exalted rites," and on it they climb their "route to the sacred, to perfection, their tortured path to holiness. They descend from this path on the whole unfulfilled, and sometimes 'precipitously' but ever more consumed by the holy fire of their faith." This guidebook is a natural history, church history, philosophical treatise, tribute to the pantheon of climbing gods, detailed climbing guide, and sometimes-scorching roast of the author and the Roman climbing scene all rolled into one.

I look myself over. My fingers are still mostly straight and my forearms as yet unimpressive, but perhaps it is true that by experimenting with this weird cult—what the author jokingly calls the "*Sacro Romano Club Alpino Italiano*," the Holy Roman Alpine Club—I risk being infused with the spirit. I don't know this yet, but over the following eight months, I will never hear the Sunday bells toll in Rome—every Sunday will be spent in rural Lazio, Campagna, or southern Tuscany, and eventually many Tuesdays too. Soon I will earn the calloused fingers and the sore forearms of the fervent novitiate. I will become a purple-kneed pilgrim on my own *via sacra*.

The day at Ripa Maiala has passed quickly. In late afternoon, I stand with an instructor, Piero, who teaches me to coil a rope over my shoulders. The sun slants in from over the sea, and it sets the rock face alight, exposing deep reds and oranges. Piero is pulling the rope over his shoulders, left right, right left, measuring out the lengths with his arms. Looking at Piero, I have the uncanny feeling that I already know him. His face is thin and his body wiry and strong. There is a certain self-containment about him. I realize with surprise that he reminds me of a young version of my grandfather, my father's father. But unlike my grandfather, Piero is always suppressing a laugh: about the Italian state, his unreliable car, the weather, anything.

I confess to Piero that he bears a strong resemblance to my grandfather.

He stifles an embarrassed laugh. "*Caspita*," he says, shaking his head. *Go figure.* He has arrived at the end of the rope, and he lays it, neatly coiled, into a blue IKEA bag.

The setting sun throws four flickering silhouettes against the rocks—Piero, me, and two others who are packing up their belongings.

"I'm forty-one," Piero says in mock despair, "and I look like your *nonno*."

❧

Every so often on weekday afternoons, Piero and I meet for tea in a Trastevere bookshop. He is curious about my research and demonstrates a kind of pure enjoyment of history. In the years since, I have met many Romans who deeply appreciate the landscape of ruins, around which they navigate their lives, for its aesthetic beauty. But Piero was the first. He revels in the past with a child's delight, stopping in his tracks when we are strolling about the city to admire one detail or another. He is an introspective vagabond in spirit, someone who does what work he must to support his life of reading, writing, and the outdoors. But he's as erudite as they come, and from what I can tell, self-taught. He's the kind of person who translates entire books for the challenge of it, whom you wouldn't be surprised to find reading Pliny in the morning and later, hiking a mountain alone by moonlight.

Piero was raised in Rome, but his parents came from Sardinia, and every few months he takes the ferry back to the island to help cultivate the family apiary. In the coming year, he will bring me unmarked jars of lavender honey after returning from these trips, and I will portion them out into my tea in small, precisely measured doses, as if I were spooning gold itself. At one of our meetings over tea in a bookstore café, Piero hands me a different kind of gift. It's the guidebook that Giulia and I were reading that first day at Ripa Maiala, *In cerca di guai*, a play on the title given to the Italian translation of Mark Twain's autobiographical work *Roughing It*. Piero is the author. I hadn't known his last name on that first day climbing and had not put two and two together. The full title reflects Piero's sense of humor: *Roughing It: Or How to Risk Your Life in the Absence of Any Danger and Feel Free While Tying Yourself to a Rope.*

Piero tells me he's at work on a second edition. For this he is composing a segment on Ciampino—where I had lived during my summer of Living Latin. At that time, I had been unaware that I was living right beside an ancient Roman quarry that had become a popular climbing destination. But when we visited the site on the second Sunday of the climbing class, the landscape felt immediately familiar. A black cliff that falls straight away from an otherwise placid plain of the Roman *campagna* dotted with umbrella pines, and a stone's throw from the Aqua Claudia aqueduct, the quarry at Ciampino is a rock wall with historical signifi- cance. It was here that ancient Romans took the basalt they needed to carve the stone blocks to form the via Appia Antica, the Appian Way, which passes by the quarry about one hundred meters away. Later Ro- mans once again made use of the basalt to form the *sampietrini* on which every inhabitant of central Rome for the past five hundred years has gone about daily life. Their extractions formed the vertical face on which to- day's visitors happily strain and groan their way through the afternoon.

To Piero, however, the Ciampino quarry offers "a vision worthy of Dante." He elaborates: "A few tens of people dangling like hanged men from as many ropes, others clinging to narrow crevices by one hand or by their big toe, others still frenetically ascending and descending like eleva- tors. I half expected to see jailers with whips, Doberman pinschers and robust armed surveillance . . . and yet: all these people had come of their own volition and were supposedly 'having a great time.'"

Looking back on it now, it occurs to me that, in that first month in the archives, I had yet to find anyone with whom to talk about history or books. In Piero I found a kindred spirit. Someone who read widely and stopped to admire ancient ruins. Someone who took pleasure in words and history and Dante. Someone who found refuge in leaving the city be- hind and pondering, often with humor, the infinite fragments of the past upon which one stumbles in the Roman countryside. I found Piero in the alpine club. And he even resembled my grandfather. *Caspita*.

22.

VATICAN LIBRARY

Next door to the Trastevere apartment is a small shop. Every few days I go there to buy the purple plastic phone cards I use to call Javier. I have to scratch off a strip of metallic film to find the code, then dial an access number, wait for an electronic voice to give me the go-ahead, and then dial his number. The long sequence of operations is a reminder of the many miles between us. There is also snail mail. Among the things he sends: clipped newspaper articles ("This might interest you"), recipes he is trying out ("Shall I make this when you return?"), and letters in which he reflects on the progress of his separation ("Things are moving slowly") and the state of his feelings ("Please have patience"). Sometimes I read his letters and rush to call him; other times I place them in a stack with all the rest and wish to do anything but. This is the hard part, I remind myself—granting him the space to disentangle from his marriage and myself the liberty to give my life in Rome a fair shake. I determine to do just that.

One evening, the phone rings. "*Telefonata per te!*" Sabrina shouts from the living room. I pick it up assuming it's Javier, but it's Paolo, letting me know that I've left my wallet in his van. I scramble over to my backpack, and it's true, the pocket is empty. He suggests we meet tomorrow at Caffè Trastevere, if that works for me. It's no problem at all, it's on his way to work.

The next morning, I traverse Trastevere to reach the café. The gold mosaics of Santa Maria in Trastevere prance and prattle in the morning sun. The small but robust crowd loyal to Bar San Calisto has already taken their seats outside, oriented toward the street like an audience awaiting a performance. Down via di San Francesco a Ripa, past the Bancomat, the dingy entrance to the supermarket, and the *supplì* shop, at the corner of viale di Trastevere I reach the café and check the name above the door to make sure I have it right.

I needn't have. Paolo is already at the counter, reading a newspaper below the fold. His attire is a panoply of no-fuss gray and black, and his padded jacket tells me he has come on a motorcycle. He greets me promptly and I claim a spot beside him at the granite countertop. Paolo asks what I'd like and then orders for us—*un caffè e un cappuccino*—to which the barman nods. Cups clink and clatter. People jostle by—paying for coffee, pastries, cigarettes, lottery tickets. Cold air wafts from the open door. The bartender hurriedly places our coffees before us, the ceramic landing on the granite with a sharp *crak-crak*.

Paolo asks me about my research, and I answer in a general way: *storia medievale, ricerca per il dottorato, Roma nel periodo di Avignone . . .* And while I talk, I also contemplate how good it feels to stand in a café in my new neighborhood in the company of another. A woman reaches between us to pull a napkin from the aluminum dispenser. I rip open a packet of cane sugar and sprinkle it over my cappuccino, then stir it just enough that the granules partially submerge in the steamed milk. Over the buzz of the espresso machine, Paolo tells me he has lived in Asia, that his father started the business in which he now works, that he likes hiking, paddling, and diving—and, he adds wryly, returning lost wallets. After we part ways, I find myself wondering why we have never really spoken before.

Leaving the archive one early October afternoon, I pick my way among Rome's small streets. I take in the details of the city while reviewing the day's work. That morning I came upon the 1337 notarial register of a certain Angelo di Nicola Grivelli, which looked promising. Where might it lead? A stroller-bound child wails while her mother roots around in a bag for something to pacify her. How can I leave the notarial registers behind if I don't yet have a clear alternative? Maybe I am not cut out for archival work at all. A store clerk tiptoeing in a display window frees a sleeveless linen dress from a mannequin's body with a flick of his finger—it falls to the floor, rippling like a puddle. It is normal to feel lost in the documents, I tell myself. Feeling lost is the necessary starting point when orienting oneself in a strange land—which the fourteenth century definitely is. The clerk pulls a cowl-neck sweater over the mannequin's head. But for how long is it okay to feel lost? What if I never find my way? A poorly parked car protrudes comically across the sidewalk. I maneuver around it. It is a pleasure to move through Rome on foot. I fear being lost in the archive, but I have no fear of being lost in Rome.

At Campo de' Fiori, the outdoor market is closed and the last vendors are already sweeping their plots. An aroma of truffles wafts over the street. The old Jewish Ghetto, where Paolo and I will soon meet, is less crowded than Campo de' Fiori. The turtle fountain burbles away unobserved. At the foot of the Theater of Marcellus, I mill about for a minute or two until I see Paolo heading around its curved base. We meet up between blocks of fallen stone.

We have been walking together, meeting for dinner, several times per week. On our outings, we talk and talk. With Paolo I feel spirited and light. He ribs me gently for a great many things—for being American (endless fodder), for the arcane nature of my subject of study, for the way I eat bread even when awaiting a plate of pasta (*proibito*, apparently). Each evening we spend together, we cover many miles on foot, and hardly ever with a destination in mind. We strike up conversations with strangers. "People are nice to me when I'm with you," Paolo says, more than once. In our interactions there is an element of charm—not his, not mine, but something like a light mineral dusting that glints in the sun.

This afternoon we pass by the synagogue, and a few blocks later, by many people, mostly tourists, seated at the outdoor tables of the Jewish Roman restaurants that line this street. The area known as the Ghetto was first defined, by mandate of a papal bull, or edict, in 1555. A wall was soon built, and three gates were added, and then a few more, and those Roman Jews who did not already live here were forced to move from Trastevere and other areas of central Rome. For three centuries afterward, the curfewed Roman Jewish population was locked inside each night, often in squalid conditions stemming from overcrowding and regular flooding from the Tiber. Now no longer enclosed—the walls were broken down during national unification in the 1870s—the area remains the center of Jewish Rome today. With its small streets, it is a good area for strolling.

Paolo and I are talking about the rising pitch of American rhetoric directed at Iraq and about his recent trip to North Africa.

"I've been thinking," he says, changing the subject. "The way you're writing about medieval Rome . . ." He joins his palms together and, moving his hands back and forth, starts to laugh. "Nothing has changed in this city in two thousand years!"

The scholar in me wants to quibble: well . . .

"What is there still to say about the fourteenth century," Paolo goes on, "especially if, as you say, the documentary evidence for that time period is so thin?" He's reviving a conversation from several days ago.

In front of us is the Portico d'Ottavia, whose compound over the centuries has contained a Roman temple, a library, school lecture halls, a church, and an outdoor fish market. Under an arch and around a corner, we happen upon an old woman seated in a plastic folding chair.

"And what," Paolo asks, coming to a stop, "can an *Americana* teach Romans about Rome?"

The woman's hands are on her lap, her feet crossed at the ankles. She greets us with a nod. I struggle to answer Paolo's question succinctly: I am still finding my footing, after all. But his question unnerves me. I ought to have an answer. The old woman says something about enjoying the *ottobrata romana*, these spectacular blue-sky October days in Rome when the sun still warms but the air at night is cool and fresh. While I fret about what I might contribute to Roman history, Paolo engages the woman, asking about the small tower behind her, where, we learn, she lives.

The tower is square. At three stories, it is not very tall. On one side it is connected to another structure of similar height, which in turn is linked to others, forming a chain that twists and turns, defining the contours of the neighborhood's narrow, winding streets. On the other side, above us, the tower is joined at the top to the ancient marble pediment of the Portico d'Ottavia. The tower's brick is exposed, and unlike its ancient neighbor, the tower reveals a history of haphazard planning: windows and doors, several of which are boarded up or bricked over, scattered at seemingly random heights. On the top floor, two green French doors are the only cheerful exterior detail. But they open, oddly enough, onto the abyss, which is blocked only by a flimsy wire shelf that is attached to the doorframe at about waist height and on which grows a gaggle of potted sunflowers. But for the green doors and the sunflower pots, the tower appears thoroughly neglected, though whether for decades or centuries it's hard to say. Conspicuous vertical cracks race along its surface, as do at least a dozen dark voids—holes—where one presumes bricks or beams used to reside. What was once an exterior stairway ends abruptly about ten feet above the ground.

I am both attracted to and repelled by this tower. It is the kind of structure—stalwart but dilapidated—that for centuries has moved the hearts of visitors to Rome, who see the ravages that time has worked on earth and stone and feel compelled to ponder the brevity of life and the vanity of human effort. The tower has this effect on me, too, though it helps, perhaps, to know that we have been primed to feel this way by the eighteenth- and nineteenth-century visitors who cemented the tradition of viewing Rome's ruins in this nostalgic light. The tower pulls on my heartstrings, but in a way that feels predictable—and is therefore, perhaps, not entirely to be trusted.

"*Bellissima*," Paolo says, standing beside me. It reassures me that he likes the tower too. That what I feel is not just some reflexive American senti- ment for the exoticized Roman ruin. When we move on, Paolo asks me how I know the old woman. "She spoke so familiarly, I assumed you had met before."

Back in the archives, I find myself daydreaming about towers. Beginning in about 1000 CE, so many were built in Rome that one historian has likened the medieval city to a hedgehog. Privately owned towers were useful to a newly ascendant urban aristocracy that wanted to strut its stuff, and they rose in tandem with another medieval architectural form, *campa- nili*, or church belltowers, which also sprouted up all over the city around this time. For noble families, towers were both defensive strongholds and conspicuous possessions, built to defend their territories and to inscribe the family name on the urban map. In the thirteenth and fourteenth cen- turies, the names everyone in Rome knew were Papareschi, Pierleoni, Frangipani, Caetani, Cenci, Savelli, Anguillara, Annibaldi, Colonna, and Orsini—and whose tower was tallest counted a lot.

But towers were also homes. *Turris* and *domus*, the notaries called them, "tower" and "home," using the terms interchangeably to mean one, the other, or both. A tower was almost always moored to the family domicile, which was linked, in turn, to others, rich and poor sharing a wall, or walls. Many poor and middling folk who lived in the towers' shadows resented them. So too did many who were newly wealthy from commerce but lacking in aristocratic lineage—to such families, towers represented a society ruled by brute force rather than by good government. The towers, after all, were symbols of power and privilege—of military might, and of a social structure that allowed the few to dominate the many. The Roman city council, when it could, legislated to limit their height. In the 1250s, Brancaleone degli Andalò, senator of Rome, ordered the destruction of over 140 towers, becoming one of the city's most renowned tower topplers and thereby endearing himself to the Roman populace. So beloved was Brancaleone that, after his death, they placed his head atop a marble column—an instinct, and an image, that is difficult for us in the modern world to comprehend, but that represented a great honor. Easier to conjure is the sound: the rumble and roar of one hundred and two score crumbling towers.

Yet even before these towers had tumbled, even when they protruded like a hedgehog's quills, or perhaps like needles from a silver ring, even then they remained dwarfed by those other stone giants that littered the cityscape: the Colosseum, the Theatre of Marcellus, the Baths of Caracalla, the Mausoleums of Augustus and Hadrian—those constant reminders that the present, no matter how ambitious, could never quite stack up to the past.

❧

In mid-October, Javier flies in for a short visit. His brief stay in the Trastevere apartment has been green-lit by Sabrina, who, of course, believes he is my husband. Three days are all we've got.

I take the train out to the airport to greet him. It feels impossible, and wonderful, that he is here in Rome, where he has never been before, and where there is so much I want to show him. On the train our hands interlock and I notice that he is no longer wearing his wedding ring. It's awkward, but from my jeans pocket I extract the ring I bought in Campo de' Fiori and ask him to wear it. Miraculously, it fits him. A shake of the wand, and we are a couple wearing wedding rings. And here, far from his Providence apartment filled with the materiality of his conjugal life, I feel almost freed from the landscape of his marriage story.

In three days, we do a thousand things. We walk through the Forum; we take long siestas in my lumpy blue bed; we eat in a bustling Trastevere pizzeria; we climb the Janiculum Hill up to the *Fontanone*—the Fontana dell'Acqua Paola—and take in its commanding view of the city and valley below; we stand, gaping, beneath the Pantheon's awe-inspiring cyclops eye. Javier takes in the city with relaxed but enthusiastic curiosity. He intuitively knows the codes, the cues, the way things work—without any explanation on my part. He likens it to Madrid, but without the family responsibilities. He becomes such a part of my experience that I want him to stay forever.

And then, just as quickly, he is gone.

꩜

Back in the archives, I have by now called up half a dozen notarial registers. Some, I discover, are easier to read than others, and I have begun to fill my notebook with notes and transcriptions. Yet I feel ill at ease. It occurs to me that if I continue on this track, I will probably spend the next few years counting and sorting the findings. The dissertation that would emerge from that effort would likely be full of charts and tables. It's not that I discount the value of such work. On the contrary, much social history is built upon methodical counting of people and possessions and tracing what happens to them over time. But what the Archivio di Stato is teaching me, and quite quickly—for I am still only about six weeks in—is that such an endeavor is not for me. I recall that the classes that have touched me most deeply have almost always been literary in nature, and I find myself longing for the kind of textual world that Dante first gave me. One in which I could make connections and inferences, unpack symbols and systems of reference, and move sequentially through layers of meaning. What I have been seeking has grown suddenly clearer. And I know now that I will not find it in the Archivio di Stato.

Before I left Cornell, Paul gifted me a book from his own shelves: an inventory of and guide to the Vatican Archives. From perusing this book, and from noting the sources cited in scholarly books and articles, I know that the Vatican Library holds many primary sources for the study of fourteenth-century Rome. There are those city statutes I have read so much about, confraternity records, private letters, chancellery letters, court cases, and a handful of chronicles. The Vatican Library feels like a new frontier.

The Vatican lies just north of Trastevere. From Sabrina's apartment, the route is almost a straight shot, taking me through the crenellated Porta Settimiana and onto via della Lungara, the road now named for its length (*lungo*), which runs along the Tiber. This narrow, straight road leads me past John Cabot University, past the bucolic grounds of the Villa Farnesina, past Rome's botanical garden and the Regina Coeli prison, past the historical scientific academy to which Galileo Galilei once belonged. At Piazza delle Rovere, I veer away from the Tiber, keeping the Hospital of Santo Spirito in Sassia—from which emerged, in the late twelfth century, the crusading Knights Hospitaller—on my right, and then onto via dei Cavalieri del Santo Sepolcro, named after the Knights of the Holy Sepulchre until I reach the bright boulevard that, were I to turn left, would lead me into the fold of Piazza San Pietro, the heart of Roman Catholic

Christendom. Skirting around it, I soon arrive at the Porta Sant'Anna, a gate that is also an international border between Italy and the Vatican City State.

There is no breezing into the Vatican Library. Gaining entrance, especially the first time, takes patience and fortitude as you progress through a series of checkpoints that seem to have been designed by a mind intimately familiar with the rings of Dante's *Inferno*.

At Porta Sant'Anna, I stand nervously before a pair of Swiss Guards in their glorious uniforms. *Abandon all hope, ye who enter here?* They regard me skeptically, but my student ID, my passport, and my letter of support on Cornell letterhead appear to pass muster, and they step aside, waving me in.

Their casual gesture is my little boat, rowed by an invisible Charon, which tips precariously as it ferries me across the River Acheron and up via Sant'Anna to the Vatican police station. In a drab little building that very adequately mimics Limbo, I wait in line while filling out the requisite forms. When called, I push my materials under the scratched and cloudy plexiglass partition and, after stamping this and that, the official hands me a paper permit. With this in hand, I proceed uneasily up via Sant'Anna to a large archway, where there awaits another Swiss Guard. As Minos does for *Inferno*'s condemned souls with his giant tail, the guard points me into the Belvedere courtyard and off to the right.

At the end of the courtyard, I push open the heavy glass door and find myself face-to-face with a Vatican official popularly nicknamed Cerberus, after the three-headed guard dog who rends and flays the gluttonous of *Inferno*'s third circle. He gruffly commands me to show my temporary permit and then sends me down to the Secretariat, where I am instructed to wait. Sitting apprehensively on a bench in the hallway, I feel what Dante must have felt as he clambered into a flimsy boat to cross the muddy Styx.

After a few minutes, I am shown inside a small, windowless office, where a huddle of library administrators, fallen angels of the archival world, ask me to explain my research. They wish to know which manuscripts I intend to examine and what specific questions I plan to pursue. Their detailed interrogation takes me for a moment by surprise, and I worry I am failing their exam and will soon be sent packing, only to see a printer in the corner rolling out my image. Returning to the main entry, I glimpse on its far end, much as Dante glimpsed the towers of the distant city of Dis, a luminescent marble staircase rising before me.

I hand my newly laminated card to Cerberus, who hunches on his stool and glares. Better do as he says: I stash my belongings in the locker assigned and scurry up the stairs to the reading rooms. Once upstairs, I sigh with relief, for I have made it into that other great walled city, the Vatican Library.

Once I situate myself, I order up a manuscript from the fourteenth century. I relish the feeling of not knowing quite what I will find and think of my friend Bob, who once found between his manuscript's pages a downy mouse pressed thin as a wafer by the centuries. Waiting, I take a seat before one of the many rows of dark wooden desks and peer over the back of a bespectacled man bent over a giant illustrated manuscript, a document far more beautiful than any of the wormholed ones my mundane research will require.

I begin to relax into the silence of this large space, into its muffled coughs and occasional whispers, and lean back to admire its austere, vaulted ceiling. Through the tall windows, I catch sight of a flock of light-pink-and-blue clouds as they hurry by, pulling in a chill worthy of winter in their wake. I rise from my chair to stretch and walk to the inner courtyard, where two men converse while strolling around a trickling fountain. I pace the courtyard, too, but in the damp November cold, I cannot shake the chill.

When I return inside, I discover that my manuscript has arrived, and a man in gray hands it to me without ceremony, recording my name and locker key number in his broad ledger. Carrying the book back to the desk, I place it on a wooden support and spread its pages. My eyes skim the words, and with such pleasure, for I find I can decipher them with little hindrance. My fingers slide across the soft vellum, and the acrid smell of the ink rises, and what eats away at the cold is my realization that, for all its opacity and foreignness, a manuscript always feels a little like home.

✑

The manuscript was a medieval copy of a work by a Roman prose writer from the first century CE named Valerius Maximus. His *Facta et dicta memorabilia* (Memorable deeds and sayings) was a compilation of historical anecdotes arranged to promote reflection and to serve as a Latin rhetorical stylebook. The tome was large and heavy and bound in leather, and I ordered it up not because I wanted to read its original text but because I hoped that the comments written in its margins might illuminate something about Rome's fourteenth century.

Back in the 1300s, the very pages in my hands had been held by Giovanni Cavallini dei Cerroni, a Roman cleric, a papal scribe, and an erudite reader and writer of history who was roughly one generation younger than Dante. As Cavallini read through this book of anecdotes, he penned his reactions and comments, in Latin, on just about every page. I spent a while familiarizing myself with Cavallini's script, moving between the manuscript and the Cappelli paleography lexicon with satisfying swiftness.

"Note that so-and-so also did this" was a common opening for Cavallini's comments. And: "Note that the same thing happened to so-and-so" and "Note how back then . . ." Cavallini was doing exactly what Professor Kaye had taught us to do in college—marking up the text with thoughts and reflections, comparing and contrasting, making the act of reading, as much as it can ever be, into a conversation. It struck me that while seven centuries lay between me and Cavallini, a whopping thirteen stood between him and Valerius Maximus.

Reading Cavallini's marginalia also made me feel a curious rapport with him, as if I had been invited into his otherwise private conversation with Valerius Maximus. That I could decipher his writing came as a relief, and I felt curiously grateful to him for allowing me entry into his document, and thereby, into his world. Some of Cavallini's comments were poetic, and even endearing—for instance, those expressing his fondness for his home city. Consider the acrostic poem he penned in the upper right-hand corner of one page, on the virtues of Rome:

Royal seat of priests
Origin of arms and laws
Mother of faith and moral exempla
Aid of allies and kings

Lower down on the same page, he meditated on the letter *R*: "Note the excellence of this letter *R* that stands for Rome." His attentive focus on the aesthetic of the city's name reminded me of the way I often regarded those same letters—*R-O-M-E*—with anticipation and no small measure of disbelief when I saw them printed on a plane ticket. I wasn't sure where exactly Cavallini was leading me, but I felt, instinctively, that his comments were taking me somewhere worth going.

Not all of his marginalia were wistful. There was this comment: "Note that because of private quarrels the republic is governed poorly." In this sentiment, he agreed with a common perception of his time: that Rome's notorious political unrest was the result of private conflicts between powerful families spilling into, and upsetting, the weak public sphere. I had come across this assessment frequently when preparing for my qualifying exams and remembered in particular the words of the famed jurist Bartolus of Sassoferrato, a near contemporary of Cavallini who taught at the law school in Perugia. Bartolus had condemned the form of government in fourteenth-century Rome as "a monstruous thing," because instead of strong civic institutions, the city had "many tyrants just strong enough that one cannot prevail over the other." By "tyrants," Bartolus was referring to Rome's great landowning families, who since the eleventh century had amassed so much property and wealth that, by the 1300s, they had dominated, and often upended, almost every aspect of Rome's governance. Most owed their rising status and fortunes in large part to the papacy and its remunerative posts, although this fact didn't always prevent them from acting at the papacy's expense when self-interest dictated. By the 1330s, when Cavallini and Bartolus were both writing, these families numbered about a dozen, and at their pinnacle stood the Colonna and Orsini. These were the builders of towers and urban fortresses and rural castles, the knights on horseback, the senators, cardinals, and even occasionally popes, and they were variously called "nobles," "barons," "magnates," and "magnificent or illustrious men" in the lexicon of the day. They were more powerful than their peers in most other Italian cities, and their power was less checked by the city's feeble civic government, whose boards of elected officials drawn from the professional and guild classes came and went, and whose existence was anyway frequently challenged, if not eradicated, by a hostile aristocracy or papacy. Cavallini noted that private quarrels had undermined the city's governance, but I knew that to be an understatement: the violence and vendettas that had long been rife between the most powerful Roman noble families had made the city, in the eyes of many, the Italian peninsula's most grievous example of failed government.

With this sobering thought in mind, I ventured further into Cavallini's marginalia and soon came upon another one that directly addressed this civic strife: "Note against Nicola, son of Lorenzo, tribune of the city, who did not permit the bodies of the Colonna lords to be buried during the day." I was already familiar with this Nicola di Lorenzo, popularly nicknamed Cola di Rienzo, from the syllabus I had prepared that summer, and of course from the story I had encountered in the Istituto Storico about Petrarch and Stefano Colonna. He was the type you bumped into everywhere, for he was a major figure, if not *the* figure par excellence, of fourteenth-century Rome, famous above all for challenging the Roman noble families that Cavallini had censured and Bartolus disdained. And yet I was still surprised to stumble upon Cola's name scribbled in the margin by the hand of one of his contemporaries. It felt as if, after months of having heard his name from afar, I was finally being given a personal introduction.

Cavallini started me thinking about the close connection some Romans felt to the history of their city. With that in mind, I became interested in looking at Cola di Rienzo through the same prism. The dissertation that was by then forming in my mind would revolve not around notarial documents and what they might say about family status or property, as I had originally thought it might, but around questions of memory and history: Who possesses it, and what form, or forms, might struggles over that possession take? Which parts of history are remembered, which are discarded or forgotten, and who gets to decide—and what are the consequences of those decisions? Given his creative use of the past, Cola was a figure I knew would be at the center of that investigation.

❧

As the subject of my dissertation evolves, rock climbing remains a constant. Every Sunday I go out with the group. Invariably, our expeditions begin with a stop for *cappuccini* and *cornetti*. One Sunday in late October, we stop in Latina Scalo, a town perched on a steep incline. Once in a while I forgo the *cornetto* and up my game, and calorie count, to a *bombolone* or *sfogliatella*. Whereas the humble *cornetto* is a terrestrial delight, *bomboloni* and—when they're very fresh—*sfogliatelle* are pastries descended from the heavenly spheres. *Golosa* ("glutton") one of the instructors calls me when he spots me, gleeful as a child with my mouth full of pastry.

I am gluttonous for so much in Rome: for *cappuccini* and *cornetti*, for *bomboloni* and *sfogliatelle*, for *cacio e pepe* and for *pasta amatriciana*, for grilled lamb and for potatoes roasted with rosemary, for boar sausages and for *supplì al telefono*, for *carciofi alla romana* and for *carciofi alla giudía,* for tiramisù that pillows like a cloud and for fresh pomegranate juice that stains the chin. But unlike *glutton*, which rings to me of a stringent dourness, of sin and contrition, in those who call me *golosa* I detect only warmth and affection. To be *golosa* is to eat with your eyes. To be *golosa* is to hunger for life, to lick the sugar or the fat from your fingers or, better, from someone else's, to capture what is sweet and vital before it dissolves, before it is swept from your plate, from your palate, and gone forever.

When the last drop of coffee has been sipped from our cups and the final flake of pastry picked off the plate, we exit the warm *pasticceria* and pull our jackets snug around us. Paolo guides the red van up a steep, winding road leading into a high valley. The villages up here—Sermoneta, Norma, and our destination, Bassiano—perch protectively on the edge of mountain ridges. They are many centuries old. Sermoneta, for example, can trace its earliest roots back at least two thousand years, to the time of Virgil, and its current location to the ninth century. Villages such as these owe their existence not to the via Appia but to a much smaller thoroughfare called the *pedemontana*. This footpath predated the via Appia and then replaced it for much of the Middle Ages, when the via Appia was sub-merged by floods. The *pedemontana* traced its way, hill by hill, from the sea at Formia, where I had visited Cicero's tomb with Reginald Foster's class, to Rome.

When I step out of the van, the sun has broken out in a clamor of rays that scatter in shards over a small town on the plain below. In his guidebook, Piero calls the cliff at Bassiano "miniature and precious as a cameo," and I can see even from below that, like a cameo, the wall has been intricately carved and sculpted by the elements. We set off through a grove of olive trees and a quarter of an hour later reach the climbing wall. The instruc-tors embark on the day's first climbs. I step into my harness and stuff my feet into my cramped shoes, whose soles are still stiff with autumn chill. I think of Javier, of how much he would have enjoyed these rocks and this early-morning light, and for a moment I feel sharply the pain of his absence. When the ropes are ready, a few of us tie in, practicing our figure-eight knots.

An instructor peers over my shoulder. "*Che brutti nodi che fai*," he says, chuckling and elbowing me gently. "What ugly knots you make!" Enrico, my belay partner, regards my knot with puzzlement. "*Dai*," he finally says, "it looks fine if you squint." This affectionate ribbing is a texture of interaction that I will come to miss when I am back in New England, where a kind of earnestness generally prevails, such that making light of a matter, even something as minor as poor knots, can come across as dimin-ishing. No one at home, for example, would call my figure-eight knot *ugly*. Instead, they might say, "Nice job, you're getting better." Something *encouraging*. But my knots *are* ugly, and laughing about them makes me feel at home in the group.

"*Vai*," says Enrico, when I am harnessed and ready, giving me the green light to climb. *Vado*. My fingers pick their way across the limestone. Wind and water have pocked the surface, creating tiny pockets and indentations, and the feel is as rough as coral. As much as it can be a physical challenge, rock climbing is a mental puzzle. The rock surface contains clues—a small crevice here, a rounded protrusion there—that you must decipher to find your way up. The trick is to not panic, to keep a calm head as you continually reorient yourself on unfamiliar terrain. The body must do its part, but on even a mildly challenging route, it is the mind that gets you up.

Over the course of the morning my fingers grow tender. But what harm Bassiano does to the skin is mitigated by the beauty and prime positioning of the wall. As the clouds give way to sun, a gentle heat spreads. The rock face warms. Birds of prey soar confidently overhead. Smaller birds trill their songs, hidden from sight. Enrico wanders around with his camera, following his artist's eye, kneeling and craning and leaning into cracks and crevices to capture the details of the afternoon light, the landscape, the rock, us.

A teenager in the class makes his way across the base of the wall carrying a white box over one shoulder. *"Pasticcino?"* he asks each person he encounters. When he gets to me, he lowers the box, and inside I see maybe two dozen small pastries. I pick one out and he goes on his way, offering pastries to anyone who wants them.

Contemplating this small but unexpected act of generosity, I experience a sudden wave of gratitude. For this teenager, offering me a pastry on the side of a mountain. For this varied group and the sense that everyone, no matter their ability or age, brings something to it. For my ugly knots and my bruised knees and my robust appreciation for pastries, all of which are cause for common laughter. For the comradery generously distributed, and for the contagious good spirits and genuine enjoyment with which many of us end each day of climbing over pizza and beer in a nearby restaurant. For the sense that no one—not the students and not even the instructors—really wants it to end. Gratitude, too, for the red van, already a place that feels like home, and for the people in it—Paolo, Giulia, Enrico, Piero, and others—who make me feel I have a place here, in this city where, just two months ago, I stood before an open window beset with the deepest sense of solitude I had ever known.

23.

VIA APPIA

Venice in February: the wettest kind of cold, and the coldest kind of wet. The rain is forever on the verge of turning to ice, barely suspended in its liquid state. It slides and drips and seeps, permeating every crevice, crack, seam, and pore. Tides of visitors crowd the waterlogged sidewalks. Umbrellas jostle along, forming an unstable canopy. They tilt without warning and send icy water scuttling down the chink between the jacket and neck.

Bob, Niall, Sophus, and I have come together for Carnival, the festive period that precedes Lent in the Catholic liturgical calendar. We are bone cold and soaked. All day long we walk, looking at churches, at public squares, the stone walls on all sides of us emanating a chill for which my uninsulated Salvation Army wool coat is no match. None of the sites we visit is heated. Among them, the Piombi prison, with its lead ceiling, is the coldest. I chatter my way through its dolorous rooms. The chill comes from every direction, seeping up from the paving stones through the soles of my shoes and creeping up my calves. Bob and Niall have more stamina. They don't mind standing an hour in a freezing church, cricking their necks at the details of who made what, designed what, destroyed what, and when, and how. I am happy to see my friends, but I miss Rome. I miss its light, its aroma of earth, its climbing routes aflame with afternoon sun, even my lumpy blue bed. I miss how well I know its streets. I miss the incipient, fragile feeling of belonging. Venice is another Italy, one where words mean different things and I am once again a tourist.

My one salvation are *fritelle di carnevale,* here called *fritole,* bite-size deep-fried dough balls that I buy three or four at a time and consume with coffee. They are warm when fresh, and the bars where I find them are warm, and the coffee is warm, and the bodies crowding the bars make them even warmer. I could stay in them all day.

I can't remember what we were talking about, but I remember I had my mouth full of *fritelle* when Niall says, "But you will never be from here."

"You'll never be from Rome, or from Italy," he elaborates. It's too late. I'll never have the experiences of elementary school, high school, those formative experiences that make a person from where they're from.

Which of course is true. Yet I tell Niall that he has not quite understood me. It's not that I want to be from Rome—it's that in some way I can't pinpoint, I am *of* Rome. That I belong to it, even if I don't exactly belong *in* it. That a part of me, or even a different me, surfaces in Rome. That there is a Roman me, and I like that person, even if we have only just begun to know one another. Roman me is *spiritosa* and *capricciosa,* youthful and spirited and happy to sleep in a lumpy bed or walk for hours with no destination in mind. Roman me feels connected, as if by some invisible wire, to the many ages of the human past present in the city's ubiquitous accretions of brick and shell and stone. I think back on a friend of my mother's who has always loved Venice. He said that what linked him to Venice was the energy. Every place, he said, has its own energy, and sometimes your energy can line up with a place even when you're not from there. Maybe especially if you're not from there. But Niall remains unconvinced, and I know that by talking about energy I risk sounding ridiculous.

Five days later my train pushes away from Santa Lucia Station, its wheels clacking reassuringly on their tracks. As the landscape of northern Italy gradually falls away, as the gray begins to burn through with sun, as the fields around us green, as the wan light grows gold—my body relaxes, I grow sleepy and content. Just over the horizon, Rome awaits.

～⌒ᒡ

When Easter came, everyone I knew vanished into the fold of family: Paolo left for Frascati, Piero for Sardinia, Giulia for the other side of the city. Even Sabrina left. She took the train to Paris to visit her daughter, leaving her mottled dog in my care. The Vatican Library was closed for the better part of the week, as were many shops, and an unseasonably chilly fog hung in the air. The holiday, which for many must have reinforced their ties to others, stripped mine away—for suddenly it felt like an illusion that I was connected to anyone, or anything, in Rome.

A few days before the holiday, my brother Ben flew in from New York City for a visit. (I'd managed to convince Sabrina, ever wary, to let him sleep on the floor of my room.) At the airport at Fiumicino, he greeted me with his broad smile and open arms. We sat side by side on the train, catching up. I luxuriated in the ease of our communications, in not having to translate between languages, gestures, modes of feeling.

As we strolled the city together, taking photos from the rooftop of Castel Sant'Angelo and from the windows of Sabrina's apartment, the pleasure I found in this ease took me by surprise. All these years, I had sought what felt hard: languages, archives, the history of a city through which my mentors could not guide me. My supposition was that the hard path yields the greater reward—that, as Mr. V had said, it *offers you the chance to discover what it is that you can do.* But during my brother's brief visit, I slipped back into the soft, warm mitten of the sibling relationship, remembering that the struggles I had chosen for myself were not the whole of me.

One night in late April, Paolo and I walk along the Tiber. It's a damp evening, and the road glistens under the streetlights, which have just come on. For a while we stop and watch the water churning around Tiber Island. Paolo has recently returned from abroad, and we have not seen each other since before Easter.

We walk through the Ghetto and cross via Arenula, amble through Largo di Torre Argentina and over to the Pantheon, where a few bored boys are trying out lackluster pickup lines on passing girls. We are approaching Sant'Ivo alla Sapienza when there is a lull in our conversation. I think of the boy and father who had traced the geometric patterns in the courtyard with their running game all those months ago. When Rome was so new to me, and I was alone.

We walk up the stone stairs and into the courtyard. In silence we admire the place's clean lines, the smell of freshly fallen rain on rock. I feel the way I have always felt in this space—that the architecture envelops me in a manner both exhilarating and soothing, its features formed of a complex but coherent geometry that liberates rather than constricts.

To break the lull, I decide to share my story. "I once saw a beautiful scene here," I say. "I was standing up there on the balustrade. It was mid-September. A boy and his father were playing a game."

I point to the white pattern inlaid in the black paving stones.

"They were following these lines. They ran down there, then parted ways, and rejoined each other over there," I say, indicating a spot near the church doors.

Paolo listens closely, traces the path with his eyes.

"The boy circled here, and the fath—"

"Sì, sì," he says. "The boy here, the father there, and then in the middle they spun around each other."

"How do you know?" It's perplexing to have my story taken from me. "I was there."

I recall the courtyard as it was on that September day, the pure blue of the sky, the halo of sun on the boy's hair, the silence but for a birdcall. My solitude before that scene.

"No, you weren't," I say. Paolo must be pulling my leg, as always. "The courtyard was empty except for them, and me."

He clucks in the way Romans do when they're telling you you're wrong, and shakes his head. He won't have my version of it.

"I was there."

I regard him skeptically.

"*Mi stai prendendo in giro*," I say. "You're making fun of me."

But he's not laughing. He points to a small curb. "The mother was sitting over there," he says. "She was wearing a striped shirt."

I look at the corner where the mother had, indeed, been sitting.

"*Parlavano francese*," Paolo quietly adds.

"Sì," I say, "French."

"I was there," Paolo says.

He points to the spot directly below where I had been standing that September day.

I regard the balustrade where I had been, back when neither of us knew the other, and both of us believed we were the sole viewer of the scene before us. A month would pass before we would meet, brought together by a rock-climbing course with dozens of participants, during whose first session we happened to sit side by side. I would happen to ride in his van, and happen to forget my wallet, which would lead us into a conversation that filled the better part of a year. Toward the end of that time, we would amble out on an evening walk and stumble, entirely by chance, upon our most unlikely story.

❦

What do you do with such a story? For a long time, I found gladness in the telling and the retelling. I delighted in its aesthetic beauty. I delighted in the connection I felt, on account of it, to the courtyard of Sant'Ivo, and to Paolo. I took pleasure in the unwitting yet perfect geometry of our scene: the triangle formed by the French family, Paolo, and me in Sant'Ivo's contained universe.

When life hands you a story, it is yours for the keeping or for the discarding. For the remembering or the forgetting. Forgetting carries its own real risks. But there are risks in keeping a story, too. Should you keep it, there is the risk—today, tomorrow, in the distant future—that you will be kept by it. Remembered or forgotten, story, history, has a power all its own.

❦

I turn to look as we round the Colosseum, but it flies past, blurred like a jack-o'-lantern hurtling through the night sky. I grip the back of Paolo's motorcycle as he guides it down streets hemmed on either side by brick walls blanketed with ivy. A week has passed since our walk to Sant'Ivo, and I am still ruminating on the stunning coincidence of that evening. We zip across the Caelian Hill, the spaciousness of its estates hinted at only by the distance between gates and driveways. Everything else—what I imagine to be gardens in slumber, driveways packed with crushed snail shells, tuff, peperine stone, and bits of ancient masonry—lies obscured from sight. But there are things the walls cannot retain: the damp air laden with the smell of jasmine and pine needles, the roar of the motorcycle as we hurtle down the stone strait leading us out of Rome.

At this late hour of the night, the streets are quiet, lit only intermittently by a lone yellow streetlamp and our single headlight. Then the surface beneath us changes from asphalt to *sampietrini* and the wheels of the bike begin to chatter lightly, vibrating and humming as if at any moment they might break into song. The path before us has been laid out by countless hands over tens of centuries. Hands now without faces, without names.

We slow as we pass under the twin archways of Porta San Sebastiano that signify the end of Rome-inside-the-walls. They tower two or three stories above our heads, each one witness to seventeen centuries of traffic. Each one signed, inscribed, engraved by that many centuries of pilgrims and tourists. "This way," one graffito points, "to the church of Domine Quo Vadis." Another, my favorite, an etching of the archangel Michael standing victorious over a drake, a serpentine-shaped dragon, inscribed after the city militia defeated an invading monarch in the fourteenth century. Michael looks out impassively, his wings symmetrically aligned as he impales the drake by driving a stake into its gaping mouth.

Over the years I have returned here repeatedly to look at the inscriptions of those arriving to and departing from the city long ago. I am attracted to the liminal feeling of this place, the sense that you're no longer quite in the Rome you thought you knew. Even though the city no longer depends on its walls for defense, something still changes when you pass through them. I experience it as a transition from closed and tight to open. And somehow, when I leave the city through the Porta San Sebastiano, I also feel I am moving back in time.

We cross the thoroughfare, empty now, that circles the perimeter of the Aurelian Wall, and continue straight onto the via Appia Antica, that most ancient of roads. Once again we find ourselves pressed on either side by high walls that glance by at dizzying speed and at arm's length. I keep my fingers wrapped around the metal bars beneath me, even if they are chilled from the damp night, even if I am starting to shiver with cold. "I'll never let you ride a motorcycle," my father, a doctor who had worked in emergency rooms, always said. My head wrapped tight, maybe too tight, in a helmet, I become aware of my breathing—for life, from fear—as Rome falls away from me, under me, behind me, when suddenly we slow. I no longer know exactly where we are, the length and speed of our trajectory having blurred my geography. The surface beneath us has changed from the classic *sampietrini* to truly ancient stones: lumpy, oblong rocks worn smooth and irregular by time. On them, the motorcycle struggles and lurches. Paolo guides us to the left, where a narrow strip of *sampietrini* offers the tires just enough purchase to continue. Thus bypassing antiquity, we accelerate once again into the night.

Cypresses and umbrella pines stream by. Three scantily clad women stand idly by the road, plying the most ancient of trades on the most ancient of roads. A field unfurls and then, just as quickly, vanishes. Walls appear, disappear, gates whiz by. We sail up a small hill, and out of nowhere rises the crumbling cylinder of the tomb of Caecilia Metella, its silhouette dark and imposing against the night sky. Then it is behind us, receding, gone. We lose our *sampietrini* again. We swerve left, aim for another narrow strip until it, too, narrows to nothing and we must again lurch across the slippery stones, worn by the feet of Roman legions, to the other side of the road, where we find more traction. Huge segments of crumbled monuments slide by, like UFOs landed roadside.

Every so often the engine guns and we jolt forward out of a rut between the stones. The road narrows again; it begins to look more like a pedestrian path than a road. And then the *campagna*, the countryside, spreads out before us, broken only by a few pikes of cypresses. A full moon has risen, pregnant and burdened, illuminating this other world in ghostly white. Paolo slows, then stops, the motorcycle. All of Rome is behind us, a distant planet mired in its own worldly cares. Between us and it lie miles of darkness. Like astronauts from another galaxy, we lower our feet, lift our visors, and take in the Alban Hills, which rise from the far edge of the plain.

I sometimes wonder whether, as Neil Armstrong took his first steps on the moon, he found himself thinking about the past. About prehistoric man, *Australopithecus*, and the Neanderthals, and how far we have come. Or about the bizarre fact of Armstrong himself, a man born during the privations of the Great Depression, disembarking from a rocket ship onto the face of the moon. Or maybe, as some have speculated, whether he tethered his thoughts closer to home, to the toddler daughter he lost to a brain tumor seven years before his moon landing. Whether, as some have said, he left her little gold bracelet to glint for eternity in the Little West crater, we will likely never know for sure. But I wonder what knowledge it gave him, traveling so far, seeing the earth like a distant planet, all its cares and hopes and fears contained on that one silent sphere spinning through darkness?

The moon I was gazing at, on this spring night of the fourth year of the third millennium, was the same moon on which Armstrong had walked. The same moon that had illuminated the paving stones leading young men carrying the pain and elation of war back to Rome. And the same moon that, before that, had glinted off the cheekbones of Neanderthals. Though shivering with cold, I try to stand still in the present, in the here and now, where Paolo stands quietly beside me, a whiff of expectancy in the air. But between the gravity of the past and the magnetism of the future, the present, so slippery, holds little traction.

Paolo begins the cumbersome process of turning the motorcycle around. Its form heaves and rocks on the uneven stones. I think of a horse, its hooves sliding, legs splaying. Paolo motions me on. I swing my leg over, take hold once again of the metal bar. With the other hand, I lower my visor. We're ready for takeoff. He pushes off, the engine kicks in. We head back toward the dark, distant planet that is Rome. The via Appia Antica constricts once again and its walls rise on either side of us. The city's gravitational force swallows us whole, pulls us back into its narrow straits and winding channels, then spits us out in Trastevere, a block from my room. On via della Scala, Paolo lowers the kickstand. I pull the helmet over my head with ungainly force. It does not want to come off.

At my feet I hear a clink. My earring has been tugged from my ear. It's small, silver, shaped like an apple. It cannot have fallen far. In the cracks between the cobblestones, I search for a telltale glint, for streetlight or moonlight thrown back at my eye. I see no such shine. We crouch and feel around but do not find the earring.

"You'll just have to come back again and again until you find it," Paolo says.

When I am back in my room, Paolo's words continue to resonate. *Until you find it.* But will I ever find it? Something more than my earring has been lost. It occurs to me that a man possibly just offered me a key to his city—to Rome, to himself, to the unfolding of a story that began in the courtyard of Sant'Ivo?—and without a word I have let it slip by. He stood with me at the foot of the Alban Hills—same place, same time, the simple geometry of a line between two people—and instead of going to him I went to the moon, and all the way back to *Australopithecus*. I went to the past and, in so doing, avoided a problem of future. Or perhaps I avoided a fact I was not ready to face. No matter how many nights I'd spent in my childhood bedroom, dreaming of a city I knew only from books, no matter how well I knew its map or how deeply I delved into its history, no matter how remarkable the stories this city presented me with, I could not with any clarity perceive the contours of a life in Rome. The shard of future that I had glimpsed—illusory or not—lay elsewhere. The earring fell between the stones.

For years, every time I returned to Rome, I returned to via della Scala to search for that earring. I have often imagined it at night, glinting in the moonlight, stepped carelessly over by people engrossed in their own lives. Years, decades, of people walking right over it.

❦

Spring came late that year. Since February, everyone everywhere—in shops, on the radio, in the climbing class—had been heralding its arrival. And yet it did not come.

On the night before I left, I didn't sleep. I had few belongings, but they were still too many for my suitcase, so I packed and repacked, deliberating over what to bring and what to leave behind. In his last letter, Javier had written that his divorce was underway, and that he awaited my arrival. Soon we would eat breakfast again in his sunny kitchen. But once again, I dragged my feet about leaving. It was only May; I had not even been in Rome a full year. I was not certain I had enough material on which to build a dissertation. I would miss my new friends, and the walls on which we climbed. I would miss my long walks with Paolo, our endless conversations, and the person—*spiritosa* and *capricciosa* and *golosa* and (almost, but not quite) *romana*—that I was in the company of him, Piero, and our other climbing friends. I would miss that part of myself, which I was just getting to know, that had begun to flourish in Rome.

And yet I was convinced that there was no other choice. My lease with Sabrina was up; her daughter would soon return from Paris. I lacked the money to stay. I had a dissertation to write. I needed a research library. I did not see any way to continue my graduate studies while staying in Rome. I did not have, and did not think I could get, a work permit. It seemed patently clear that remaining there would spell the end of my academic career. I did not know what a shared future with Javier might look like, or if such a thing would even materialize. But as fleeting and fragile as it was, I held on to the possibility of it.

On my last morning in the city, the sun rose bright and warm. Birds chirped, trees burst into bloom. Spring had finally arrived. It felt like some awful kind of revenge. Paolo drove me to the airport in the red van.

For the first time, my feet grew hot in my leather boots, which until this day had been the only pair, besides climbing and running shoes, that I had needed all year. Paolo accompanied me to the check-in area. He had a grisly expression on his face, as if he had just witnessed an accident, and I probably did, too. When I was ready to go, he kissed me quickly on my forehead, as a father or an uncle might. Then he spun swiftly on his heels and walked away, in a straight line, without looking back. I boarded the plane and took my seat, incredulous that I had boarded a plane, that I was facing out toward the runway, and that Rome lay behind me.

~∞

Rome gave me a story.
A story is a gift,
and a burden.

Part IV

24.

If Only I Could
Live in Their Times

.

Back in Providence, I began to clear the ground on which to build my dissertation. First and most urgently, I needed a research library, but the only one to which I had open access was back at Cornell. Brown University offered borrowing privileges to a select few, depending on affiliations. Was I faculty at Rhode Island School of Design? No. Was I a medical doctor with board certification? No chance. Was I a member of the American Mathematical Society? Well . . . thirty minutes and forty dollars later, I most certainly was.

I checked out a few armfuls of books from Rockefeller Library and brought them back to Javier's apartment—which was now, very tentatively, *our* apartment. So tentatively, in fact, that I went on viewing other rentals because maybe it really was, still, too soon. His divorce now underway, Javier occasionally slipped into periods of mourning, during which I gingerly stepped around him, giving him the space to process his loss. Outside of those delicate, painful periods, the new routine we took up that summer, of writing, biking, cooking, and rock climbing, was filling out with budding friendships with his colleagues and our explorations of Providence and Rhode Island. The commitment we expressed to each other, furthermore, felt rooted in honesty, and this appealed to me as a

solid foundation for a relationship. Slowly, we began building a life together.

I began, too, to build a dissertation, following the thread of the questions I
had been developing in Rome: How did medieval Romans understand
their relationship to their city's past? Did the past "belong" solely to members of the commercial elite and aristocratic families, those literate classes
who either owned books or had access to them in monastic collections?
How much did others know about their city's ancient past, and what, if
anything, did it mean to them? I began to poke around the sources, trying
to get at this question this way and that.

As 2004 slid into 2005, my dissertation began to take shape. It grew
into a structure with a roof, windows, and doors. The subject it came to
explore was historical memory: I was looking at how, in the early fourteenth
century, the idea of Rome as founding city of an empire was repeatedly
invoked, often by Roman nobles, to attract support among the populace
for political movements, even though many of these movements ultimately
eroded the rights of the people in favor of the aristocracy. Put another way, I
was interested in the ways a mythologized memory of a "golden age" of
the past was used in the struggle for political and social power. I concluded
that culture, by which I meant learning, knowledge, and the arts, was a
central arena in that struggle for power. Conversely, the dissertation was
also about forgetting—oblivion at the level of collective memory—and
what we gain, and lose, when we forget.

The figure that loomed largest in those pages was Cola di Rienzo,
for it was he who spoke most eloquently about the relevance of Rome's
past to the struggles of his own day. I was interested in what he had to
say. But although I could not hear it back then (keeping Cola and his
story at the proper distance taught me by my discipline: up in my head,
safely distant from my heart), I know now that I had begun a secondary

conversation with Cola, too. It has taken me two decades to begin to decipher it.

~~∽~~

Born in the flood-prone bend of the Tiber to a tavern keeper and a washerwoman, Cola was probably the last kid born in 1313 whom anyone would have bet on to take a memorable stance on Rome's past or future. The sources don't tell us precisely how it happened, but after the death of Cola's mother during his early childhood, Cola left Rome for Anagni, a hill town southeast of Rome, to live with a relative. There he gained an education solid enough to prepare him for his future career as a notary.

As had been plain to me in the archives, the work of notaries made the wheels of medieval Italy go round, and Cola was well positioned to be of service. But he wanted more. In addition to acquiring the workaday Latin necessary for his profession, and the liturgical Latin that he surely heard in church, he immersed himself deeply in texts from classical and late antiquity—texts that only the most ambitious students of Latin would have read.

Among them were Virgil's *Aeneid*, Lucan's *Pharsalia*, Ovid's *Metamorphosis* and *The Art of Love*, the poetry of Statius. These texts were already a thousand years old, written in an older, classicizing Latin, and many were composed before the emergence of Christianity. They taught Cola the subtleties of Latin syntax and style. And with their meditations on mythology and history and poetics and natural philosophy, they colored how he saw and thought about his world. By the time he left Anagni and returned to Rome at age twenty, the boy born into poverty on the silted banks of the Tiber was well on his way to becoming an expert in antiquuities.

———

Now I allow myself to ask: How do middle-aged pagan poets who write in dactylic hexameters and elegiac couplets about a world that no longer exists speak to a devout teenage Catholic boy who speaks Romanesco and who lives seven or ten centuries down the river of time?

Give me a glimpse into that black box, that I might perceive how these things happen, why we are driven to pursuits that arise from within us and that few around us, and perhaps least of all we ourselves, can understand.

Tell me the story, Cola, that none of us can tell.

When Cola returned in 1333 to the city of his birth, it little resembled the powerful *caput mundi* depicted in his readings. Vastly depopulated, Rome was mired in a long economic slump. Many ancient buildings were in a state of collapse. With the papacy's departure nearly three decades earlier, the city's noble families had lost their primary avenues to institutional advancement and, in the power vacuum that ensued, had become only more entrenched in their violent struggles. Their conflicts, many of them multi-generational cycles of vendetta, played out on city streets, often pitting one neighborhood against another. One Florentine visitor described Rome as a "den of thieves" and the Romans as "a people disposed to bad deeds." The impoverished Roman populace, tired of turbulent politics and humiliated by the city's loss of stature, hungered for stability and relevance.

Soon after he returned, Cola began taking a public stand on the issues facing his city. A contemporary chronicler, known to history only as the "Anonymous Roman," described Cola's "beautiful speech" and noted with awe that he had been "nourished on the milk of eloquence." By his late twenties, Cola was already widely considered the best orator in Rome, and this, combined with his qualifications as a notary, his charisma, and his deep-seated belief that Rome was overdue for a revival, made him an attractive candidate to represent Rome's interests before the pope in Avignon. In late 1342, he was selected by a newly formed civic government—a panel of elected magistrates (it would be short-lived) that had overthrown the two papally appointed senators from noble families—to head a delegation to the papal court. Among Cola's tasks were to convince Pope Clement VI to return the papacy to Rome, and to request that the pope move the next Jubilee year up from 1400, where it was currently set, to 1350, so that living Romans might derive some benefit, whether financial, spiritual, or both. In his speech, Cola appealed to Rome's ancient splendor, and he advocated for commerce, taxation, laws, and a just society, while criticizing the Roman noblemen for their wanton and destructive lawlessness. Pope Clement was mesmerized by Cola and asked to meet with him every day.

Cola won other admirers in Avignon, too. Petrarch, whom he met at the papal court, would quickly become his closest friend and most ardent supporter. "My heart was all inflamed as you spoke," Petrarch wrote of their first conversation. Later, on the poet's visits to Rome, the two friends were known to take long walks through the Forum, reading the inscriptions on fallen ruins and musing about the contemporary state of the Italian peninsula, as well as on ancient Latin poetry and Roman history. "If only I could live in their times!" Cola sighed.

For inspiration and knowledge, both Cola and Petrarch looked back over a thousand years to the history and culture of ancient Rome. Such cultural access was not easily opened to men of their ilk, and each had to overcome familial and social barriers to attain it. Not surprisingly, both men first pursued practical professions: while Cola was a notary, Petrarch studied law. For those from families like Cola's, literature and history were luxuries. But in excelling at Latin, in mastering Roman history and literature and epigraphy, Cola joined Rome's most elite families on their own turf. He conquered that turf; he made it his own.

Petrarch's family was not poor, but like Dante, they had been exiled from Florence. As they wandered from Italy to the papal court in Avignon in search of employment, their fortunes hung in the balance. Petrarch's father, a notary, was so discomfited by the extent of his son's passion for ancient literature that he once threw the family copies of Cicero and Virgil into a fire. But like Cola, Petrarch persisted, becoming among the most learned men of his time. Despite constant wandering, he assembled a library so voluminous and renowned that great noble families, and even entire municipalities like the city of Venice, fought for possession of it upon his death.

"Read whenever you have any spare moments," Petrarch exhorted his new friend in 1337, and "if you can't do so conveniently, have others read to you."

In Avignon and in Rome, did you and Petrarch stay up late into the night, cooking, drinking wine, talking about history, until one or both of you fell asleep on the couch, or on the floor? Did time seem plentiful to you then in a way it never would again? Did you sit around a table debating the differences in the styles of your Latin? Or discussing those new words, alchimia, elixir, algebra, *and so many others, that were finding their way into Latin by way of Arabic? Did your friendship change your lexicon, make it bolder, deeper, richer? Did you do these things for the sheer pleasure of being in each other's company, sitting in taverns—talking, angsting, laughing, sighing—until closing time, only then trudging out, bracing your bodies against the chill of the Roman night?*

Cola and Petrarch used their knowledge, their passion for the past, to build a vision of Rome's future. And because Cola articulated this vision better than any other of his time, he became the hope of a generation of idealists, including Petrarch, that dreamed of a unified Italy long before (and after) that idea was common currency. Both men despaired of Italy's divided, warring city-states and what they saw as its fallen ideals. Both looked to ancient Rome as salve and solution.

Cola dreamed of a Rome that could win back its status as *caput mundi,* head of the world—even if that "world," to him, was limited to Italy. In his vision, Rome would become the head of a federation of Italian cities. In an age in which many municipalities in Italy were both larger than Rome and fiercely independent, possessing fortresslike walls and citizen militias, Cola's plan was extraordinarily ambitious. In his vision, his city would once again be a guiding force on the peninsula, Roman citizens would free themselves from the depredations of the Roman nobility and govern themselves through elected councils, fiscal reforms would allow the wheels of commerce to roll smoothly, and legal reforms would make the streets safe while ensuring that noblemen and commoners received similar, and fair, treatment before the law.

This rebirth of good government, as Cola envisioned it, also had a spiritual element of religious renewal and reform. Like many of his contemporaries, including Dante and Petrarch, he was deeply versed in the rhetoric of prophecy popularized by the twelfth-century preacher Joachim of Fiore, who had divided history into three ages: the age of the Father (Old Testament), the current age of the Son (New Testament), and that of the Holy Spirit, an impending new age of spiritual contemplation and the fulfillment of Christian ideals. By reviving Rome, Cola dreamed, not only would he restore the city to its political pride of place, but he would usher Italy into the third, and final, age of history—an age of peace, justice, and reconciliation.

Through his intelligence and his charisma, Cola convinced a startling number of people, many of whom had been deeply skeptical at the outset, that his vision was attainable. In public and in private, he promised to lift his city from the mire of his times.

In your most solitary, private moments, what form did your vision take? Was it a weightless, crystalline planet, with pinnacles of torchlight and great expanses of darkness? Did you feel the energy of those filaments, as thin and strong as silk thread, pulsing forward and back across centuries and millennia? Or did it take a different form? Could you visualize the alchemy by which you would transform your muddy present using the substance of a golden past?

In the spring of 1344, Pope Clement rewarded Cola with a promotion. As notary of the city chamber, Cola would serve the needs of Rome, but his appointment at the pope's discretion would keep the young parvenu closely aligned—the pope hoped—with papal interests. While many looked at Cola with increasing reverence, others regarded him with contempt. Roman noblemen, in particular, both feared and disdained him. At a dinner party in Avignon in 1345, the young, aspiring Cola chided the Roman nobles for being bad citizens, for prioritizing their private agendas over the common good. In return he received an insult he never forgot: a member of the Colonna family slapping him, literally, in the face, and publicly ridiculing his far-fetched dreams of reform. "With his little coat on his back," the Anonymous Roman wrote, "he stood in the sun like a snake." So exposed was he, so young, indigent, and naive.

Cola quickly earned a reputation for personal style that outshone even the most extravagant nobleman. Like a Liberace of the 1300s, Cola became known for his frocks of red velvet, or layers of white silk, and fur trims, which he paired with fancy stockings, stacks of bracelets, multitiered crowns of silver and gold, and elaborate hats, one of which was topped with a bird—the dove of the Holy Spirit—made entirely of pearls. These outfits made Cola visible and memorable, and as he developed his innate talent for public spectacle, they also communicated his political messaging.

But because neither the clothes nor the status nor even the power of the sword would ever be enough, knowledge remained the most powerful tool in Cola's arsenal. And he instinctively knew how to combine that knowledge with spectacle to achieve his political aims. He orchestrated one such defining event in 1345 or 1346, when in his early thirties.

Dressed in layers of ethereal white and wearing a complicated, multitiered headpiece out of which protruded a silver sword, Cola ascended a dais in the Basilica of Saint John Lateran. Gathered before him were the city's most illustrious men. Behind him stood an ancient bronze tablet measuring over five feet tall and almost four feet wide. For centuries it had lain on the basilica floor, but for today's display, Cola had erected it for all to see.

Unlike plaques produced in the 1300s, which were inscribed with a minuscule, or lowercase, Gothic script, the one behind Cola bore Latin words in majuscule lettering. There were no spaces between the words, moreover, and many of those words were abbreviated in ways no longer commonly understood. But since returning to Rome twelve years earlier, Cola had often strolled the Forum, examining the ancient marble, teaching himself to read their lettering and abbreviations, and attempting to understand them in their historical context. He became one of the first epigraphers of his time, and as far as we know, he was the only person in Rome capable of both reading the tablet's words and deciphering their meaning.

With no shortage of dramatic suspense, Cola explained to the assembled crowd that the tablet commemorated the act whereby the Senate and people of Rome had conferred power and authority upon the Roman emperor Vespasian in 69 CE. Just beside the tablet, Cola had placed painted visuals that likely depicted the ancient Roman people, senators, and emperor—all dressed in fourteenth-century style—engaged in this symbolic vesting of authority. Between his powerful words and his inventive use of visual art, Cola's point would not have been lost on the men in attendance. In their day, it was highly contested who—whether the pope, a distant emperor, a handful of noble-born Roman senators, or an elected body of citizens—was the rightful ruler of Rome. But if we look to history, Cola seemed to say, the chain of authority is clear. Emperors had derived their authority from Roman senators, who in turn derived it from the Roman people—the ultimate source of political authority. He lamented that the Romans of their day, to their great injury and shame, had squandered this authority.

This debate, about the source of political authority, was hotly contested in fourteenth-century Italian legal circles. But rare was the spectacle of a tavern keeper's son, in elaborate costume, parsing Latin epigraphy before a rapt group of Roman noblemen.

Did you follow unerringly what you loved most? Did you pursue it even though its outcome was uncertain, and even though it likely made little sense, at least initially, to those who knew you best? Were you a ship steaming toward a horizon that only you could see?

Might you have been, in another life, the son and grandson of Milwaukee plumbers? And is it possible, Cola, that history is like a whale whose body slices the water's surface before diving deep and disappearing, until at long last surfacing elsewhere, very far away, to draw her next breath?

In Cola's vision, the infighting of the Roman nobility would be quelled and Rome's fallen status in the eyes of the world would be redeemed. In May 1347, when many of the city's noblemen were on their agricultural estates outside the city walls tending to the first harvest, Cola attended an all-night vigil in his home parish of Sant'Angelo in Pescheria. The following morning, Pentecost, he emerged from the church in full knight's armor, leading a procession of his supporters bearing arms and banners. Together, amid increasing fanfare and the raucous support of the gathering crowds, they proceeded to the Capitoline Hill, then, as it remains today, the site of the Senatorial Palace. There he and his men ousted the two sitting senators, a Colonna and an Orsini, who fled.

In a speech before the assembled crowd that Cola deemed a "parliament," he asserted that on that day, May 20, 1347, the Roman Republic had been revived. He called himself "Nicholas the severe and the clement, tribune of liberty, peace and justice, and liberator of the sacred Roman republic." This new title resuscitated the ancient office of tribune of the plebs—the plebeian-elected officials whose task it had been in the Roman Republic to advocate for the people and check the power of the Senate. One of his first acts as tribune was to temporarily banish the noblemen to their rural estates. And so, without a drop of bloodshed, Cola claimed to have ushered in a new age of peace.

Petrarch was elated. In a long letter addressed to Cola and the Roman people, the poet wrote: "Italy, which only recently lay listless and enfeebled, with head bowed to the ground, has now risen to her knees." He likened Cola to Romulus, the mythical founder of Rome, and to Brutus, who by assassinating Julius Caesar "gave Rome liberty." He also informed Cola that the news of his successful uprising had spread like wildfire in Avignon, where people were passing Cola's letters around with such zeal as if they had been sent "by an inhabitant of another world." For many, euphoria was in the air.

Not so for Stefano Colonna, who upon hearing the news from his rural estate on Pentecost Sunday, jumped on his horse and, despite being eighty-two years of age, rode nearly seventy miles over several days to reach Rome, declaring upon arrival in his neighborhood that "he did not like what had happened." Cola let him stew for a day and then sent him a reminder of his banishment, a note that Stefano tore to pieces before realizing, surely with no small measure of astonishment, that he actually needed to leave. Which he did, but only after making a pit stop just outside the Aurelian Wall to gulp down some bread in his grief.

With the noble families sulking outside the city, Cola made quick strides. He and his supporters drafted a set of fifteen ordinances that defined the new republic's laws, articulated its commitment to the nuts and bolts of governance, and asserted, above all, that the source of political authority lay in the people rather than in any single entity. The Ordinances of 1347, as they are known, prescribed the approach of the new civic government to applying law and justice; to reforming the city militia and addressing issues of security (such as, notably, curtailing the powers of the noble families by appropriating their control over castles, bridges, ports, and gates); and to defining the government's involvement in works of mercy and charity. When Cola heard that the Roman noblemen were (predictably) conspiring against him, he boldly recalled them to Rome, where, following the model of Florence and other Italian cities, he compelled them—Stefano Colonna included—to swear an oath of fealty to the new government. One after another, many submitted.

In the months following his coup, Cola bolstered the provisions he had outlined in his speech with the force of law, military might, and public spectacle. He organized processions in which he rode on horseback dressed in sumptuous, symbolic attire, distributing coins to largely adoring crowds. He introduced fiscal reforms that directed the flow of money into public coffers, applied the law to Rome's powerful families, and promoted his vision for urban renewal, which was inspired in part by the spiritual movements of his day.

Cola knew that if his government was to endure, it would also need political allies from outside Rome—and not just the pope. Securing support from other Italian cities would also enhance Rome's stature on the peninsula and allow Cola to usher in the new age beyond the city walls. Many of Cola's early diplomatic efforts were successful, to the extent that multiple cities in Tuscany, such as Siena and Perugia, sent knights to aid Rome's military defense, while others sent monetary tribute. The more distant cities of the north were less responsive to Cola, though, and some even outright dismissive.

Even still, Cola's aspirations went beyond mere troops and tribute. For early August he planned a Roman synod aimed at restoring Rome's leadership on the peninsula and invited the cities of Italy to send representatives. Many came. The city they arrived at was festooned and celebratory.

"All Rome was happy, it laughed again, and it looked like it had returned to better years past," wrote the Anonymous Roman.

On the evening of July 31, as representatives from much of Italy looked on, Cola underwent an elaborate knighting ceremony he had planned at the Basilica of Saint John Lateran. There he took the customary ritual bath in an uncustomary way: in the porphyry basin that, according to legend, had been the baptismal font of Emperor Constantine in 337 CE. Many of those present—and, when he heard the news, the pope in Avignon—regarded the brazenness of Cola's act with incredulity. Not only did the baptism of the first Christian emperor feature heavily in Christian art and symbolism, but the idea that Cola, in likening himself to Constantine, was reviving Roman imperial ambitions was threatening to many, and perhaps most of all to the pope, who strongly preferred the city to remain complacent.

There is evidence that in his words, too, Cola was growing bolder. In a remarkable speech given at Saint John Lateran the morning after his ritual bath and knighting, he imperiously declared that the right to elect the emperor belonged to Rome, to its people, and to Italy, and that any emperor, king, elector, prince, or duke who disagreed must appear in Rome to argue his case. He then drew his sword and waved it toward the three divisions of the world (Europe, Asia, and Africa), saying, "This is mine; this is mine; this is mine." These gestures had precedent in imperial coronation ceremonies, but that mattered little: the optics were bad. The papal vicar, stunned and dumbfounded, commanded Cola to rescind his words. But Cola directed the band to play, drowning out the vicar's voice with the blare of trumpets and drums.

Two weeks later, on August 15, the Feast of the Assumption, Cola staged his own coronation ceremony. Representatives from six major Roman churches each presented Cola with a different symbolic crown, and Cola apparently also donned a hat topped with a dove, symbol of the Holy Spirit, made of pearls. The full title Cola now claimed was "white-clad soldier of the Holy Spirit, knight, severe and clement, liberator of the city, zealot of Italy, lover of the world and tribune augustus." That night, he held a sumptuous feast that all ranks and stations of Roman society were invited to attend. Among those few conspicuously absent were the Colonna and Orsini families.

In Avignon, Pope Clement was beside himself. He was appalled by the news of the knighting ceremony, by Cola's attempt to hold a synod of Italian cities with Rome as capital, by his unauthorized appropriation of titles, and by his decision to levy taxes on towns in the church's jurisdiction. He reminded Cola, tactfully at first, that Cola was working at his behest. Yet within one week of the Roman synod, he launched a quiet campaign to depose Cola. Only one of Cola's crimes—his ambition—had been spelled out by the pope. The other crime—his competence—went unsaid, but it was perhaps the graver of the two. The fact was, the papal curia did not want a resuscitated Rome or a unified Italy, for either one would weaken the papacy both politically and fiscally. There was no scenario in which the pope wished Cola to succeed.

Cola was in an impossible situation, having no choice but to continue working with Pope Clement. At the same time, he must have sensed that the pope had begun to oppose him. In fact, the pope had already betrayed Cola in secret by fanning rumors that the upstart leader was delirious with power. Contemporaries apparently picked up on this messaging, because by August and September 1347, multiple chronicle accounts begin to portray Cola as psychologically fragile and prone to wild flights of paranoia and visions of grandeur.

Throughout the late summer and early fall, Cola remained as determined as ever to manifest his vision of a new Rome. To this end, he continued trying to win the support of a small group of the highest-ranking noblemen—most of whom were from the Colonna and Orsini families—who had still not sworn loyalty to his government. At a sumptuous dinner on the Capitoline Hill that he organized for this purpose one mid-September evening, Cola clashed with Stefano Colonna. Dripping with condescension, Stefano fingered the hem of Cola's robe. "*Per ti, tribuno,*" he said. "For you, tribune, it would be more commendable to wear the plain clothes of a poor man than these pompous garments"—skillfully insulting him by deploying the informal *tu*, used for familiars, children, and servants, while also ridiculing his lower-class background, his flashy dress, and his lofty ideals.

But Cola was no longer the political ingenue "with his little coat on his back," no longer alone, like a snake in the sun. Shortly following Stefano's comment, Cola followed one well-known script of medieval Italian political diplomacy by promptly imprisoning more than half a dozen Colonna and Orsini dinner guests, including Stefano himself. He then threatened to execute them as traitors (an act he likely never planned to carry out, even though Petrarch endorsed it) and sent confessors to their prison cells to convince them that their end was near. Only at the last minute did Cola release the subdued noblemen, at which point he asked them to swear loyalty to the Roman commune before the public, which had gathered at the foot of the Capitoline. When the noblemen acquiesced, they were praised and notified that the public had forgiven them when they had confessed in their prison cells. Cola gifted each nobleman a fancy robe and a banner, conferred honors and offices on them, dined with them once again, and then processed on horseback with them through the streets, signaling to all the city that reconciliation had been achieved.

What Cola presented as reconciliation must have felt, to the noblemen, like humiliation. They had already conspired, and failed, several times to have him assassinated, and by autumn, despite their recent oath of loyalty, they had joined with the pope to defeat him. On the down-low, they began fortifying their castles, gathering supplies, and waging small battles against the Roman city militia that was under Cola's command. Six months after the coup, in late November 1347, the noblemen staged a military uprising. As it unfolded, eighty-two-year-old Stefano paced helplessly out on his country estate, where he awaited news of the outcome. But everything that could have gone wrong for the noblemen did. Just outside Porta San Lorenzo (today's Porta Tiburtina), Cola's militia killed more than eighty men allied with noble families, and three generations of Colonna men—including Stefano's son, nephew, and grandson—lost their lives in the space of several hours. Of his victory over the noblemen, Cola pronounced, with little evident satisfaction: "I have cut off an ear from the head that neither the pope nor the emperor could touch."

Immediately following the battle, Cola consolidated his victory over the now-vulnerable Colonna family through what might appear as coldhearted displays of power. To start, he refused to allow the bodies of the Colonna men to be removed from the muddy puddles in which they lay. When finally he relented, the corpses were carted to the Church of Santa Maria in Aracoeli, atop the Capitoline, where the Colonna women had gathered outside to mourn. Cola shut the women out of the church. In a final coup de grâce, he denied the dead men a daytime burial, shaming the preeminent family for the third and final time. He did not, however, eke military revenge on the defenseless family. A few days after the battle, Cola coolly described Stefano as "old, unhappy, living on, and half-dead." Even the proudest Colonna had been thoroughly chastened.

Cola and the Roman commune had won a military victory, but it came at the expense of a costly moral defeat. After the battle outside Porta San Lorenzo, Cola's claim to have ushered in a new age of peace lay in tatters.

For years to come, the bloodiness of that battle would continue to repulse Cola. He had lost the support of Pope Clement months earlier. Now he would also lose Petrarch, who had been influenced by the pope's rumor mill, which was now calling Cola "the precursor of the Antichrist" and urging Romans to "shun him as a sick beast that contaminates the whole flock with its disease."

A few weeks later, amid the blare of trumpets and an outpouring of public sympathy, Cola resigned his post in tears and went into hiding in Castel Sant'Angelo. It was the middle of December. In a stunning display of grace and respect, Stefano Colonna commanded that "the peace previously made between so many by the lord tribune Cola di Rienzo" should not be broken: there should be no reprisals, no revenge. Just as Cola had spared the defenseless Colonna following battle, Stefano now ensured that Cola's family and supporters received similar protection.

The papal legate acted with no such restraint. He began proceedings against Cola almost immediately, declaring him an outlaw and a heretic. Cola's portrait was painted on the Senatorial Palace, dressed as a knight but strung upside down: a *pittura infamante*, a defamatory portrait, a public shaming.

In January, Cola fled the city at night. Exchanging the laurel leaves of his tribune's crown, as he put it, for the forest leaves of the wanderer and pilgrim, he took refuge in the mountains of Abruzzi. As Dante had once been, so was Cola now: in exile.

What was it like, that first December night in Castel Sant'Angelo, that mausoleum of an emperor a thousand years dead? The moon, waning crescent. Did you walk up to the roof of that great drum, press your cheek to the cold stone, and look out across the darkened city? Did you think back on that moment you first read Dante's words on loss and banishment?

> *You shall leave everything you love most dearly:*
> *this is the arrow that the bow of exile*
> *shoots first. You are to know the bitter taste*

of others' bread, how salt it is, and know
how hard a path it is for one who goes
descending and ascending others' stairs.

For consolation, did you murmur his Tuscan words aloud: questo è quello strale, *and* come sa di sale, *and* come è duro calle lo scendere e 'l salir per l'altrui scale?

How great was the weight of your solitude?

Cola's story does not end with exile. He reemerged into public view in August 1350, after two and a half years of wandering. He arrived on foot at the imperial court in Prague, whereupon he was imprisoned—to his dismay—for heresy.

The world around him had changed. The month that Cola left Rome, in winter 1347, the Black Death, which would kill more than half the residents of many cities, reached Italy through its ports. Rome was not the most devastated, but nor was it spared. Around the same time, a series of earthquakes toppled Rome's monuments and towers. Even the roof of the Basilica of Saint John Lateran came down. To many, the apocalypse seemed nigh.

Still a prisoner, Cola was transferred from Prague to Avignon, where Pope Clement VI soon died. Ever the master of rhetoric, Cola won the esteem of the new pope, Innocent VI, who sent him back to Rome to try his hand at reforming the city a second time. It was 1354, seven years after he had first marched to the Capitoline Hill and proclaimed the Roman Republic revived. Cola's dream remained the same. But the man chasing it had changed, or perhaps he hadn't changed enough. A familiar story played out, as the Roman nobility closed ranks against his efforts at reform. Within months, Cola was betrayed by a consortium of noblemen allied with the Colonna family, as well as from within the ranks of his former supporters.

Seven years after his successful rise to tribune, Cola once again stood in the Senatorial Palace atop the Capitoline Hill. But this time, instead of gazing upon a rapt gathering of Rome's citizens, he saw and heard a crowd clamoring for his demise. Cola ditched his sword and helmet, threw on the cloak of a commoner, clipped his beard, smudged his face, and, thus disguised, joined the demonstration. But his rings and shiny bracelets gave him away—his love for opulence undermining him one final time. Someone tore off Cola's cloak, revealing the green silk jacket with gold trim that he was wearing underneath, and his blue stockings "like those barons wear."

No one had the courage to move until one man, a certain Cecco dello Viecchio, stabbed Cola, at which point the pent-up fury of the crowd was released. Cola died atop the Capitoline, the same hill on which he had lived his finest hour.

There was still more to come. The crowd dragged Cola's body through the city and up the via Lata, the street on which Stefano Colonna and Petrarch had taken their walk almost twenty years earlier. There, in front of the Colonna palace, he was strung upside down. People threw stones at his body, defiled it. It hung outside for days.

Finally, Cola's remains were taken to the Mausoleum of Augustus, where the city's Jews were assigned the infelicitous task of setting them alight. His ashes were tossed into the currents of the Tiber, which carried them past his childhood home and out and out until they joined with the salty sea.

There, a lone fisherman in a rickety boat may have glimpsed the glistening body of a whale risen from the deep, ever briefly, to carry Cola's ashes into the great beyond.

Of what did you dream, as a boy lying in your parents' tavern? In your mind's eye, did you see a saturated kind of sunlight? Did you hear the chirping of birds, the patter of shoes on stone? Did you dream that you would one day speak the very words that Virgil had once spoken? That you might summon a past you knew only from books? That with paper and ink, and the knowledge they carried, you might bring your fallen city back to life? Deep down, did you really believe you could revive what was so long gone, that you could be a bridge between those worlds?

You had a story, Cola. That story was a gift. And a burden.

25.

AMERICANA

In September 2005, a little over a year after returning from Rome, I successfully defended my dissertation. Although the university wouldn't officially confer the degree until January, I was essentially a PhD. In late October, I would travel to Venice to participate in the German Historical Institute's medieval history seminar—where historian Patrick Geary would ask us why we wished to devote our lives to the Middle Ages. After that, I would return to Rome on a research grant for the month of November. Javier, on a teaching sabbatical, would join me.

Through my brother's girlfriend, we found a room to rent near Porta Latina in the apartment of a coquettish Roman woman in her sixties who flirted unrelentingly with Javier and who seemed to regard me as a pesky intrusion on their new life together. It worked out well—while I was out at the Vatican Library, Javier worked on his book, and then the two of them cooked up delectable meals to which I returned, tired and hungry, at the end of the day. *Saltimbocca alla romana* one day, seafood paella the next. I relished my reimmersion in quotidian Roman life: the produce market twenty steps from the apartment, the bar at the corner whose coffee cups clinked cheerfully each morning as I passed, the cobbler's shop just a block away where I could resole my shoes and boots, the weekends we would spend climbing in the Roman countryside. And although we were living just a few blocks away from Paolo's apartment, we wouldn't see him for the length of our stay. One of his closest friends had fallen terminally ill, and he was at his bedside.

In what felt like a stroke of fortune, I managed to arrange a meeting with a distinguished professor of medieval Roman history. A friend of Piero's connected the two of us, and to my surprise, in the final week of my stay, the historian invited me to meet him at his home.

I had seen this professor once before, at a conference in Rome I had attended a few years earlier. Organized around the topic of the Roman Middle Ages, it was my first conference in Italy. I was the only American there, and also, I think, the only graduate student. Fifteen or twenty scholars, men and women whose names I knew from books and journals, sat on heavy chairs arranged around a large oval table. I, and the few others who did not fit at that table, sat on metal stacking chairs that had been dispersed throughout the room, a few here, a few there, facing every which direction like lonesome, disoriented travelers. The scholars presented their papers and then discussed them as a group.

The conference had a kind of intimacy, in that the scholars were deeply immersed in the same small world. There was animated debate, for example, about whether the term *senatorial aristocracy* was useful, and about what features distinguished the medieval Roman nobility from the noble families of other Italian cities. The terminology was familiar to me, and I had been mulling over these same questions for three years. So it was strangely disjunctive to be so inside this world on paper, and so outside of it in every other way.

The two days I spent in the conference room did little to change that. There were no registration lists, no name cards, nothing that would document the fact that I had ever been present. I might as well have been observing the conference through a two-way mirror. During coffee breaks I milled about, hovering at the edges of small groups engaged in conversation. Like the others, I held my ceramic plate in one hand and drank espresso from a little cup in the other. But I was too shy to break into their circles, too unsure of my Italian, too young, too American, too inexperienced, too socially unconnected, too self-conscious, and possibly too female. Eventually I resigned myself to sitting on one of the many modern white sofas that dotted the break area and opening a book, any book, to pass the time until the next session. Over the course of those two days, though, the names I recognized from the card catalog gradually morphed into the figures, albeit still beyond my reach, of actual people.

During sessions, the professor—I could never have imagined then that one day he would invite me to his home—sat expansively at the center of the table, one arm draped across the back of the seat next to him. From that position he presided, occasionally leaning in over the table and reaching toward others when making a point. As the group debated the cultural capital of Roman noble families and how it changed between the eleventh and fourteenth centuries, he was articulate and vocal. He could also be cutting. He was charismatic, trim, and handsome, and with his sandy hair, he appeared younger than many of the other scholars around the table.

I had noted in my readings that this professor's scholarship exuded a comfort with the scholarly literature of many languages, American English included. His cosmopolitanism distinguished him, in my eyes, from some of his Roman counterparts, whose work seemed more deeply entrenched in the specifically Italian academic milieu. He was versed in a historical world I recognized, an international landscape I hoped I would one day be part of.

Meeting with this professor would be the first time I talked to an Italian scholar about my work, and I was excited at the opportunity. But even before meeting him, the old question surfaced in the back of my mind: What can an *Americana* tell anyone about Roman history? What could she say that an Italian had not already said? How could I know anything about Rome that an actual living, breathing Roman did not?

This turns out to be a fundamental question, one that I now understand actually *does* direct the different types of work that American and Italian historians tend to do. Scholars who live in Italy and who have been brought up in the Italian educational system have broad and regular access to archives, and as a result they often know their way around them with a depth of knowledge that can take newcomers years to attain. With a strong command of paleography, they have excelled at producing the edited editions of primary sources that, once published, are so valuable to other scholars. They also have the benefit of an innate familiarity with some aspects of the medieval world that have been preserved in the culture around them. No one needs to explain to a Roman teenager, for example, that *la lupa* is a symbol of their city, or that to be a notary was to belong to a highly esteemed profession.

By contrast, scholars working in America and other countries outside Europe must navigate a historical world that lies far outside the realm of their everyday experience. Without regular access to archives, they must limit their research plans to what they project they can get done in a specific amount of time—say, over the summer break or during a sabbatical or fellowship year. Because of this relative distance from the archives, some scholars working outside of Europe have also, I would say, been inclined to center their work around contemporary theory.

At the time I was setting up the meeting with this professor, however, I had not consciously dwelled on these differences, and any deviations I noted in myself from the standard I saw around me I interpreted as my own weaknesses. But, nervous as I was, I steeled myself. I had a dissertation under my belt. It was time to share my work and begin making connections.

❧

"Leave plenty of time to get there," advised my mother, who was visiting at the time. Yes, yes, I nodded, of course, plenty of time. With the smug satisfaction of a job well done, I closed the gate behind me and struck out onto the sidewalk near Porta Latina a full half hour earlier than necessary.

At the bus stop, I scanned for bus 118. Nothing. But only half a block away was the cobbler's workshop where I had left my boots to be resoled. The weekend forecast was for rain, and although my boots were not waterproof, they were warm: brown Spanish riding boots that hit just below my knees. A leather band around the top had been perforated with small geometric shapes, then laid over a white layer to create an intricate pattern. When buying the boots, I had endured the incredulous scorn of a Madrid equestrian shop salesman who seemed offended that I liked the boots simply for their style and that, no, I would not be doing any actual riding in them.

I checked my watch and five minutes had passed. Still no bus in sight. But looming ever larger was my innate desire for efficiency, combined perhaps with a dose of self-sabotage. Sprinting over to the cobbler's shop, I came up just behind an older woman swaddled in a voluminous fur coat and a clear plastic rain bonnet. Carefully, she stepped up the single stair, balancing herself against the doorframe, while I slid reluctantly to a halt.

The cobbler greeted the woman familiarly and went about locating her shoes, extracting them from a large stack and placing them into a crumpled plastic bag. With his muscular, blackened hand, he extended the bag to her like a chicken grasped by the neck. And she, reaching up with her own tiny, liver-spotted one, retrieved it. She plunged in a furred arm and rooted around, glancing outside and shaking her head as if the weather had dealt her a personal insult. One by one, she pulled out her shoes: one pair of blue Prada stacked heels, and one pair of very long and pointed canvas flats with a yellow flower print. Did she really wear these shoes? Humming with satisfaction, she flipped them over to examine the work. As she ran a finger over their edges, the cobbler waited patiently, resting his palms on the counter and looking out at the glistening street. I followed his gaze and, in the blink of an eye, caught sight of my bus sailing by.

With my boots finally in hand, the bus stop now felt colder, damper, more forlorn. I pulled my earbuds from my pocket and turned on my iPod Shuffle. Johnny Cash began serenading me with his litany of regrets as I, watching the minute hand of my watch tick ever forward, meditated sullenly on my own. An accomplished historian had invited me to come speak with him and now I was stuck, by my own doing, on an empty sidewalk while my bus sped on without me toward his home.

When the next bus finally pulled in, panic was batting around in my chest like a bird hell-bent on freedom. I was going to be late, and there was nothing I could do about it. I looked at my boots on the seat beside me. Why had I wasted valuable time picking them up? And what would it look like, showing up for a meeting with an extra pair of boots in a crummy bag? Why had I not thought of this sooner?

As soon as the driver swung open the bus doors, I bolted and ran several blocks before realizing that the street I was looking for was nowhere to be found. Retracing my steps in this pre-smartphone era, I ran the map over in my mind. Two blocks straight and then one block left, wasn't it? Or was it, as I now feared, one block straight and then two blocks left? I ducked into a bookstore and beelined for the travel section, flipping hastily through maps of Rome to find the street I needed, and then was off again, blowing past the cash register and galloping down the street I had just come up. How had I missed it? His street was right there. I hooked a left and ran uphill another block. And there it was: his building.

I took a few seconds to catch my breath. Don't huff and puff into his intercom, I reminded myself. I removed my earbuds and stuffed them in my jeans pocket. When I felt sufficiently calm, I pressed the button for his apartment, and moments later, his voice, slightly staticky and electronic, directed me up. I began climbing the stairway up to apartment number . . . wait, what *was* the number? I had been so fixated on controlling my panting that I had not paid attention. What choice did I have but to climb as slowly as humanly possible, praying he would open his door and save me the embarrassment? Slowly, dutifully, I ascended the stairs, all the way to the very, tippy, you've-got-no-choice-but-to-turn-around-now top. It was on the way down that I finally encountered him.

"Coming from upstairs?" he asked, perplexed.

"It's . . . an American custom," I answered, hoping my joke would put an end to his inquiry.

He looked just like I remembered him from two years earlier, with one notable exception: he was wearing furry slippers, so furry, in fact, that it looked like a small animal—a marmot, maybe, or a possum—had wrapped itself around each of his feet.

As an undergraduate, the first time I was invited to a professor's home was in my sophomore year—a Christmas *glögg* party at which I discovered by process of elimination that I was the only undergraduate who had been invited. The professor was youngish and Swedish and had a distinctive flair that made his classes entertaining. Wearing his signature clogs and a long pink scarf draped over one shoulder, he and his colleague—a hip American scholar who wore a lot of leather and denim—led us energetically through the paces of modern European history. One of their memorable lessons concerned the divisions of Europe. This was 1995, and when you talked about division in Europe, you generally still meant the Berlin Wall. Even though it had been down for half a decade, the wall still defined the way we, or at least I, thought about Europe.

"What is the most important division in Europe?" they asked, brimming with expectation.

Many hands shot up. East and west? North and south? Catholic and Protestant? After we had hazarded all the usual answers, the professors projected a map onto the screen. No, the *real* divisions of Europe, they showed us with unconcealed delight, were defined by habits of alcohol consumption. The *real* map of Europe was divided by two mostly horizontal lines that created three geographical divisions: the vodka zone in the north, the beer zone in the middle, and the wine zone in the south.

My history professor came from the vodka zone, but his Christmas party was organized around *glögg*, the Swedish version of mulled wine, which I had theorized, correctly or incorrectly, to be the cultural by-product of Viking invasions of southern Europe in the Middle Ages. With my facile handle on the history of alcohol, I showed up to his *glögg*-fest. My old high school friend Dave was visiting that weekend, and he came along too. The sharp smell of hot wine greeted us at the door, and after following "Lasse" (as he told us to call him) down the long entry hall, we landed in his mostly empty living room. He then skipped off merrily into the kitchen, which was jam-packed with professors I had taken courses with or seen in passing, including my adviser, who waved to me with a big smile from amid the crush of bodies near the stove.

Sensing that the kitchen was no place for us, Dave and I befriended a bowl of clementines and the professor's music collection, which we pored over as if it were an intensely absorbing work of art. Not far from us, in the center of the room, were four chairs arranged in tight circular formation. They had been commandeered by four women dressed in black and gray who were intently debating the particulars of tank warfare in World War I. Giving them a wide berth, we lingered in the corner for what seemed an appropriate amount of time, after which Dave and I gave each other the signal and headed toward the door. Our host saw us, thanked us for coming, and held the door open with a smile. Dave left, and as I was about to pass through, the professor stopped me and kissed me on my lips.

Dave froze, stunned.

"Was that a Swedish thing?" he asked as we exited the building.

I had no idea. Nor was I certain I wanted to know the answer. Better just to pretend it had never happened. This strategy seemed successful, in the sense that the professor never brought it up and it never happened again. I was not entirely silent, however. The event became a story I recounted to the other history students, those who had not been invited to the *glögg* party and who were eager to hear what it had all been about. My report was in part a boast, about being the only undergraduate we knew who had been invited, and in part a field report, in which I returned dutifully to my kind with observations about the professorial fauna in its native habitat. I was also, I think, asking for guidance. When I got to the part about the kiss, I gauged their responses. A few laughed, but no one seemed to think much of it. The enigma of the kiss remained just that.

It wasn't until college graduation that I next set foot in a professor's home. To celebrate, our adviser had invited me and the rest of his small group of advisees to his townhouse down in Chelsea. He and his wife had arranged a small buffet for us in their living room. We sat in a circle and talked about history, and about our futures, the contours of which were still entirely malleable. I told them that I was heading up to Ithaca to live with my boyfriend, who was beginning a PhD in mathematics. My friend Tamar, with whom I'd shared a prize for best senior thesis, would be going to Jerusalem to work at the Cinematheque. To both of us, Professor Kaye felt a little like a father— serious but also comfortable and funny. Historians, professors—they were not yet real to me. They were inspirational figures, people I might emulate but never actually approach. That May evening, I stepped out of my adviser's home exhilarated by the first unfurling of what felt like real adult life.

⁓

Now, seven years later, I was one month away from officially receiving my doctorate. I was, in all but title, a historian myself. Just before leaving for my research trip, I had written and sent my first applications for academic jobs—thirteen in all, to a variety of colleges and universities across the U.S. I felt eons away from the sophomore doing her best to remain invisible at the *glögg* party, and from the graduating senior talking about the future over a plate of cheese. And even though I had been to many professors' houses while in graduate school, those early episodes were still alive in my memory, defining the spectrum of outcomes I might expect.

I set my boots down by the entrance and followed the professor down his hallway. The living room was casually furnished, as I remember it—a blue velvet love seat and a few armchairs, a floor lamp casting a warm glow. There was a framed photo of him with a teenage girl I assumed was his daughter. It was a family home, with the usual casual clutter and lived-in feel. I had the sense of being in a small hive whose inhabitants were out buzzing about, soon to return.

Would I like a *birra*? he asked. No, I said, water would be fine. I knew he would object—the way Italians often did with me—as if someone who chose water over beer or wine were vaguely untrustworthy. "*Solo acqua?*" he asked. I stuck to my guns. With a resigned shrug, he stepped under a wide arch into the kitchen, where I heard the refrigerator seal unstick. "*Frizzante?*" I liked sparkling water but did not want to impose. No, I said, thanking him, "*va bene l'acqua dal rubinetto*"—even though I was certain that he would find my "tap water is fine" the true mark of my disappointing character. Whatever underpinned my austere choice of drink—Anglo politeness, possibly, combined with graduate student deference, and also a dollop of fear that I might come across as anything other than professional—I already knew it was not helping me here.

The fridge door banged shut and he emerged from the kitchen with a beer in one hand and a glass of water in the other. Pointing to the love seat, he gestured for me to sit. It was a small piece of furniture, quite petite for two, and I was surprised when he sat down next to me. Our knees touched. He took a sip of beer and leaned on the backrest, resting his other arm over the back of the seat with comfortable authority, much as he had positioned himself at the conference two years earlier.

"So I heard you have written a dissertation about Trecento Rome. That's an interesting choice."

I thanked him and took a sip of water.

"What's the title?" he asked.

"'Rome Before Avignon,'" I replied. It was a relief to begin the conversation on terra firma.

"The same as Brentano's book?"

I swallowed hard.

"Oh no, obviously not, *mi scusi*." How careless! "I meant 'Rome *During* Avignon.'" *Rome Before Avignon* is a well-known book by the Berkeley historian Robert Brentano, on whose title I had based my own.

He nodded slowly, the arch of a single eyebrow communicating both surprise and suspicion. Who, after all, misstates her own dissertation title? He was curious, he went on, whether I had command of the languages necessary to pursue this field as a career.

My Italian was by now in pretty good shape—not perfect by any means but, well, here we were conversing about medieval history in it. I didn't mention this, but I could also talk my way up and down a mountain in Italian. All of that vocabulary from the rock-climbing course was still my principal language for talking about climbing, and it comforted me to know that in that vertical realm, Italian was, and would always be, my mother tongue.

But he was not referring to Italian. Nor to Hebrew, which I could still, several years after breaking up with my Israeli boyfriend, speak and read with relative ease. Nor French, which I had studied for seven years beginning in middle school. Nor Spanish, which I was learning to speak with Javier.

"By which I mean," he clarified, "Latin—of which I find few Americans have sufficient command . . ."

Oh, Latin—a language so malleable and powerful. With the intensive summer course at Cornell and two months with Reginald Foster under my belt, I had clawed my way to intermediate. But I was certainly no Latinist. In a few minutes flat, this professor had identified a major weak spot and pressed right on it. It was an easy button to press because graduate school, if it teaches you nothing else, impresses one lesson quite effectively: that you can never know enough. In my answer, I hemmed and hawed, recounting the courses I had taken, which made me sound exactly like what I was—a novice.

"*E tedesco?*" he continued. "German is the most serious weakness for Americans, as I see it."

All the while, his eyes were sharp and lively, as if our conversation really interested him. Was he enjoying this grilling? I couldn't tell. I had no other relevant experience, no prior contact with the Italian university system, to help me assess how this was going. Maybe this was just how he spoke with young scholars. Maybe this was his normal set of questions. Maybe if I were just *better*, I wouldn't be having such a hard time.

What could I say? Once again, he had put his finger right on it. I was weak in German. *Real medievalists*, I was starting to accept, began training in the cradle. Whereas by contrast, I had done all my German work in graduate school. Who was I kidding?

I enjoyed German. My kind instructor at Cornell, Frau Lischke, came from Hamburg, and she pronounced the language with such gentleness that it sounded like a poem, like at any moment she might lift off the ground into a pillowy susurration of Schubert *lieder*. I loved studying the language with her. But be that as it may, I had not pursued it long enough, or lived it in the way a language must be lived to be learned. As Javier, who taught Spanish, liked to joke, "to really learn a language, you have to take a lover." Alas, I had no German lovers. This sad fact must explain why I could make it through a German academic article only with clenched teeth and a dictionary chained to my wrist. But the effort always left me exhausted, and without a trace of the elation—*süße Liebe*—that I felt when speaking it, or hearing it, in the presence of Frau Lischke.

"My Latin is okay," I spluttered, "and my German, well, it's true, it could be better." I shifted uncomfortably. I took another sip of water. In my mind, I was compiling all the reasons I could never do the thing I had just spent nearly seven years training to do. The evidence was so clear—this professor had simply helped me to see it. Did it occur to me that not one of the accomplished professors on my committee had an impeccable command of all three languages in question? Naturally it did not.

"Well, what's really interesting is that you picked the fourteenth century," he continued. "Why, of all the periods of Roman history, did you pick that one?"

Well, maybe I wasn't dead meat just yet. Finally! Here was a question I felt good about answering.

"Oh, the fourteenth century is so interesting," I said, with sudden breezy confidence, "even though there are so few people who work on it. With the pope away in Avignon for almost a hundred years, I thought the period raised an important question: What is Rome without the papacy?"

The professor discarded the second half of what I had said and seized instead on the first. "But there are so *many* people working on the fourteenth century! If you had wanted a century that no one worked on, you should have chosen the fifteenth."

I was perplexed. The fifteenth century marks the beginning of the

Renaissance in Rome, and from what I knew, there was no shortage of scholars working on that period.

"Well, there's always so-and-so and his crowd," I said, mentioning the name of a Roman historian whom I had perceived as central to the conversation about the fifteenth century.

And *plunk* goes the stone, whence it sinks to the bottom of the lake, never to be retrieved again. His face dropped, and there ensued a considerable silence during which I wondered what I had said wrong. This other scholar, too, had been at the conference two years earlier, though in my memory he had arrived late, or left early, or maybe he was a distant memory because he sat at the far end of the table, or was quiet. I couldn't remember. Whatever the case, it didn't matter. The professor leaned forward and sibilated, slowly and precisely, presumably so I would not miss a word of it: "*Lui non vale nulla.*" Literally, "That scholar is worth nothing"—although this literal translation communicates neither context nor tone. A better translation would be "He is a completely worthless bastard."

What are we to do in situations like this, when we realize, too late, that we have stepped into the dank, fertile soil of someone else's resentments? With no idea how to proceed, I employed the most obvious tool at my disposal: I grasped my glass and tipped it back, buying myself some time. But somehow—yes—that glass never made it to my lips. In one go, I poured nearly a full glass of water down the front of my white button-up shirt and onto my lap, from where it made a slowly expanding puddle on the cushion of the blue velvet love seat.

The professor leaped to his feet, startled. "I'll get something!" he exclaimed, the slippers scuffing as he beat it hastily to the kitchen.

He returned with a huge wad of paper towels in hand. I dabbed at my shirt while thanking him profusely. It was mostly in vain. Though the towels were soon soaked, my shirt seemed as wet as ever. When I had finished trying, he offered to throw away the soggy mass. I remember thinking that I could not possibly hand this accomplished, charismatic historian a wad of wet paper towels. I remember thinking that maybe all was not lost, that maybe I could still salvage this meeting.

"Oh no, that's quite all right," I said. As if to shrug off the whole mishap. Maybe we could both conveniently forget that this had ever happened. While he watched, I stuffed the entire mass of wet towels into the front pocket of my jeans. It was a slow process, given that my pocket was not all that big. He looked on with astonishment.

"*Non si preoccupi*," I said, patting the widening wet spot on the side of my thigh. "It's nothing. Nothing at all." There—could we please move on?

A many-seconds-long pause ensued, during which he stared with evident disbelief. When he raised his eyes, it was clear he had made a decision.

"You know what? Why don't you just send me a copy of your dissertation?"

I knew this was both a failure and a way out. He went over to a small table that held a phone and a tablet of paper and began writing down his mailing address. At that moment a realization dawned on me.

"*Aspetti!*" I said, feeling a little like a phoenix rising from the smoking embers of our conversation. My dissertation was right here, on my iPod. I had uploaded it a few weeks prior to take it to the printing shop. I would transfer the document to him, and we would get off on a new foot. He lifted his pen, probably weighing the odds of what extending this interaction might bring. I pulled the thin iPod Shuffle from my other jeans pocket and dried it on my sleeve. He relaxed the pen, hesitantly agreeing to download the document.

"My computer's down the hall," he said. He led me back down the corridor where I had first entered and into a room on the left. On our right was a very tall and wide wall of books. I find it difficult to remember the rest of the room, so determined was I not to look at anything except the bookshelf. Nevertheless, to the left stood a bed and just beyond it, a smallish desk with a laptop. His study was also his bedroom.

Circumventing the bed to get to his computer, he lifted the cover and pressed the power button. It began to hum and buzz. Motionless, we waited. The computer was clearly an old model, one that takes an eternity, sometimes two or three or seventeen, to boot up. In my memory the room had stone walls, undecorated, and windows only very high up, like a church, or a prison. I tried not to look anywhere except at his books. As it turns out, it was like gazing upon a group of friends. There was Eugenio Dupré Theseider's *Storia di Roma*, and André Vauchez's *Roma medievale*, and Sandro Carocci's *Baroni di Roma*, and many others, all on the same shelf. These were books I had been reading for the past six years, many of which I owned. Looking at this professor's wall of books, I saw a reflection of my own bookshelf back in Providence. It was the only time I had ever—*have* ever—seen these same books, *my books*, all together, in someone else's private library. I felt a surprising stirring of kinship. I was so at home, and at the same time, so very far from it.

At long last, the computer was booted up, its screen bright as a beacon. I uncapped my iPod and he plugged it into his computer's USB port. Only then did I remember that the week before, I had deleted it to make room for image files of scanned archival documents.

"Oh." I began explaining that actually, somehow, the document we had been patiently waiting for was not, after all, on my iPod. That it *had been* there, but that it was *no longer* there, and that I had forgotten because I had made that change *so recently*, whereas before, it had been there for *so long*. And I was, of course, *so sorry*. Would he still like me to mail it to him?

He turned up his palms and shrugged, in a gesture that said, *Sure, whatever*. As we were leaving the study-bedroom, a woman—his wife, I presumed—entered the front door. Seeing me, she stopped in her tracks and looked me up and down, pausing several beats too long on my wet shirt. "*Buonasera*," she said icily.

"Let's get your stuff," he said quickly. He led me briskly back to the living room, where I retrieved my bag, and he handed me a small piece of paper with his university mailing address. I left my empty glass on the table and headed for the door.

With an astonishing sense of relief, I heard the door close behind me. All that mattered was that I was out. The evening's humiliations translated into a burst of physical energy that sent me running down the stairs and out into the street. A misty rain was suspended in slow-motion descent. It felt sublime to run, as if I might be able to outrun, and thereby obliterate, what had just happened. My feet carried me swiftly through the dark streets. Tears welled in my eyes, but I could not identify whether their source was comedy or tragedy. Strange guttural sounds rose from my throat, neither laughing nor crying but a hybrid of the two. A kind of loud gulping that, should anyone have seen or heard me, they must certainly have thought I was mad. I remember wanting, really wanting, to believe that what had transpired was funny, and I offered myself the consolation that one day it would make for a good story. When I got back to the apartment, I would recount it to my mother—how we were going to laugh! The *sampietrini* were slippery under the thin soles of my shoes and I reminded myself to be careful of falling. Which thought brought me to an abrupt halt, my heart dropping to my feet.

The boots.

For about ten seconds, I entertained a variety of fantasies. That I would leave the boots in the apartment and they would go unnoticed for the rest of time. That they would become the family umbrella stand. That they would disintegrate into thin air. Yet I concluded that leaving them there was worse than not leaving them, and slowly, heavy of heart as a penitent, I retraced the steps of my liberation. Reaching the building, I pressed the call button of their apartment. His voice.

"The boots?"

"The boots."

I trudged up the stairs, this time to the correct floor. He was waiting at the door, his wife peering out coldly from behind his shoulder. He extended the bag, and I took it with a small smile and a nod of the head, as if this, too, were normal. I thanked him, thanked them.

"*Buonasera*," they said in unison, just before the door clicked to a close.

This time I had no pent-up energy to dispel. In its absence, I felt depleted, humiliated, abjectly disappointed in myself. The story might not be that funny after all. I took the stairs slowly this time, and walked, dejected and yet also incredulous, to the bus stop, the boots weighing down my arm.

The bus came quickly. A small stroke of fortune, for suddenly I felt so very tired. The mist had already permeated my jacket, seeped in at the shoulders. Inside the bus, there were no seats left. But at least it was dry. I placed the bag with my boots between my feet and grasped the overhead bar for stability. Off we chugged into the Roman night. Three women seated before me observed me uninterestedly. Their arms were wrapped identically around their purses. They wore similarly dark circles under their eyes, the badge of hard work, or earthly cares. I could not wait to be home, to fall asleep, to forget the evening's ludicrous events. As we began the wide, sweeping turn around the Colosseum, my body pulled to the left. Then the bus driver jammed the brakes, and I very nearly lost my footing. Through the rain-speckled windshield, I saw a trail of red brake lights that snaked out in front of us as far as the eye could see. Traffic jam.

Held hostage with my thoughts, I went over what had happened in the professor's apartment. My late, inelegant arrival, my incredulity at being in his home. Then there was the love seat that was too small, his questioning of my skills, and the use of my nationality as a categorizing filter. Unfair. He had been stacking the bricks against me. He had pressed my most sensitive buttons. He had arranged our meeting on his terrain, and in furry slippers, no less. He had scrutinized and interrogated me and, in the process, highlighted my weaknesses. I had spilled my glass of water because I was nervous and cowed by his authority, by the fact that he was older and a man and Roman and that he did not have to think about verb forms or whether he should address me formally or informally and what form that takes when you must leap up suddenly and apologize for spilling water on what was in fact very nice velvet.

What could I have done differently? I wondered. I might have instead said:

Mi perdoni professore, sembra che io abbia versato tutto il bicchiere d'acqua su questo suo bellissimo velluto blu! "Forgive me, Professor, it appears that I have spilled my entire glass of water on this lovely blue velvet of yours!"

Or perhaps, I thought, it would have been better to say:

Ma dai, com'è successo? Impossibile! "Oh, come on! How on earth did that happen? Impossible!" and then inspected the glass for imperfections that had caused such an unlikely accident.

It was, of course, the first expression—the earnest apology, formal in its grammar and prudent in its acknowledgment of personal fallibility, that came to me more naturally. But the second response was probably more Roman, and would likely have gone over better. It acknowledged the ridiculousness of the situation and exteriorized blame in an absurd, borderline comical way. A real Roman might even have looked around the room, for a bat or a bird, or the Holy Ghost—anything to explain the outrageous appearance of water on the love seat.

Instead, deeply ensconced in my role of the deferential graduate student, I'd apologized and fretted. *Mi perdoni professore . . .*

Though I had submitted my dissertation and within a month would hold a PhD, the evening with the Roman historian had vividly revived the worst aspects of being a graduate student: the long-winded answers, the inability to cut to the chase and state the core of the issue with confidence, the tendency to speak and write in an endless series of dependent clauses, to allow others to define the parameters of the conversation. Spending much of my twenties in graduate school had given me great freedoms: to live in

Rome, to develop meaningful friendships and to live the life of the mind, all while acquiring a considerable body of knowledge and—although it would take me a long time to recognize—a host of practical intellectual skills. Yet it had also accustomed me, early in my adult life, to feeling powerless. For six years after graduating from college, I had relied on my graduate student income, accustomed myself to the limitations of making do on fifteen thousand dollars a year, and to taking out loans when I came up short.

Just as important, I had been dependent on a triumvirate of older scholars, all men: for accepting me to graduate school, for appraising my work, for molding my professional person. In the beginning, I had assumed without question that they took those duties seriously. That they took *me* seriously. But slowly, incrementally, over the first two years of graduate school, that assumption had begun to erode. It eroded slightly when one of my professors suggested that it might help if I unbuttoned my shirt before going to speak with another about a grade. And a bit more when a professor said he wished he could spend his next birthday in bed with a twenty-nine-year-old—my precise age at that time. And then a little more when another fell asleep and snored during my first lecture, for which I had been preparing for weeks, and afterward, when the students stood and clapped, reproachfully said, "They never clap for me," and suggested that if I wanted to give a *really* good lecture, I should look to my male colleague and friend as an example. And still more when I chose to pursue Roman history and was dismissed with "Wouldn't we all like to spend time in the sun?"

As a graduate student, I was free in many senses of the word, but I was also dependent and powerless in ways it would take me a long time to perceive. That dual state, of freedom combined with powerlessness, became so habitual, so familiar, that eventually it became the most comfortable place to be. And there was an important question I had yet to ask: How seriously did I take myself?

〜✍〜

As the bus idled in the river of red brake lights, my nose started running and I rooted around for a tissue. With relief I remembered the wad of paper towels in my jeans pocket. I wiped my nose and, when I pulled the paper away, was shocked to see it stained with a clamor of bright red. *Really, a nosebleed, now?* I pressed the paper to my face. Already wet, however, it could not absorb the blood, which began running in rivulets into my jacket cuff. I became acutely aware of the other passengers, of their stares, and of those close by, who shifted to distance themselves from me. Now, in retrospect, it seems strange, even oddly dystopian, that no one on that bus offered me a seat, or a clean, dry tissue. That all of us on that night bus watched with morbid fascination as the wad of paper towels paled from red to pink, as the blood, creeping along the paper fibers, met and mingled with the water that had spilled from the glass.

The blood wound its way down my forearm. So strange. A bloody nose is not a common occurrence for me. Mulling it over then, I began to suspect it was telling me something. But seldom does my body speak in symbols. Why, of all times, was I bleeding now? I went over the evening again.

I knew full well that whether or not the Roman professor's generalizations about Americans were fair, I had furnished him with an abundance of evidence that fit his theory: I was just another American graduate student, with all her usual shortcomings. Our meeting had been a fiasco. But whose fault was it? He had shown up in slippers, true, but who can say for sure that he had not been trying to make me feel at home? He had peppered me with questions about my qualifications, indeed, but that is how historians often speak to each other.

Much of graduate school had felt like a game of one-upmanship, a contest of who knew the most, who could find the fatal flaw in the argument.

It had often seemed to me, in academic discussions, that those who could criticize and take down a historical argument enjoyed more credit than those who could connect and construct. This professor lived in that world, too. Could I really fault him for that? Finally, it was true that he sat me on a small love seat, in his home during the evening, when no one else was home. Now that I have taught in the classroom, now that I have children, I know that those with authority have an array of choices about how to wield it. That how you position yourself and where you sit or stand in a room alters its chemistry. I know now that *home, evening, love seat, alone* were choices, and on that evening I felt, to my distinct disadvantage, their cumulative effect. But I had come of age, professionally speaking, in an environment where the rules had never been clear, where relationships between professors and students were not yet critiqued—at least, as far as I was aware—through the prism of power. And with him, I had also faced a cultural divide, which further undermined my confidence about assessing the situation with clarity. Nothing he did explicitly violated the rules as I understood them. Though maybe that was because, as far as I knew back then, there really were no rules.

Over the next few years, I told the story of my meeting with the Roman historian over and over—to family, to friends, at parties. I played it for comedy, and it delighted me when people laughed. *What a fiasco!* they'd say. As two years turned into three turned into five, though, the story began to feel less funny. Later, when I left academia, I stopped telling it altogether. Every so often, though, I thought back on that nosebleed. Was it a key? If so, what was the lock? What was it I had not been able to see?

It has taken me more than a decade to decipher it. A decade living outside of academia and the life of the mind. A decade spent much more, I can only conclude, in the physical realm. A decade in which I experienced two pregnancies and two births, two years of nursing infants at my breast—motherhood in itself a kind of school of the body. When you're pregnant, you're always listening for clues, checking in with what's inside your self. The brush of a movement, or no movement at all? A hiccup, a burp, a luxuriant stretch. What you eat, what you drink, what chemical compounds might lurk in the walls of your home, in your fridge, in the very cells of your body, which up until now you have more or less blithely disregarded. You get accustomed to losing control, to the fact that now your body has a mind of its own. Whatever your feelings about it, you must go along for the ride.

As your belly grows, you are cheered on by women whose bodies begin to impress you. How come no one talked to you about birth in these terms before? These women use words you have never heard in relation to childbirth: *empowering, ecstatic, miraculous.* In your births you come into contact with a power you never knew your body had. Your tectonic plates shift, you are a rushing jet stream, a whirling circumpolar current, a giant massif stacked rock on rock, an atom so densely packed you dare it to explode. You learn to take such pride in your body's work.

Your mind stands by as witness. Right now it is there to support the body, to visualize the body's path forward, to convince it of what is possible. Concepts float by, untethered to physical reality. You try to latch on to the concept of "mother," but you sense that to this new creature, you are still simply "flesh," the source and sustenance of life. You think, for a moment, of *la lupa*, of the infant twins clutching ever at her body. You let the thought go. Right now you are a mass of muscle, a conglomeration of cells made to feed the hungry. Your baby finds his way clumsily to your breast. In the coming eight weeks, as you learn to nurse him, your nipples will be so raw, will burn so fiercely, that the thought of the next feeding will send a tremor through your body and a cold sweat down your face and neck. Women with kind eyes will patiently observe you and adjust the baby's latch and position, and they will offer you such solace that you will weep with gratitude. *They are angels*, you will foggily think, *angels descended from heaven*. Every week you will weigh the baby, count his ounces like gold coins, all of them, you realize, a bounty derived purely and exclusively from your body's work.

After two childbirths, after years of nursing babies at the breast, what is a little nosebleed? I might easily have forgotten it. Except that it had been a sign, an undeciphered symbol. The scholar in me, still there more than a decade later, couldn't let that go. And I had finally acquired the tools to read it.

As sign and symbol, the nosebleed spoke of vulnerability and shame and, somewhere far beneath, of failure biding its time.

To be clear, shame does not concern herself with trifles such as my petty failure to communicate well that evening in the professor's home, or to assert who I was as a historian and scholar. Likewise, shame had nothing to do with arriving late, forgetting that I had removed my dissertation from my iPod, spilling a glass of water, or having to return for my boots. Those were embarrassments, sure, but they were smaller than shame.

No, the shame was in perceiving, as tenuously as one might sense the beating of a butterfly's wings in a distant forest, that I might well fail. And I was steeped in a world in which failure came with an inherent fall from grace, from the moral victory that was the pursuit of knowledge. *You can always go to law school and make money*, as my adviser's mantra went. And what is the residue of the fall from grace but shame?

The nosebleed, I would come to understand, was portent and premonition. Of how powerless I was as a newly minted historian, and how deep into my person that powerlessness had seeped. Of how far I was from home, how little tangible support I had from my mentors, how few were my academic contacts in Rome, and how closed their circles felt to me. It spoke of the shame I felt under the cold gaze of the professor's wife, and the assumptions I perceived her to have made. And it betrayed the fragility of my own false bravado of believing for so long that I could do it all on my own, on meager stipends floated by federal loans. It exposed the impossible standards I had set for myself—that I could write Italian history as if I were Italian, that I could become, at thirty, a bridge between distant academic worlds, that I should have perfect command of half a dozen languages—that would freeze me in my tracks, leave me no other option than to fall short. That night my body, years ahead of my mind, perceived the depth of that powerlessness. I believed I was on the cusp of becoming. But my body already knew it wasn't to be. And so it bled.

26.

CHECKLIST

The day after my meeting with the Roman historian, my mother and I emerged from the tunnels of the Catacombs of Domitilla. We had spent the last ninety minutes deep in this ancient burial ground, feeling our way through eternal twilight in a labyrinth of tunnels hewn by hands nearly two millennia before our arrival. Older than the labyrinth is the tuff, the foundation of rock on which all Rome sits. This rock was born forty thousand years ago when nearby volcanoes erupted, spewing fine sediment that settled, layer upon layer, upon the ground. As my mother and I emerged from this netherworld, the musty air clung to our clothes, hitch-hiking a ride back to the land of the living. We squinted our eyes against the sun's low rays as the planet tilted us irrevocably toward winter solstice.

"Well," announced the man who had been grouped with us on the tour, "I'm almost done." He was wearing a mod little yellow backpack.

My mother and I regarded him uncertainly. "Done with what?" she asked.

He waved a piece of paper on which he had written out a long checklist. "Today is my fourth day in Rome and I've seen almost everything of consequence."

He gave one final look over the list, as if to make extra sure that he had not forgotten anything.

"Yep," he said with a look of satisfaction, "just about everything." Stuffing the paper in his jacket pocket, he turned and went on his way, his little yellow backpack bobbing cheerfully behind him.

A few paces later he spun around, grinning broadly.

"So long!" he waved. "Next stop, Istanbul!"

My mother and I watched as he receded along the via Appia Antica until he blended with the surroundings and disappeared from view.

For a moment, I envied the man's blithe cheer, his satisfaction at a job well done. I envied him his little backpack bobbing behind him as he walked, practically skipping, away from us. I was reminded of the moment two years before when, looking for an apartment to rent, I had envied children, and even the fictive mistress of some unnamed politician, who knew where they would sleep. I would never know how to be like the man in the yellow backpack, so apparently light, unencumbered, and satisfied.

But of course, neither did I want to be. My place was in the labyrinth, hands out in the dark, searching for that hidden chamber where lay, as if entombed, *what it is that you can do.*

27

TEACHING ROME

The following year, I embarked on a two-year position teaching history at a liberal arts college in Boston. It was exciting to stand at the front of a classroom, with students taking notes and asking questions. It felt like a responsibility, a happy one, to take them through the corridors of history, trying to help them perceive the architecture of its infinite, connected rooms.

In my desk drawer I kept a folding ruler with two thousand years of Western history marked along it on an incremental time line. When fully extended, the ruler was seven feet long. I would stand in front of my students holding it horizontally before me, like a tightrope artist balanced on the high wire. On one end was ancient history—Egyptians, Greeks, and Romans. Together, they covered about two feet. On the other end, occupying fourteen inches, was everything that happened in the West after Gutenberg printed his first Bible in 1455. The remainder of the ruler— close to four feet—was the Middle Ages. A thousand years between the sack of a city and the printing of a book.

The students would stare at the ruler from end to end before resting their eyes somewhere in the middle. "The Endless Ages," said one. "But wait," asked another, "in the middle of what?" The ruler tries its best to hide the chaos. With its hundreds of events neatly pressed, ordered, and lined up, it wants you to think you can grasp it, perceive its beginning and its end. But you cannot even hold it straight. It is not a rod. It is one flimsy piece of wood after another, its segments held together by cheap hinges. When you try to hold it straight, it wobbles. Its ends sag into a downward arc. Inadvertently, the ruler shows us what the past really is: a chasm, an abyss. There is no such thing as a middle.

~~~

Toward the end of my teaching contract, I sign up to teach a three-week summer course in Rome. Javier and I have been married almost a year and are expecting a child. I arrive in Rome during the last week of May. My pregnancy is in its eighth month, and for this one week, before the students arrive, Rome is all mine again. Only now, I am sharing it with this new being. I think of my professors Tom and Libby, who spent sabbatical years in Rome and sent their children to Roman schools, and dream that the future might hold something like that for us, too. I think about all the ways this baby is experiencing Rome. Maybe, from last night's dinner, it now knows what a Roman artichoke is. Same goes for *cacio e pepe*, lamb, and *vignarola*, my favorite spring stew. The baby's first encounter with Rome will be culinary.

Over the past four years, Paolo and I have kept in intermittent touch. One afternoon, we make a plan to meet on the Capitoline Hill. I spot him standing under Marcus Aurelius, and we make our way toward each other. He compliments my belly, which these days precedes me wherever I go.

"Boy or girl?" he asks.

"Every old woman in Rome is quite sure it's a boy." It's 2008, but when it comes to baby sex predictions in Rome's fruit and vegetable markets, it could just as well be a thousand years ago. (They were right.)

We sit on a bench and talk. I soak up Paolo's old familiar face. The afternoon stretches languidly before us. I already know what we will do: wander and talk and talk and wander, and eventually get hungry and eat something. No plan. It is June, and Rome is sweetly alive.

Next week, twelve undergraduates will arrive from the States. Just before them, Javier will fly in. The college has given us an apartment in Trastevere. His siblings will come from Madrid to visit, and while I teach, they will get to know the city. It will be my first time teaching in Rome. I look forward to it, even though the thought of teaching while so visibly pregnant is strange.

We stroll down Michelangelo's long stairway. We pass the statue of a hooded Cola di Rienzo, who gestures in the direction of the Vatican as if to say that he's still not done, that Rome still needs him. We are heading toward Largo di Torre Argentina when Paolo's cell phone rings. "*Sì, grazie, grazie, sì*," he says, and comes to a halt. With his head he motions back up the hill.

"You left your cell phone in the care of Marcus Aurelius," he says.

We retrace our way up the stairway.

"How did they know to call *you?*" I ask.

"*Intelligente*," he says, pointing to his temple. "She looked up the last number you called."

"*Intelligentona*," I say, making up a word to poke fun at Paolo's yen for suffixes. "Smart cookie."

"This doesn't happen in Rome," he says, shaking his head. "*Solo per te.*" "Only for you."

The following afternoon I take a seat at the Basilica of San Clemente. With its cool and quiet, the basilica offers immediate relief from the sweltering afternoon. On the bench beside me I lay down my notebook, in which I have been assembling teaching notes for the following week. I lean back and exhale.

A cough from a few feet away surprises me, and when I turn to look, I see that a man is regarding me intensely. He is late middle-aged, with bushy eyebrows and unkempt curly hair.

"*Mi dispiace signora,*" he says, apologizing for bothering me. But he must tell me something, something very important.

What could this man need to tell me?

He gestures to my belly. Everyone here has an opinion about it. By now, it comes as little surprise that the man in the Basilica of San Clemente has something very urgent to relate to me regarding my pregnancy.

"I must tell you," he says, "that the mosaic floors here carry very potent energy."

Energia potente.

"Potent energy?" I ask.

"Yes," he says, "you know, for the baby."

He advises me to remove my shoes and walk barefoot on the tiles. I weigh the pros and cons, assess the man's potential to harm me (conclusion: minimal), and ask myself, *What's to lose?* I unstrap my sandals and slip them off.

"Now walk," he says, almost triumphantly.

I walk. The mosaic floors feel smooth and cool beneath my feet, their surfaces worn down by close to a thousand years of footsteps. They crest slightly here, slope gently there. They undulate. It's marvelous.

I nod to the man, whose eyebrows quiver. "*Splendido,*" he says, rubbing his hands together and chuckling.

28.

No Map, No Virgil

Sometimes things don't pan out. You can pour six years of your life into study, and you can teach at a college for several more until that contract—which you stumbled into by dint of a miracle—expires. During those first years of study, it might have seemed that you were exactly where you should be. You delighted in learning and reveled in your friendships. Before the winter holidays you baked cookies for your professors and left them in their mail slots with notes of gratitude. You were so young, so naive, that you didn't realize how much of a girl this made you. The cookies *and* the gratitude.

By the end of your classwork, you perceived the shape of history; you could hold up that crystalline globe before revolving it, like a magician, this way and that. You made mistakes of youth. You neglected to plan strategically, you allowed yourself to fall briefly into the arms of a professor—a falling, a failing, that will haunt you ever afterward because you will never know the full extent of its consequences. You flew to a faraway land and oriented yourself in its systems. You lived in another language, among people you did not know, with no preexisting networks to support you. You didn't do it perfectly, it's true. You never found a trove of documents to call your own. You never quite got over feeling lost in the archives, like any document you had before you was a piece of drift-wood in a vast ocean. Instead you wrote a dissertation based mostly on published sources and called it a day.

But the Roman professor liked your dissertation, didn't you know? He wrote to you one day, his name popping up in your inbox, that name you never thought you'd see again, saying that he wished to have it translated into Italian and published in Italy. Your work would fit right into that series on medieval Roman history published by the Istituto Storico Italiano per il Medioevo, where you sat in those early days like a captain poring over a map of the high seas. You imagined your book residing there, among those names that felt as familiar as old friends.

In the years following, you submitted countless job applications and paid your own way to the interviews on the other side of the country, hope and ambition rising and falling with each passing season. Before the interviews you removed your wedding ring, as female candidates were advised, so that traces of family life did not arouse fears among the hiring committee that you were more wife and mother than scholar. The men who interviewed you kept their wedding rings on, however, as did the young male candidates waiting in the hallway for their interviews. You knew these unwritten rules were not fair, but you put on your best smile. Again, too much of a girl? You found out, in hushed tones, from a member of a hiring committee who wanted to help you, that in a mentor's letter of recommendation, he praised the quality of your smile in the first sentence. There were spelling errors, too. Deep down, you were growing so very weary of these judgments of older men—about your work, your marital status, the endearingness of your smile.

When you did not get the job, or the next one or the next, you chewed on what went wrong. Not enough publications, perhaps. (Perhaps because that Cornell professor, when you'd asked him for advice on publishing, ridiculed the idea that you, a graduate student, might put something in print.) And, of course, there was the long shadow cast by that relationship, whose external effects and repercussions remained invisible to you, but whose internal effects—the paranoid and corrosive self-doubt that everyone, students and faculty alike, held it against you—would never quite go away.

When 2008 came, you lamented that the financial crisis wiped out the funding that would have enabled your dissertation to be translated into Italian, and then you lamented some more when the following year they pulled the plug on the whole project—your book would not sit beside the others at the *istituto*, after all. And in the end, you had no job. And you had no tools to process failure. In your six years as a graduate student, no word was ever spoken, not even at a whisper, of those who left academia.

The term *transferable skills*—so prevalent now—had not yet been coined. Nor did you have a map to tell you where to go from here. No one wanted your PhD. In fact, you quickly learned, you had to erase it from your résumé before any hiring manager would look at you. And even then, no one could make sense of your story. All that work you had done now worked against you. Your failure seemed singular. Whether others, too, had failed, you had no idea. If so, like you, they seemed to have simply disappeared from the face of the earth. You were alone. Invisible. Lost. And you didn't even get a Virgil.

29.

NEW WORDS

After academia, I am dead tired of scholarly articles, journals, footnotes. In fact, I want nothing to do with the written word at all, in any form. I have gone too far. I am parched for life. Too much ink has turned me acidic. I cannot bear to read a book.

The idea of a paragraph, like a concrete block on my chest, exhausts me.

I want my sentences untethered.

Someone says, "Read *The Da Vinci Code*. You won't be able to put it down."

I put it down.

I put all the books down.

I take my son on walks. We look at leaves and puddles and squirrels. We hold snow in our hands and watch it melt.

I use my rudimentary sewing skills to fashion a crude little jacket for him to keep him warm.

Strangers ask where they can buy one.

Before long, I have a little business.

A factory in Boston agrees to make a small production run.

I make lists: fabrics, trims, packaging supplies.

Fill the car with jackets and drive to New York City.

Drop in on baby stores, unannounced.

Sell the jackets.

Return home, satisfied. The car empty.

A store in Switzerland buys them. And a bunch of stores in Japan. And Korea.

I send a few to friends in Italy. One of my little jackets goes to Rome.

I like to think about that jacket bobbing under umbrella pines. And hiking up the nearby mountains. Keeping a baby warm.

In the beginning, it is easy.

Every time a store agrees to carry my little jackets, I feel less vulnerable. I am making my own way.

I begin to live in concrete words. A business that manufactures cold-weather garments for babies. *Manufacturing*: a word so bound to the archaic labors of the *manus*, the human hand.

New words pile up in my journals: factories, converters, 2009 trade show calendar, labels, trims, insurance, safety commission, projected sales, marketing, design, identity, packaging, cutting tools, textiles, cut yards, elastic, lawyers, strategy, features, applications, core values, competition, market definition, differentiation, resources, ideal customer, video, business plan, safety testing, cellulose polyester, yield calculation, accountant, keywords, logo, disclosure agreement, import/export center, .com, .net, .info, web copy, print copy, wireframe, copyright, commission, torso mannequins, sales permit, invoice, grosgrain, cord locks, interfacing, block ads, seam allowance, serger, profit & loss.

I relish this new language and the freedom it signifies.

If there are wearisome abstractions, academic ponderings, I whittle them down, reduce them to their most practical component parts.

I chew these words like hard candy. Not worrying about the day they might break my teeth.

30.

FABULATION

I still have all those books. The Dupré Theseider and the Vauchez and the Carocci. They occupy a bookshelf that, seven feet tall, dominates one corner of the living room. I worry about the shelf tipping, and I know I ought to tether it to the wall. I have worried more than once that my shelf of books on Roman and Italian history will fall and crush my child, or me. I think about getting rid of the books, but I don't. Once, a few years ago, I went over the shelf with the intention of culling the collection. But even that wasn't a success. Of all the books, I managed to rid myself only of a tiny pile, maybe eight or ten books total. It was unsettling to realize that the shelf had become a shrine. And just like a shrine, it is grounding, tethering me to a place and time that no longer exists. I could light a candle in front of it, and it would make a kind of sense. The day I dismantle it, it will be both a loss and a liberation.

Standing before that tall shelf, I think back on the dreadful evening with the Roman historian. Instead of recounting the story as I have always told it, though, I imagine the evening as it might have gone, now that I know how many academic careers have gone the way of mine, now that I understand what an impossible task I had set for myself. We are waiting in that long silence as his computer boots up.

"Okay," I say, "let's accept your premise that American scholars often fall short in languages. What contributions might we best make, then, to Italian history?"

He doesn't miss a beat. "Which language is your weakest?"

"German."

"Focus on the other two, then," he says, "and spend a summer in Germany if you can."

"Forget it, I'll find a translator."

He raises an eyebrow. "You Americans think everything should be easy. You want everything fast." He thinks for a moment. Then this infinitely more helpful version of a Roman history professor says, "What you've got to do is learn how to use the archival material that we Italians are transcribing. Few of you can compete with us on sheer quantity of archival research—we have the training, and we have the archives right here at our fingertips. It's our home turf."

"So how do I use it?" I ask. "How do I make your turf my own?"

"That's your job to find the answer," he says. "But remember that feeling disoriented is a necessary part of making your way through the past."

"I had no Virgil," I say.

"Your professors can only take you so far. You must look and look until you begin to perceive the story. You must, in fact, embrace being lost."

"You think I gave up too quickly."

He shrugs. "I don't know. But the fact is that Rome is teeming with scholars from all over the world going through exactly what you did. No one, when they first get here, knows what they're doing. And when they leave the profession, that loss belongs to all of us. We haven't been able, up till now, to make full use of that plurality of voices. We're all still separated by our national institutes. The Italians are as guilty of this as anyone.

And you Americans, too. You hole yourself up in your American academy up there on the hill and don't talk to anyone but yourselves."

"But I'm not one of them," I protest. "They rejected me."

"Finalists can hardly claim rejection," he says. "And how different are you, anyway? You came to my conference two years ago and you spoke to no one," he says.

"No one spoke to *me*."

"Few of us are good at speaking across divides," he says. "I'm not your adviser but I'll give you some counsel. Next time you go to a conference, reach out to an attendee before you go and set up a meeting. You'll get your foot in the door. You'll see how it'll open up."

"Okay," I say, "but you opened your door to me, and look what happened. I've had to speak articulately in a language that's not mine to an authority figure twenty years my senior about a history that's also not 'mine,' while being grilled about how I stack up to your national stereotypes. At night, on a love seat, in your home, while you're wearing furry slippers."

"This is what I wear at home."

"Hardly professional, though. And we just met."

"All right. But this floor tile is freezing." He removes the slippers and places them beside the computer stand. His actual feet look tiny by comparison, bare and vulnerable.

"And the love seat?" I prod.

"The love seat? I concede it was not the best choice."

"Worse than that."

"That bad?"

"Yes. It was unnerving."

"You ruined the velvet. Anyway, you Americans and your 'personal space.'"

"True, but we just met. Is this how Italian professionals behave?"

He looks—perturbed? Annoyed? Perplexed?

"I'm not your student," I say, "but let me give you some advice. Pay attention to the messages you're sending young scholars, especially women. And if you go on inviting them to sit beside you at night, in your empty home, so close that your knees are touching, do not be surprised when they decide instead to stay holed up in their national institutes."

He looks bashful. "Point taken."

His computer blinks and he is about to insert my iPod Shuffle when I remember that I recently removed my dissertation copy from it. I tell him I'll send it by email instead, and I have walked into the hall to gather my things when I come upon his wife, who has just closed the front door behind her and is giving me a stony glare.

"I'm sorry about your love seat," I tell her. "I was careless and spilled water. On myself, too," I say, gesturing to my shirt.

She glares at her husband.

"Haven't I asked you to stop meeting with your students at home? And why are these riding boots blocking my hall?"

"They're mine," I say, picking them up, "thank you for having me. I have to go."

I wish them a good night, and before turning to leave, I hand the professor the mound of wet paper towels that I have been holding all along. "If you could please throw these away for me," I say, taking a few clean, dry tissues from a box by the door, thinking to myself, *Just in case.*

Part V

31.

THE PIED PIPER

I awake to the sound of a flute. Bright, melodious, insistent, it tugs me out of jet-lagged sleep. Groggy, stumbling toward consciousness, *I am still here.* Fragmented memories from last night's wedding party: a portly man in a cummerbund playing a white tuba, deer heads mounted on oak plaques, partygoers peering over the guest book, whispering. A vague memory of feeling unsettled, out of sorts. It is early September. It is 2015. *I am still in Rome.*

I pull at the heavy curtains, squinting. Four stories below, illuminated by a cascade of morning sunlight, a young man stands alone under a high arch. He has placed a small pot of money at his feet, and though the alley is narrow and untrafficked, a few passersby have stopped to listen to him play. A pied piper.

I place my phone on the sill and turn on the microphone. My time in Rome is short; sometimes one must stockpile memories. As I race to dress, my hotel room begins to feel like a holding pen. The *sampietrini,* and all the life I have lived and not lived on them, are down there, and I am up here, and the distance between is unbearable. In that moment I wish for a parachute, long to skip down the stairs and go back more than a decade to a life—in Rome, about Rome—that I have left behind.

Over the next few days I walk the streets for countless hours. I wander as if through an interior landscape, Rome less a living city now than the topography of my mind. From the Janiculum Hill and its swaying umbrella pines down to the underground tunnels of the catacombs, the dark, cool chambers of Mithraea still running with water and the memory of people long gone. I gravitate to the most ancient places, sites beneath the surface of the earth where secret springs gurgle from mossy crevices, where crumbling brick meets humid soil. I see, very clearly, my own bones mingled there. I visit places that once meant something to me and photograph them, hoping that capturing them in my albums will help me hold on to them when soon, inevitably, I have to leave again. I wear sunglasses, my sense of loss running down my neck and settling into my scarf, moistening my collarbone.

~∂

I was invited to Rome for a wedding. Five years have passed since 2010, when I was last in Italy for an academic conference held in Fiesole, outside of Florence. Even then I was two years out of academia, but could not turn down the invitation to an all-expenses paid trip.

All summer before the wedding I look forward to returning to Rome, though I also notice in myself a hint of guardedness, a slight drag on my enthusiasm, like a cross-current skimming the bottom of a hull.

I have left the world of history far behind. For years now, I have been someone else: someone who counts inventory and organizes photo shoots, someone who packs orders and decides on web page layouts. From the airport I arrive to the city by train. Each stop is familiar, the map still imprinted in my head. Parco Leonardo. Fiera di Roma. Ponte Galeria. Muratella. Magliana. Villa Bonelli. Roma Trastevere. From there, the tram to Largo di Torre Argentina, and then it is only a quick walk to the hotel where I will find my mother and stepfather, who have also come for the wedding.

The city looks much the same as last I left it. But as I walk, the city streets consume me. They rise up all around me, and in them I am confronted with visions of the person I used to be but am no more—all the way back to the *tartufo cioccolato* and the comment in my teacher's tightly looped red cursive.

 ∽

The restaurant where we eat the night before the wedding is not even ten minutes by foot from the hotel. More like five, I assure my mother, promising I will get us all there. My stepfather, who is nearing ninety, is apprehensive and prefers to call a taxi.

"That's really unnecessary," I insist. I'm embarrassed to take a taxi such a short distance.

We set off with time to spare. I get the first part right, but when there's a fork in the road, I doubt myself. I look up at a street sign and catch sight of my mother frowning at me.

"You said you knew the way," she says.

I get flustered. The streets begin to look the same: narrow, poorly lit, each one decisively right until it starts to look, somehow, wrong. A curve to the left—shouldn't it be to the right? My certainties crumble. The map I once knew so well distorts, like images around the edge of a magnifying glass. My stepfather, whose eyesight is severely limited, sets each foot cautiously on the cobblestones. My mother holds on to the crook of his arm, looking accusingly at me. I am angry with myself—for my excess of confidence, for my pride. Just as corrosive, I perceive that I have lost my hold of Rome. The city has slipped away from me. I am no longer a historian of Rome. I have no reason, now, to speak Italian. What used to feel like mine is no longer. What I still have in spades, however, is the same old need for it.

I lead them one block farther than necessary, and we have to circle around to get back. But we end up at the right place, and on time. Guests are chatting happily under an ivy-covered awning.

"Our guide got us lost," my mother tells the hostess, loud enough for everyone to hear.

On this evening, two prewedding dinners take place simultaneously in different locations: one for the parents and their friends, and another, elsewhere, for the bride and groom and theirs. The wedding guests are either far older than me or much younger. The bride's parents are dear friends of mine, people with whom I have felt such a long and continuous affinity that sometimes they have felt like surrogate parents. And so even though my age doesn't line up, I have been invited to the parents' dinner. The plan is logical: at the young people's dinner, I don't know a soul anyway. I offer myself the meager consolation that, age-wise, I am still closer to the late-twentysomethings. But it doesn't help. Nothing does. It is pathetic to even be counting.

Walking into the restaurant is excruciating. A sea of faces I don't know, faces I perceive to be those of accomplished individuals. Expensive clothes and jewelry, chins held aloft with composure. I have recently turned forty. My academic career has vanished, my little business is struggling. Words like *inventory* and *projected sales*, once shiny and new, have lost their luster. And now this wedding, which promises to be beautiful and lavish, hurts me all over as I waft about among strangers in a city where I was once someone else—someone young and free and *spiritosa*, someone who now feels so long gone but who I am sure, quite sure, must be here somewhere, maybe just around the next corner. I feel out of place in this elegant restaurant. It is not my Rome. I don't want to be wearing heels or have my hair blow-dried. I want to be walking with my friends to nowhere in particular, talking for hours, eating a warm *torta della nonna* from a midnight bakery while sitting on a curb, laughing.

I am seated at the farthest table from the entrance with four kindly couples the age of my parents. I feel the contrast of my relative youth, my solitary female–ness. The conversation, safely bland, turns to grandchildren, so I mention my children, who are four and seven.

"And who is watching them?" asks the woman next to me. She wears a clamorous yellow necklace and is the only one at the table, besides me, who seems unhappy.

It takes me a moment to follow her question.

"My husband?"

"Oh, isn't that nice of him to babysit so you could go to Rome," she says.

I bristle at her words. *Babysit*, because my husband is not *babysitting*, he is—as he would insist—being a father. And *Rome*, because the *Rome* I assume she means—*glamorous* Rome, *Anita-Ekberg-in-the-Trevi-Fountain* Rome, *oh-darling-isn't-it-just-so-captivating* Rome, a modern-day Grand Tour Rome where actual Romans mainly appear as servants and drivers and for comic relief—is not the Rome I miss or want, and so I clutch all my feelings about Rome tightly to my chest and try to summon a smile and let the conversation push on to someone else.

I manage well enough until the same woman begins raving about the artichokes—the "Jewish artichokes," as she calls them—on her plate. How much she loves them, and how every time she comes to Italy she *Just. Must. Have. The. Jewish. Artichokes.* But these are not Jewish artichokes— which are cut in half, smashed flat, and deep-fried. What we have on our plates are *carciofi alla romana*—artichokes in the Roman style. They have long stems and are prepared by quartering the artichokes, then braising them in white wine, olive oil, and water, with garlic and mint.

My pulse has begun to race because I feel somehow pitted against this woman and now I feel I must correct her miscategorization of the methods of Roman artichoke preparation. But the others listen to her with attention, poking their artichokes and saying, *Oh, how interesting* and *That's marvelous.*

The old pedant in me rises up, the one who cannot tolerate a mislaid detail. It is my duty, at this table, to fight for truth.

"These are not Jewish artichokes," I say, to no one in particular.

The woman looks startled.

"Why, of course they are," she says. "I've had them a million times."

"These are *carciofi alla romana*," I say, feeling like a jerk for sailing in on my truth wagon, and for doing so in Italian, to boot. "Roman artichokes. Jewish artichokes are different. They are flattened and deep-fried."

No one knows quite what to say.

"I used to be a historian of Rome," I say.

Silence reigns at the table, and I feel like more of a failure than ever.

The wedding reception is sublime and disorienting. It takes place at Circolo della Caccia, an aristocratic social club in Palazzo Borghese. With its stringent requirements for membership, it is one of the most exclusive clubs in Rome. Under a lavish ceiling, bucolic pathways of pink and green tendrils sprawl languidly across tables a hundred feet long, spiraling up the sides of silver bowls and candelabra. The Audrey Hepburn–beautiful bride makes her rounds while women in exquisite dresses buzz this way and that. Waiters in white jackets with black lapels and bow ties attend right and left as the warm, laden air of early September wafts in through enormous gilt-framed windows swung open to drink in the night. Some kind of jazz band, with a lot of brass and a white tuba, plays. One half of the wedding party appears accustomed to the location, nonchalant to the point of boredom. The other half marvels at the floors and ceilings as they inhale the musty, mysterious air of aristocracy. Did you know, they whisper over champagne flutes, you need seventy-five percent aristocratic bloodlines to join this club? Framed photos of the kings of Spain and England line the hall, as well as those of many men, photographed on horseback, hailing from Roman families I studied, families whose names go back many, many hundreds of years—some of them, more than a thousand.

The person who counts inventory and organizes photo shoots has no hold over me here in Rome. Without even a hint of protest, she melts off my face, peels off my body, as if all she had ever been was an outer layer of skin applied for warmth or disguise, and on the marble floor of Palazzo Borghese I leave her behind in ragged strips. I feel skinned, as if the core of my being were exposed for all to see.

༒

At the wedding dinner, over a magnificent plate of truffle tagliatelle, I ask the woman seated next to me, a dark-haired woman in her fifties, where she is from. She points casually upward: her in-laws live in the private apartment upstairs.

Upstairs in Palazzo Borghese? Well, then.

She is friendly and introduces herself, her thousand-year-old family name sliding off her tongue like an oyster from its shell.

"You're here alone?" she asks me in Italian.

"Actually, I'm with my mother," I explain, gesturing across the table through the thicket of vines and tendrils. My mother is engaged in animated conversation with the woman seated next to her.

"And . . . bride or groom?"

"I'm a friend of the bride's stepmother," I say. Somehow, upon inspection, this feels inadequate. I feel immediately delegitimized, as if I were usurping the place of my seat's rightful guest, who is a woman, undoubtedly more beautiful than me, with a better name, who speaks a different language, and who has a natural and uncontested right to inhabit space at this table. I think of the whispering voice of Stefano Colonna the night that he dined with Cola on the Capitoline Hill, and imagine him fingering the hem of my dress. *For you, tribune . . .*

A tall, gray-haired Italian man, in a gray suit with gray glasses, seated two seats down from me turns out to be a scholar of the American Revolution. He asks me about myself, and I report that I used to be a historian of medieval Rome. He raises an eyebrow, and we talk around our Borghese friend, who nods politely every so often to avoid seeming bored, about Rome during the Middle Ages. I find myself making an energetic case for why it is interesting. But no sooner have we embarked on this conversation than my old question stirs in its grave: *What can an Americana teach Romans about Rome?* Seven years out of academia, and here it is—popping up at a wedding, of all places, over a sublime plate of truffle pasta. This time I see an opportunity to gain perspective on this question that has vexed me for so long.

"Did you ever worry," I ask, "that as an Italian your credibility as an authoritative voice on American history might be questioned?"

The man takes another bite of tagliatelle and shakes his head. "I always felt," he says, chewing, "that I had something valuable to say."

Five years have passed since I have seen my friends from the Alpine Club, and in the days following the wedding, I meet up with several of them individually. Piero has moved to Verona but happens to be in Rome to distribute the newest edition of his climbing book. He arrives on his bicycle to meet me in Trastevere and we catch up over pizza. Enrico and I take a walk, looping over three of Rome's seven hills. He has fought a long legal battle at work, and the toll it has taken is visible in his bearing. His cheerful face betrays a new whiff of gravity. When Paolo and I arrange to meet, I ask where. "*Sotto casa tua,*" he says. The customary place, in front of my old rented room on via della Scala. The next afternoon, I hear his voice before I even turn the corner, then spot him waiting on the cobblestones as he has so many times before. He is walking in his usual little circles, his phone to his ear. After he finishes his call, we set off walking and talking and, after a long while, sit down for a drink on a narrow, dusty side street. With pride, he holds up his phone to show me a photo of his partner—a beautiful woman sitting on a patio—and their dog.

My friends. In the last half decade, they have aged, their hair has begun to gray. All of our lives have changed in some significant way. They are regular developments of regular lives. But I am shaken. In my life in Rhode Island, time has crept on, slowly and almost imperceptibly to me. But in Rome, it seems, time has leaped forward in one great bound.

The wedding was aesthetically beautiful, and it was a window into a side of Roman life that I had never before seen. But it was not my Rome, and I wanted my Rome back. My Rome of cobbled streets slick with rain, of the acrid smell of ink on vellum, of reclining under umbrella pines, of reading rooms silent as tombs, of disapproving archivists and the begrudging access they bestow to the limitless troves of knowledge they guard, the Rome of the past that imprints itself so forcefully on the present; my Rome of one-room rentals, limestone rocks, and grassy hillsides, of meandering free of any destination, my ragtag bunch bearing backpacks weighed down with climbing ropes and wild boar sausages and cream-filled pastries, the pernicious mud of iron-rich soil clinging mercilessly to our shoes, of bookstores and teahouses and glowing light at winter sunset, of cliffs that descend to a cavernous sea; my Rome of loneliness mixed with the thrill of togetherness with people I cared for, and then left. It was a Rome in which nothing was mine, and in which the whole city was. *Romana*, those who cared for me had called me. Although of course I wasn't, and could never be.

32.

COUNTING

I had been trained as a historian. I had become a historian. Then I had become someone else. You would think I had thought enough about time. Since college, I had read and discussed theories of time at length. Time as a circle, time as a river, time as a parabola, time as an endless upward trajectory. Yet here I was, at forty, railing against time itself.

It was as if I had blinked and, in that instant, life happened. Since leaving Rome in 2004, I had received my PhD, taught for two years, then had a baby. I held him in my arms, cooing at the sight of his ten fingers, his ten tiny toes. I stopped reading. For the first time in many years, I wore bright colors. With diminishing hope, and eventually diminishing interest, I continued applying for academic jobs. When none panned out, I started a business. Then I left academia for good and had a second child. Although the narrative had taken some hairpin turns, the progress of life felt mostly orderly. Time crept forward. The past was clearly the past, and the future, the future.

During this long blink of the first years of motherhood, I stopped thinking about faraway places. Or more truthfully, that faraway place. That Rome. *Here* was life and *now* was love. And that lasted. Until I went back. And remembered.

It was the remembering that split me into pieces.

At the end of my meeting with Paolo, I had thanked him for the many gifts he had given me over the years, the greatest of which was making me feel at home. That expression of gratitude was long overdue. But then came something I did not expect. On the coattail of my words rode in a decade of feelings. They emerged as I was walking back to my hotel, and all at once, as if they had been shuttered for years in a broom closet and suddenly freed. They buzzed around me like a great swarm. I could hardly breathe.

In Rome, and later, at home, I began to count, and to mourn, all the things I had lost. I grieved my beloved city and the unrelenting march of time that had pulled me from it; I grieved, finally, the dead end of my academic career; I grieved the impossibility of coming back, of going back, and wondered at the bristling contradiction between my happy home life and this sudden sad clutching at a time gone by. And most deeply of all, I grieved my lost self, the girl who had followed, even if by a wandering path, the unfurling thread of her own unlikely pursuit. At the same time, I brimmed with gratitude for the gift of this place that had almost been my home, and even for the grief, which, perversely perhaps, proved the worth of the loss I felt.

Acknowledging this loss was not easy. I was married to a man I loved. We had two small children. I had close friends where I lived, and a feeling of connection to the world around me, a home whose windows flooded with morning sun. Dwelling on grief felt indulgent, and potentially hurtful to those I loved. And yet I could see no way around it. The grief was everywhere. It grabbed me by the throat and stole my breath. It hunkered down in my stomach and spit out my food. It demanded that I listen to it, deal with it, barter and trade with it. It took up residence in my mind and in my heart, making infernal calculations and Faustian bargains about how to recover a self that existed only in the past. *When I had journeyed half of our life's way, I found myself within a shadowed forest.* And the only way out, as Dante well knew, is through.

After the wedding but before leaving Rome, I walked back to the courtyard of Sant'Ivo. I sat down cross-legged in the corner, in the same spot where the French mother in the striped shirt had sat almost twelve years earlier. I did not know what to do with the memory of that September day, with the sheer, monumental coincidence of it. It felt like a gift, and a torment. For the first time, I could see that in leaving Rome, in leaving academia, I had left an integral part of myself behind. But that person was still here, in the courtyard of Sant'Ivo, forever looking out over that balustrade.

I counted the things I had. They were more than trivial. My husband, the man with whom I had glimpsed a future after only twenty minutes of conversation at a party. Never before had I believed in tales of instant love, but the universe, which often proves my assumptions wrong, had presented me with just that. And then there were our children. Our young boys, their shoulder blades as delicate as almond slivers, their smooth boy bodies that still sought mine in the night. All this—warmth and beauty and bodies nuzzled in sleep—was mine.

And yet. I was overtaken by the need to recover my old tracks, to step back in time. As illogical as it was, I struggled to reconcile the warmth of the present with the need to hold on to, to incorporate, to possess, an ever-receding past. Past. Future. Present. Yesterday. Ten years ago. Tomorrow. A thousand years ago. I considered these words, these concepts, from all sides, trying to understand what they meant. How is it that a historian can lose her sense of time? Feel young and ancient all at once? If only I could stay in Rome, I thought. To figure it all out. To calculate precisely what had been lost and what gained, what was dear and what had ceased to be. To be able to say *that was past* and *this is present.* For the film between the two had slipped away.

———

I longed to go on sitting in the courtyard at Sant'Ivo. I longed to stay in Rome. But I did not. I could not. Clutching my bag of tufa stone, tiny conch shells and pine nuts, my body strained its way to the train station. Roma Trastevere. Villa Bonelli. Magliana. Muratella. Ponte Galeria. Fiera di Roma. Parco Leonardo. Each stop farther from where I wanted, or needed, to be. Each stop cinching the elastic tighter, pulling my insides into knots. My mind rebelling.

At the airport, I waited at the gate, looking like anyone else, I suppose, though my heart had turned to lead and plummeted to my feet. When it was time, I dragged my lead heart onto the plane, sat holding it and examining it the way one might a sick child. Once again, incredulous at the fact of being on a plane whose nose was pointed toward the runway, with Rome behind me. And then the jet propelled me and several hundred others across the heavens and set us down gently in the New World, my old one. I stuffed my damp scarf into my purse, walked back into my house. Into the leaping embraces of my children. Into the arms of my husband. Into the pleasant joyful boring satisfying unsatisfying chaotic loving everything of our daily routine. Into the person I was in the present, whoever that was, rather than the one I once had been, or thought I might one day be.

33.

YOUR STORY

Here is a test anyone can try. Think back to a critical life juncture, let's say, a fork in the road where you made the decision to take one path instead of another. Ideally you have at least five or ten years of distance from this event. Now think of the narrative you have built up around making that decision. You know exactly why you chose that path, right? Why you took that job, married that person, left that person, moved across the country, decided not to move, dropped out of that program? Most likely, you have that story down pat. You have told it and retold it. *This is what happened*, you have told your friends, family, acquaintances, over dinner, at holidays, over drinks.

Now let's say you keep a box of old letters somewhere. And maybe a small assortment of mementos you have accumulated over time. If you kept a journal, even better. Don't discount the digital—dredge up those old emails, those photos on that hard drive, that CD in the drawer. Best if these things are all a bit dusty. Now take an afternoon, at the very least an hour or two, to sort through them, everything pertaining to that period in question, the period of the fork in the road. Look at every last email, letter, photo, memento, diary entry. Allow yourself to feel lost. Read the things people wrote to you and, if you can, what you wrote to them. Look at the movie tickets, restaurant receipts, college papers, cassette mixtapes, those photos you saved that don't really fit in any album, and ask yourself why you saved those but not the rest.

Does your story hold?

34.

INTO THE CREVASSE

For a while, I remained tormented by the desire to go back in time. I panicked at the thought that I had deviated from some course I was supposed to take. The phrase *supposed to* haunted me. Was I supposed to have been a historian? Was I supposed to have lived in Rome? I did not believe life was predestined, so how could such a thing as a right or wrong track even be possible? Everything was out of sync. I was deep in Dante's wood.

After I returned home from the wedding, everything in me continued pulling me back to Rome. It was there, I thought, that I could find out what really mattered and retrieve that person I had left behind. For months afterward, I remained gripped, seized, by a fierce desire to go back. Quite suddenly, my life at home felt so very small, and Rome, the past, so very big. I would go for a walk, or a run, and find myself immobilized, leaning against a tree whose leaves were bursting into autumn flame while, as if in the updraft of their consuming blaze, I gasped for breath. In these moments, it was as if the Providence air were not enough—it was not the *right* air, had not the correct composition of nitrogen and oxygen to sustain my life, and in it, I worried in these moments that I was suffocating, that I would quite literally faint, and fall. Rome I pictured when I first woke up; *Rome*, I chewed on the word while making myself eat; *Rome*, I repeated endlessly while trying to fall asleep—if only the invocation of its name could bring it back to me. Every newspaper was studded with land mines: people—none of them me—who were in Rome, or who had recently returned, and whose pervasive good spirits and blithe travel advice seemed nothing short of perverse. Why were they there and I wasn't? But returning to Rome just a few months after attending the wedding felt like a giant, nearly impermissible indulgence—the ties of motherhood and marriage and practical reality tethering me to another place, another time, another version of myself.

Javier, all the same, encouraged me to go. He reminded me of a documentary we had seen together in which a climber falls into a deep glacial crevasse and breaks his leg. In despair, the climber realizes that his only chance of survival lies in the inconceivable: to descend into the crevasse in the hope that, by way of the darkness, he might find a different path out of the ice. Going in deeper, Javier said, is sometimes the only way to find your way out. Among all the words ever spoken to me, these remain among the most generous and courageous.

I took the first official steps to close my business, whose operations I had been gradually winding down since returning from the wedding in September, and in late January I flew back to Rome for a two-week trip. From the plane I looked down on the Alps, blanketed under snow, and Italy north of the Po River, dense with fog. I watched as the landscape greened, as the sun goldened, as the patchwork farmlands around Rome once again came into view. I rented a shabby apartment just a few steps away from Sabrina's old place with its blue bedroom. She had sold it, I'd heard, and moved somewhere cheaper and quieter. I began to write. In late mornings I went to the market and bought *broccoletti*, fresh pasta, and chickpeas. Then I walked the city, which was chilly and foggy and moist. I longed to sink into the soil, disappear into any of the city's hedge mazes and never emerge. I visited the Baths of Caracalla, where seventy years before, Grandmother and Grandfather had gone to hear opera. There I stole into a roped-off area, where I sat down cross-legged among ancient bricks fallen on the unforgiving earth, nettles stinging my thighs and calves through my pants, fingering tiny mitre shells and balls of tufa stone as I listened to an aria of chirping birds. In the evening I returned, shivering, to the apartment and cooked the pasta and the chickpeas, and while I slurped up their warmth I listened to the bells toll and watched at dusk as lights lit up the facade of the great fountain, Il Fontanone, at the top of the hill. It was as if I had never left. There was only one difference: how quickly the days slipped past now, time sieving through my fingers like that ancient spring cascading under San Clemente, proving to me with every passing second the absolute impossibility of return.

~~~

Ultimately, the job of the historian is to help us, collectively, to hold on to time. To sew its fragments together into something that makes sense, like a quilt we cover ourselves with in the dark. *Look at this quilt,* we say. *As long as we have it, we know who we are.* We know where we come from, and because of it, we think we have the tiniest inkling of where we are going. In the morning we might toss it off, leap bravely forward into the unknown, but when night comes, we clutch it to our necks and console ourselves with the sounds of our own stories: "because . . . and because . . . and because." The narrative changes over time, we sew it and resew it, and sometimes we fight about what should go where, which patches have been neglected, which others are monopolizing the center. But most of the time, we take it for granted, and night after night it keeps us warm and dry.

I walk to Sant'Ivo alla Sapienza and sit down again in the corner. Almost twelve years later, they are still here, the boy and his father. They have not changed. From the ground level this time, I watch them as they run side by side, following that straight line of white stones. I notice the harmony in their movements. The boy does not struggle to keep up with his father. The father trots comfortably at his son's side. They cannot see me.

"*Tu vas par là, et je vais par là.*" The boy's words—you go that way, I'll go this way—bounce off the walls, tracing their own angles around the courtyard like balls in play.

The boy and father head off in separate directions, each following his own line. The rubber soles of their shoes shuffle on the stones.

"*Fais attention o tu tomberas,*" calls the mother, beside me, from the sidelines. Careful you don't fall!

The boy reaches the end of his line and makes a left turn toward the center of the courtyard. "*J'arrive, papa,*" I'm coming! "*J'arrive!*"

They reach the center—a white circle—at the same time. The father lifts the boy into the air and spins him joyfully around.

The boy's laughter reverberates. He looks down at the shoes of his father, who has stepped back onto the black.

"*Tu es tombé dans l'océan,*" the boy says. You fell into the ocean.

In this courtyard, time stands still.

Every day after writing, I venture out on long walks. Most days, the heavy January mist hangs over the Tiber until well into the afternoon, the *sampietrini* still glistening with the previous night's rain. People speak in hushed voices. The Ponte Sisto, the pedestrian bridge linking Trastevere to Rome's center, so frequently crowded in good weather, sees only isolated passersby. Everyone walks briskly, their jackets pulled tightly around them. A tattooed man sits at the top of the bridge's gentle arch playing an acoustic guitar, his sleepy chords hovering briefly in the air, then drifting down to the river. The Tiber looks familiar—under the low clouds it flows green gray, nearly the color of the Atlantic where it curls up to the shore not far from my home in Rhode Island. Looking at the river, it seems no time has passed at all.

I walk by the medieval tower where the old woman once spoke to me and Paolo. In twelve years, the tower's outer appearance has remained almost completely unchanged. The woman's sunflower pots still populate the shelf by the uppermost door. But the blossoms have shriveled, and the stalks, now the color of wheat, are bare. A sign is posted on the door: *Vende: Torre medioevale.* The tower is for sale. The list price: one million euros.

A few weeks ago, a cousin texted me from California. We have been out of touch for years, but these days, as sometimes happens in periods of transformation, old threads have been surfacing right and left. I told her I was going back to Rome. I wanted to go in winter, I explained, when sometimes, on a chilly damp night, the city feels almost desolate. *Rome in January is poetic and divine,* she replied. She voiced my longing with a precision that took me by surprise. Between running a business and raising small children, life often felt like an unending series of logistical decisions, or a prolonged problem-solving exercise. There was pleasure at times in those things, too, an embracing of the here and now. But when I saw my cousin's text, her words stopped me in my tracks: *Rome in January is poetic and divine.*

That the medieval tower has come up for sale feels prophetic. Standing before the door, I copy the real estate company's phone number onto a piece of scrap paper. Against all logic, I begin to feel that it is mine. When I return to the privacy of my apartment, I call to inquire. The realtor suggests we meet the next day for a viewing. I am going to see the tower from the inside.

꧂

I sometimes wonder whether we know more than we think we do about our lives' trajectories, whether the lines on which we travel come endowed with a few fixed points. Most of the time, they are invisible to us, or we are too distracted to notice them, but they trace our movements under the earth, or over it, or pierce us right through our hearts. When I imagine these invisible trajectories, I see another layer of meaning in Quasimodo's "*Ognuno sta solo*," the first poem in Italian I ever memorized. We are alone on the face of the earth, and the evening will be upon us before we know it, but the *raggi di sole*, those rays of sunlight, are the trajectories of our lives, mooring us, *trafitti*, impaling us even, upon some essential line, despite all our earthly wanderings, and rooting us to the same point on the distant horizon.

"I feel like I'm being carried along by a current," I told a friend.

This worried her, for in the modern world, and particularly in my country, there is great value ascribed to the notion that we are the masters of our own destiny—an assertion that medieval Romans would have found puzzling, if not funny. But nothing felt more right to me then than this feeling of being carried. For I felt then, and I continue to believe now, that by some unspoken partnership between the constellations of the heavens and my own mind and heart, I was sliding back onto one of those fixed lines. Like the climber in the crevasse, I had to feel my way through the labyrinth and shed my fear of the dark. I knew I would not be going back to academia per se—such a return would be nearly impossible, and neither did I want it. But I needed to go back to Italy, to Italian, to writing. I was a blistered pilgrim, after all, limping back to her own self. I was a surge of water, careening down the channel of an aqueduct, spilling with abandon into that great basin. I was seized by a need for the poetic and the divine—words that, in this context, might seem frivolous. They were anything but. Recovering the poetic, the divine, felt like a matter of life or death.

⌒∂⌒

A few moments before three thirty in the afternoon, I arrive at the foot of the medieval tower. Paolo, whom I texted the moment I secured a tour, joins me. The agent, a dapper man in his early thirties, greets us briskly and unlocks the door's two locks. He gives the door a little push, and it swings open into a pool of darkness.

"*Fa' la ricca americana,*" Paolo jokes, and I laugh uncomfortably at the idea of playing the rich American lady, come to find herself a piece of Roman antiquity for the taking.

Inside, dusk reigns. The entryway has no windows. A metal stairway, its thin banister painted green, leads upward, where closed shutters and boarded-over windows hold the weak January sun at bay. The chill is penetrating. There is nothing else on the ground floor—not a mat, nor an umbrella stand, nor a table for placing your keys. Right off the bat it seems a stark life, living in a tower.

We ascend the first set of stairs. The tower's state of disrepair is immediately unsettling. A jagged stump of a beam hangs uselessly over the stairwell. The real estate agent reels out the usual narratives of how the place could be spruced up, tales of future and potential. We reach the second floor, a bedroom. A modest, conical glass chandelier hangs from the center of the ceiling, tossing a light so scant that it barely extends beyond the fixture itself. Paolo walks to a small framed photograph hanging over a bureau. As the agent pushes the window shutters open, light filters in, illuminating the photo's subjects: two women side by side. Paolo points to the older of the two.

"It's her," he says.

My memory of the woman's face is less confident, and I struggle to connect the countenance with the woman from twelve years ago.

The large wrought-iron bed that dominates the room must have been hers. A lime-green sweater—handmade, by the look of it—still lies folded near the pillows. Just off the back of the room is an irregularly shaped door. I step through it to find myself in a dark, cramped bathroom whose ceiling is so low I am forced to crouch. There are no straight lines—the room, if you can call it that, looks like it has been carved out of the structure using a bucket or a trowel, the way the inside of a snow cave might, or a sand-castle. I return to the bedroom and look out the window, finding myself face-to-face with another broken beam, this one protruding from the exterior. Just behind it is the ancient arched brickwork of the Portico d'Ottavia, which by comparison appears intact and marvelously sound.

We return to the stairway. The railing is cold, almost freezing, to the touch, the light dim and gloomy. At the top of the stairs we come upon the green French doors. The agent pulls them open and there, on the wire tray, are two pots of sunflowers. Former sunflowers, really, dried now and bent and cracked and broken. To the left opens the tower's only other room, the living room, and at its far end, a roughly triangular kitchen. The kitchen looks almost as much a hodgepodge as the bathroom, wedged irregularly into the tower's corner. The countertop is piled high with sundry kitchen items whose details I try to absorb in one long, devouring glance: a stack of plates (dinner and salad, in settings of twelve), a thick roll of paper towels, a pewter candlestick, a cut-glass bowl, a silver tray, and two ornate teacups set on saucers. The personal belongings make me sheepish: I feel like an intruder, seeing things that it is not my right to see. In compensation, perhaps, I experience the fleeting urge to take up residence in this tower, to live sparingly among its owner's few possessions, and in that way to honor her. To honor her, perhaps, by becoming her.

All the while, I cannot stop thinking about how hard living in a tower like this must be. The constant traipsing up and down stairs. The pervasive chill contained by four thick walls. The way the wind must blow through its cracks and crevices on windy nights. The lonely peril of that dark stairwell. Despite the neatly made bed, and the handmade sweater still lying on it, despite the teacups with gold motifs set on dainty saucers, the tower feels more like a refuge—from war, from threat, or from other privations—than a home. Some clock in here has stopped, and long ago.

Paolo summons me back to the living room, a dark, high-ceilinged space with a second set of French doors. The agent presses a button on the wall and an ornate brass chandelier lights up, its exposed bulbs throwing harsh, unforgiving rays against the room's graying walls.

"*Guarda*," Paolo says, pointing to one of the walls.

Behind us the agent has opened the doors, and afternoon sun now drapes in wispy threads across the room. Starting at the height of my hip, the wall before us slants inward—not smoothly, like a slope, but rather in a series of ridges. The fourth ridge creates a mantel, on which are stored a few objects: a small terra-cotta pitcher, a decorative brass sugar bowl, and a torsion pendulum clock, immobile, with three chrome balls under a glass dome. I also spot an ornament in the shape of a Star of David, which I connect belatedly with the mezuzah I only half noticed down at the entry—the old woman was Jewish.

It takes me a moment to discern why the wall encroaches in this way upon the room, but Paolo, who has figured it out quickly, knocks on it to demonstrate.

"Behind this is the Portico d'Ottavia," he says.

I have to change my frame of reference to perceive what he is describing. On the other side of the plaster is the ancient Roman temple's pediment, the large marble triangle held up by columns. Each ridge pressing farther into the living room wall is a layer of stone. What we see is the shape of the ancient architecture in relief. Above the shelf holding the pitcher and the clock is a short vertical expanse, followed by more ridges and slants that, taken together, precisely mirror the features of the pediment as seen from outside. So the tower does not just lean up against the Portico d'Ottavia—it has also swallowed parts of it, absorbing its features into itself. Inside the living room, what we see is negative space.

I am struck by the possibilities for what this means. If, say, you were to live all your life inside this tower, and never once step outside, you might think the design of the wall was natural, that it had to be that way, because that was the only reality you knew. Walls are sometimes flat and straight, you might say to yourself, and sometimes they undulate inward.

Sometimes you can place a clock on them, and sometimes you cannot. But you would never know why. Had you not stepped out onto the street, you would never have known that what gave your living room wall its distinctive shape, what made it yours, was a vast history pressing in on it from outside. You would not perceive the extent to which the present, with which you consider yourself so intimate, has been sculpted by the past.

35

SACRED GROVE

I am no longer a historian. And yet, as I write this, I still find myself circling around the questions that haunted me back when I first became one. *Why are you dedicating your life to this? What is at stake for you?* As I try to make sense of my own life's path, these questions follow me on my walks, they hover over me at night. Is the answer simply *Because I loved it?* And *Because Dante led me there?* Why *should* we bother with the lives and experiences of people so long dead? Why forcefully—and sometimes luridly—extract the joys and sorrows of the past, the uncountable acts of unimaginable violence and the rarer acts of compassion or reconciliation? Why revive the noisy jostling of the powerful and the quieter struggles of the vulnerable from the dusty shelves on which their stories have finally settled, like volcanic sediment hardening into rock? Why delve into the "scandal that has lasted for ten thousand years," as Elsa Morante famously called it? Or excavate the "one single catastrophe which keeps piling wreckage upon wreckage," as Walter Benjamin so memorably painted history, in the elusive search for a causal chain of events? Why sit in the archives, struggling over letters and words, shivering with cold, wondering if your time and labor will amount to anything, or whether the narrative you seek will forever elude you? And what if that narrative, should you find it, turns out to be a sham?

Perhaps the answer is as simple as the iconic mountaineer George Mallory's terse reply when asked why he wanted to climb Mt. Everest: "Because it's there." It is true that the past is always there, behind us, about to catch up and overtake us, and—if we are not careful—swallow us whole. Such a fact is not to be discounted. But the past can swallow us only if, succumbing to our instinct to flee, we neglect to turn around. If we do not look it honestly in the face, and assess the people we once were, neither to valorize and amplify nor to castigate and erase but to confront, to the best of our ability, how we have arrived where we are. We must grasp the shape of the past that defines by its very contours the structure of the room, otherwise known as the present, that we inhabit.

Nietzsche might have raised his hand in protest of this thought. For, as he wrote, "when the historical sense reigns *without restraint* [emphasis his] . . . it uproots the future because it destroys illusions and robs the things that exist of the atmosphere in which alone they can live." The past, in other words, can suffocate the future—*future* being a currency in which historians normally do not trade. Germany, as he saw it, was suffering "from a consuming fever of history" that had hobbled the impulse to action that he saw as the hallmark of a healthy and vigorous society. Nietzsche wrote these words in 1874, when German historians and philologists—such as the Latinist Ludwig Traube—were indeed engaged in a whirlwind of history writing.

Unlike the historians of Nietzsche's day, I never set out to study history for explicit reasons of national or personal identity. If anything, I have been most curious about the history of places beyond my individual horizon, both in space and time. Some might see in this a kind of escapism, and perhaps they would have a point. But in the Middle Ages I found a world deeply different from my own, one that I had to struggle daily, hourly, to understand. And this, I would say, was not without value, for it expanded me, as a scholar and as a person, to wend my way through systems of knowledge, as well as cultural norms, languages, and modes of being, that were, to me, foreign. All that solitude—I had sought it out.

The environmental historian Bathsheba Demuth has written eloquently about how imagination is one of the historian's most critical tools. She cites, for example, the imagination necessary to construct a narrative from disparate archival documents. And then there is another kind of imagination, one born from an intense familiarity with the dizzying array of human experience bequeathed by studying the past. This is the ability to imagine ourselves outside of the particular circumstances in which we happen to have been born and raised. Demuth's defense of imagination as a critical tool of the modern world is a viewpoint with which Nietzsche, perhaps surprisingly, might have agreed. His solution to the paralysis of history, he wrote, was art: "Only if history can endure to be a work of art will it perhaps be able to preserve instincts or even evoke them."

In my own studies, I had pursued a question about disaster: What happens when a city, a people, falls upon its worst of times? Back then, I was looking at the question from a social and political point of view, and I ended up with a study showing how historical memory can be a powerful tool in societal conflict. But then I experienced my own worst times, a period of pervasive self-doubt in which it seemed to me that all the foundations I had laid—for my professional life, for my relationship to a city I loved and in which I had thought I would one day live—had come to naught. The first and simplest thing I found in the past was solace, the knowledge that I was not, would never be, alone. Dante had walked through his own *selva oscura*, descending into his crevasse, as it were, and climbed the hill on the other side. In my own difficult moments, Dante's words on the page were the first companions to which I turned. I admit it was a strange sort of solace. It was so distant, and yet undeniably real—so tied, as it was, to my earliest self. In rereading Dante, I was rereading myself.

And in the past, I also found recovery. Funny, that word's two senses— one, to heal, and the other, to take back. My recovery, it turns out, was both, for only by taking up that old self—the person who read and wrote and sought out the *poetic* and *divine*—could I mend my ruptured inner life. The act of recuperation, of looking backward to the past and recovering the shards of a person so seemingly long gone, was the only way for me to step forward into whatever future awaited.

As Orpheus well knew, this backward glance is not without its risks. For just adjacent is that other instinct, sometimes so convincing in its possibility, to revive or resuscitate. This is the instinct that Cola knew so well, the instinct that allowed for his dizzying rise and then, as might have been expected, his precipitous fall. In my own case, that same instinct sang its siren call, trying to persuade me that I could move back to Rome—just hop up and go—and step back into my old, worn shoes. This is the illusion—mellifluous, deceitful, and hollow—that the unexamined past sometimes offers.

❦

On the final day of my two-week trip, I return to the park on the Janiculum Hill. I've got my old shoes—those from 2003—slung over my shoulder in a bag. I follow the path that skirts the Villa Doria Pamphilj, whose potted citrus trees now hang heavy with fruit, climbing the wide stairway and crossing the expanse of the soccer field, which at this hour, late afternoon in early February, is empty but for a far-off couple and their dog. The ground beneath my feet is already beginning to stiffen with the onset of night. From the field I wend my way down the path into the grove of umbrella pines, the place in Rome I find the most solace, majesty, joy, and melancholy. Among this grouping of trees set on a hill, so calmly vertiginous they are somehow holy. In this tranquil sacred grove, altitudinous, muscular, divine. Sheltered by this verdant sanctuary whose conifer roof spreads out above earthly life like a miniature celestial realm. This grove, this gathering, speaks to me of all the people I have ever been, pulling the past into the present and joining them together into one. Some of these selves I know, and some I don't. I find myself, a wanderer in a wool skirt, and myself, a girl of eighteen following the ink trail of an idea, and myself, a soul outside of time suspended above the earth and below the first star, and myself, a cluster of bones nestled deep in the loamy soil. Not ravaged by time but caressed by it. As if eternity lived here, right here, on this bed of grass, under the paws of that white shepherd dog (*Bella! Bella!* her owner calls. *Dov'è Useppe?*) chasing a red ball between the rows of lithe trunks.

It's not just myself I find. Something ancient buzzes here. Or other-worldly. A conclave of the dead, perhaps, a parley of all the people who have ever been, and are, and who will one day be, our brothers and sisters, all of them, joined to us in time. Sex is here, and death, and the first cry of new life; the thrum of love and the march of war. Ours is the hum beneath the soil, ours the current buzzing through the torsos of these trees. These trees—beings in their own right—who are capable, with their beauty and poetry, of summoning tears, and hope. *Pinus pinea*, words of common prayer.

The sun has nearly set. In an old, formal garden, I find a semicircle of niches, many inhabited by small statues. At each end of the semicircle, though, are several that stand empty. From my shoulder bag I retrieve my old shoes—the mustard leather ankle boots that my mother, seventeen years ago, bought for me in a Coolidge Corner shoe store and that I wore throughout my research year in Rome. Their soles are worn now, their arches flattened. But they are still beautiful to me, and I must summon the will to bid them farewell. I place them down in an empty niche, a fitting place of rest, so that they stand neatly parallel, side by side, facing out into the garden. The last weak rays of sun are scattered by the lowest branches of the surrounding trees. I zip my jacket up to the collar. It is getting chilly.

When I leave the park, I am lighter, less encumbered. I have said good-bye to some old part of myself, who will stay on in this garden, in this niche. Not that I won't miss her. But I know her path ends here.

36.

BEATRICE

When Dante the pilgrim reaches the threshold of the earthly paradise, he lays eyes for the first time on Beatrice, who stands with regal bearing aboard a chariot. Dante invoked her at the beginning of the poem. It was she who summoned Virgil to lead Dante through the dark wood, down through the rings of *Inferno,* and finally up the mountain of *Purgatorio,* which he has climbed with great effort, searching for footholds, his fingers sore and callused from its pocked rock. We, the readers, have been waiting for Beatrice for sixty-three cantos—nearly nine thousand lines. We have waited so long that stumbling upon her now feels like a revelation. Dante recognizes her instantly: by sight, as well as by the "hidden force" that emanates from her. The same feelings abruptly ignite as when he had been a young man in her presence. His breath is taken away. He describes himself as *trafitto,* transfixed. He trembles, nearly falls apart. He remembers his youth and the great power of his old love. Simply laying eyes on Beatrice pushes Dante back to an essential part of himself that he had long forgotten.

In shock, Dante turns to tell Virgil of Beatrice's effect on him but discovers to his dismay that his beloved guide has vanished. There has been no quick kiss on the forehead, no spinning on the heels, nary a word of goodbye. What can the pilgrim do but cry? Hold his leaden heart in his hands and regard it like a sick child? And keep talking, talking to Virgil, his *dolcissimo patre*, sweetest father, as if he were still with him. *Virgil, Virgil, Virgil*, he says thrice in the space of three lines—lines of mourning, of grasping, of frantic hope that issuing a flow of words, a river of his name, might bring him back. And so, in the moment that Dante gains what he has long dreamed of, he loses what he had—progress and loss, attainment and forfeiture, tied at the hip.

Dante! Beatrice calls out, rousing him from his stupor—her first word to him and the one and only moment in *The Divine Comedy* that the poet's name is spoken. *Quit your crying*, she commands. *You'll soon have plenty else to cry about.* Beatrice, it turns out, is no passive, silent, lyric lady weaving violets into her friends' hair—that exquisite, sterile fruit of the male imagination. She is not even nice. She would never bake cookies, nor mutter *Mi perdoni, professore.* Who or what is Beatrice, then? She is an *ammiraglio*, as Dante describes her—an admiral, standing at the bow of her chariot, slicing across the scene, managing her subordinates, commanding admiration and respect. She is a stern mother, *madre superba*, who speaks forcefully and at length while Dante cries and cowers in shame. For nearly fifty lines, she rebukes him: for weeping like a baby, for following an untrue path, a *via non vera*, for forgetting her after she died, for being immature—a baby bird—and loving many women, for wasting his talent as a writer, and above all for refusing to learn from her death that even the most beautiful and perfect mortal flesh is corruptible and transient and therefore a diversion from the true good. A laundry list of failings that, incidentally, narrates Dante's personal history. Upending all tradition of the time, Dante makes Beatrice confessor, priest, prophet, and teacher of theology. And he did this while basing her on a real woman who lived a real life in the city where Dante grew up and where her family still lived.

Beatrice is so many things that she can see Dante from all sides. And her unsparing account of his wasted talents and many shortcomings forces

Dante to examine the true nature of his life's path. While his mind registers her narrative, it takes him a while to own it. He remains stationary, rendered speechless, his knees practically buckling under him. But then his body—contrary, perhaps, to our expectation—offers him a way forward. *Mille disiri più che fiamma caldi*, he writes, "a thousand desires hotter than a flame," press him to her. Those desires make him gaze into her eyes, and in her eyes he glimpses, at long last, a reflection of the divine.

The hungerings come first, the firing of synapses second. The person—whether the teacher, the beloved, or the muse—is the mirror in whose reflection we are shown the pathway. She holds the keys. He holds the black box. She utters the words that hover in wispy filament. He raises a toast, *Dum vivimus vivamus!* They change your lexicon, make it richer, deeper. They offer you an elixir both medicine and magic. Feel this, notice this, listen to this, all this that I have held poetic and divine. They instruct us in the art of seeing, of hearing, and set us down the path of discovering what we can do. At the root of that journey, before all its gains and losses, is desire.

37

ASCENT

One October morning, less than a month after coming home from the wedding in Rome, and before returning in January, I dropped my older son off at school. On my way home, a van pulled out of a driveway in front of me. It was a red Volkswagen van, the same model and color that I had clambered into on that first day of the climbing course. Paolo's van. Somehow, even though I'd passed this driveway almost every day for the past year, I'd never noticed the van before. Seeing it elicited in me both happiness and melancholy, and the simultaneity of these feelings no longer surprised me. Almost every morning thereafter, that same red van pulled out in front of me as I was heading home.

One day I decided to follow it. It drove quickly—I had to race to keep up. I followed it through Pawtucket, then Providence, from north to south, passing all my usual haunts: the bakery, the pharmacy, the toy store, the public library, the public high school, the private school, the university, and on. I followed as it traversed my neighborhood, until it veered onto the on-ramp of the highway. I knew that what I was doing was ludicrous, and I resisted pursuing it any further.

For the remainder of the school year, the red van appeared before me nearly every day. Each time I spotted it, I experienced the overwhelming sensation that I was chasing my past. Fruitlessly. Senselessly. And even if I did not want to, even if I refused to follow, there it would appear, careening off to some unknown destination. And I would be transfixed by this chimera.

After a very long time, by which I mean about two years, I managed to forget about the van. And then one day, passing its driveway, I noticed it was gone.

❧

My family lies napping as the ceiling fan pushes the humid summer air into a whir. I close my eyes and take a walk in Rome. Before me, two marble stairways form a V. The one to the left leads up to the Church of Santa Maria in Aracoeli. The one to the right, known as the *cordonata*, leads to the Senatorial Palace, the Capitoline Museums, and the equestrian statue of Marcus Aurelius. I climb the stairway to the right. Halfway up I pass a bronze statue of a hooded young man, one hand extended and the other holding his sword. I nod to Cola di Rienzo, my old friend, whose bracelets must have clinked as he last glimpsed the earth in just about this very spot. The steps under my feet are wide and generous and make for a comfortable climb. Designed by Michelangelo, they are less steep than modern stairs, easier on the body. If you were to consider only stairs, you would have to discard the idea of human progress. I walk up, thankful for the strength in my legs, the hum in my heart, and for all the hungerings that, again and again, have made me seek this place. Near the horizon I can still make out the *selva oscura*, Dante's dark wood, with its tangle of thorns and brambles, its branches bare under a silent sun, and all the pain and all the good I found there.

Soon I reach Michelangelo's piazza, a wide-open square that offers up the sky while pressing you in its earthbound embrace. In the center, Marcus Aurelius sits atop his horse, gesturing westward with outstretched arm. I admire the horse's bronze belly, its perfect hooves, the seated emperor's muscular calves, which seem to bounce in their stirrups from the power of the horse's movement.

I think of the day that Cola was dubbed knight over at Saint John Lateran, remembering that this statue had been present there to witness it. Back then, everyone thought that the horse's rider was Emperor Constantine. To celebrate his knighting, Cola had the horse filled with wine. Celebrants filled their cups from the horse's nostrils, dancing away to the idea that Cola would be a new Constantine and usher in a new age.

They were wrong, about both Cola and Constantine. But the statue's survival lies in their very error. Had early Christians known that the emperor was Marcus Aurelius—a pagan—they would likely have melted the statue down, as they did so many others, for the bronze. We like to think that mistakes are to be avoided at all costs, but sometimes our errors are what ultimately save us. Losing the straight path, the *diritta via*, is sometimes the only way to become who we are.

Less than a mile from my home in Providence, Rhode Island, stands a replica of the Marcus Aurelius equestrian statue. It is the only replica in the world outside of Rome, and it stands on a shady green hill at the center of the Brown University campus. The statue is rooted here; after a hundred years, it is part and parcel of the campus. I have often visited it, standing beneath its height and heft and following the emperor's eastward gaze. By my calculations, this Marcus Aurelius is looking straight toward Rome. Even now, rooted as I am, I remain familiar with this gaze. It spans geography and time. I know it because it is my own.

Acknowledgments

Writing this book, while requiring a kind of solo travel into my inner cosmos, has also brought me into contact with many talented and generous people. Since the origin of this work lies in his classroom, I offer my first thanks to George Viglirolo for showing me the power of a teacher to open a door to new worlds.

I am grateful to those who helped ferry this work to the printed page. Bill Clegg, thank you for championing this book with expertise, humor, and wisdom. My sincere thanks as well to Simon Toop and everyone at the Clegg Agency.

At Viking, my gratitude to my exceptional editor Lindsey Schwoeri for believing in this book and for approaching it with care, diligence, and kindness. Your extraordinary skill has allowed it to bloom. Allie Merola, your deeply insightful reading encouraged me to develop some facets of this book that mean the most to me. Thank you, above all, for urging me to go further with Beatrice.

I would like to acknowledge the International MFA program in Creative Writing and Literary Translation at Vermont College of Fine Arts (VCFA). To Evan Fallenberg and Xu Xi, I offer my deepest thanks for that life-changing experience and for your excellent mentorship. Evan, I remember with appreciation the day you visited and told me about your remarkable new program. Ira Sukrungruang, Jacky Colliss Harvey, and Robin Hemley, writers and mentors *extraordinaire*, thank you. Philip Graham, heartfelt gratitude to you and Alma Gottlieb for friendship, mentorship, and more than I can list. Thanks, too, to Michaela Anchan, Antony Dapiran, Paul Rozario-Falcone, and Xiao Zhang for illuminating conversations in Reykjavík, Hong Kong, Montpelier (Vermont), and Lisbon.

To my Providence writing community: Stephen O'Shea, Jill Pearlman, and Hester Kaplan, I am grateful for your early guidance. My enduring thanks to the members of my writing group—Bathsheba Demuth, Paja Faudree, Sarah Frye, Nate McNamara, Liz Rush, and Jodie Noel Vinson— all of whom were crucial to this book's development.

My gratitude and *ringraziamenti* to Saleem Abboud Ashkar, Susanna Angelillo, Alberto Bianchi, Ali Kenner Brodsky, Dedda DeAngelis, Rebecca Haessig, Anna and Cyrus Highsmith, Joan Pierre, Anna Shusterman, Michelle Smith, Luisa Weiss, and Rosella Zarkin for support, sustenance, and conversations that helped resolve difficult portions of the text. Annabelle Frost, thank you for striding with me down our first Roman sidewalk and for staying close ever since.

To historians, I offer my gratitude. Niall Atkinson and Bob Fredona, thank you for your long friendship, and for critical feedback on historical sections. Any errors are due to my own stubbornness. Tom Cohen, thank you for years of mentorship and friendship. Ron Musto, your exemplary study of Cola has been vital. My sincere thanks to Jonathan Mandelbaum for permission to cite his father Allen Mandelbaum's translations of Dante and Salvatore Quasimodo. Finally, I would like to acknowledge the Digital Dante project hosted by Columbia University's Department of Italian and its Center for Digital Research and Scholarship.

In Rome, I offer my gratitude to the Club Alpino Italiano. Piero Ledda and Enrico Zhara Buda, *vi ringrazio*. A tip of the hat to the Vatican Library for being a repository of wonder; and to the DigiVatLib project, which is making the library's collections accessible to anyone with an internet connection. The *OWL* (*Online Window into the Library*) newsletter has kept me informed.

My enduring gratitude to those who taught with passion and dedication: John Ahern, Joel Kaye, Caroline Bynum, Amnon Linder, and the late Reginald Foster.

No writer can flourish without resources. For books, workspace, and professional circles, I thank the Providence Public Library, Providence Community Libraries, and LitArts RI. Thanks as well to the Providence Athenæum for allowing public access—a little desk in a quiet alcove is sometimes all a person needs. The Little Free Libraries that pepper my neighborhood occasionally presented me with a book I didn't know I needed. Small miracles, reminding me that libraries of all kinds are enormous cultural assets that deserve our constant public recognition and support.

To my family I extend my sincere thanks. Elgie and Frank Holstein, I appreciate your insights into your parents'—my grandparents'—experience in Rome. Rachel Lee Holstein, my gratitude for your mystical phrasing of Rome in wintertime. Ben and Nick Holstein, Anna Curtis, Stef Wertheimer, and Sherry Moss Holstein: my deep thanks for supporting this book with enthusiasm, even when I raised difficult or divergent memories of our family. *Agradezco de todo corazon a mi familia de Madrid y Barcelona, y sobre todo a mis queridos suegros Ángeles Córdoba y Paco Fernández de Alba.* My heartfelt thanks to my father, Ned Holstein, for supporting my MFA at a late juncture and for greeting this book with pride. Your love for literature and history has found a place in me. And to my exceptional mother, Lynn Frisbie Holstein, for teaching me from my earliest days to love language and art and creative expression. Time and again you have opened the vistas of my world.

Finally, I express my infinite gratitude to my beloved Fran, who has walked every sunny peak and dark valley of this book. Your attention to caring for others, your support of my writing life, and your unwavering belief in me are my bedrock. May we be old by the time we reach the island; may we understand together what these Ithakas mean.

Kiko and Elias—you are my heart, my gift, my Rome.

Notes

3. Dante Led Me Here

21 **Nel mezzo del cammin:** Dante Alighieri, *The Divine Comedy: Inferno*, trans. Allen Mandelbaum (Berkeley: University of California Press, 1980), 1.1–3. Unless otherwise noted, all English renditions of *Inferno* cited in this book are from Mandelbaum's translation.

4. A Family Story

29 **"Inside the isolated city":** Elsa Morante, *History: A Novel*, trans. William Weaver (Hanover, NH: Steerforth Press, 2000), 364.

38 **The *Vulcania* made transatlantic voyages:** "Visitors for the Festivals: 1,000 Arrive at Haifa," *Palestine Post*, April 10, 1933, nli.org.il/en/newspapers/pls/1933/04/10/01/article/43.

39 **Now the *Vulcania* would ferry:** *Vulcania* passenger manifest, May 17, 1940, inci.org.br /acervodigital/upload/listas/BR_APESP_MI_LP_106480.pdf.

39 **The *Vulcania* was busy:** Italy had four so-called *navi bianche*, or "white ships"—*Vulcania, Saturnia, Duilio,* and *Giulio Cesare*—transatlantic cruise ships that were retrofitted in the manner of hospital ships and together transported nearly 28,000 Italian citizens back to Italy in the years 1942–43. Pamela Ballinger, *The World Refugees Made: Decolonization and the Foundation of Postwar Italy* (Ithaca, NY: Cornell University Press, 2020), 78ff.

40 **On the long trip home:** Ballinger, *World Refugees Made*, 97ff.

6. All Hungerings

50 **Dante shivers at the sight:** For this discussion and others, I am indebted to the immense public resource provided by Professor Teodolinda Barolini and the Digital Dante Project hosted by Columbia University's Department of Italian and its Center for Digital Research and Scholarship. Any (mis)interpretations are my own.

59 **Each alone on the heart:** Salvatore Quasimodo, *The Selected Writings of Salvatore Quasimodo*, trans. Allen Mandelbaum (New York: Farrar, Straus & Cudahym, 1960), 135. Gratitude to Jonathan Mandelbaum for the permission to reproduce his father's translation.

7. Searching for Dante

64 **In Dante's bones, the two:** Guy P. Raffa, *Dante's Bones: How a Poet Invented Italy* (Cambridge, MA: Belknap Press, 2020), 202.

65 **Frassetto embarked on a yearslong:** Discussed in fascinating detail in Raffa, *Dante's Bones*, 203–8.

65 **More than eighty years later:** A detailed description of this process can be found in S. Benazzi et al., "From the History of the Recognitions of the Remains to the Reconstruction of the Face of Dante Alighieri by Means of Techniques of Virtual Reality and Forensic Anthropology," *Conservation Science in Cultural Heritage* 7 (2007): 379–409, https://conservation-science .unibo.it/article/view/1262.

66 **"Don't search for my mandible":** Raffa, *Dante's Bones*, 205.

8. DOLLAR BY DOLLAR, WORD FOR WORD

70 *When I had journeyed half:* Inferno 1.1-3.

71 **Ah! It is hard:** *Inferno*, 1.4–6.

10. ARRIVAL

79 **Writing to his friend Wilhelm:** Sigmund Freud to Wilhelm Fliess, 3 December 1897, *The Complete Letters of Sigmund Freud to Wilhelm Fliess, 1887–1904*, ed. and trans. Jeffrey Moussaieff Masson (Cambridge, MA: Belknap Press: 1985), 285.

79 **His inability to arrive:** Freud to Fliess, ibid., 285.

80 **In the 1897 letter:** Freud to Fliess, ibid., 285.

80 **"I am not sufficiently collected":** Freud to Fliess, 23 October 1898, ibid., 332.

81 **"Learning about the eternal laws":** Freud to Fliess, 27 August 1899, ibid., 368.

81 **In *The Interpretation of Dreams*:** Sigmund Freud, *The Interpretation of Dreams*, trans. A. A. Brill (New York: Dover, 2015), 393.

81 **The power that Freud attributed:** Janice Hewlett Koelb, "Freud, Jung, and the Taboo of Rome," *Arethusa* 48, no. 3 (Fall 2015): 391–430.

81 **"I found it difficult":** Freud to Fliess, 19 September 1901, *The Complete Letters*, 49.

82 **Specifically, he likened the accretion:** Sigmund Freud, *Civilization and Its Discontents*, trans. Joan Riviere (Mineola, NY: Dover Publications, 1994), 6.

82 **Freud challenged his readers:** Freud, *Civilization and Its Discontents,* 6.

82 **He could not do it:** Freud, *Civilization and Its Discontents*, 6.

11. AMERICAN BEATRICE

98 **Back in 1939, when Orkin:** Ruth Orkin, *A Photo Journal* (New York: Viking Press, 1981), 15. My gratitude to my mother, Lynn Holstein, for finding this book for me and straightening out some of the facts related to Orkin's cross-country trip.

98 **"We were literally horsing around":** Ronnie Koenig and Laura T. Coffey, "'American Girl in Italy': Remembering the Woman in This Iconic Photo," today.com, May 5, 2018, today.com /news/remembering-ninalee-craig-american-girl-italy-photo-t128438.

99 **"Public admiration . . . shouldn't fluster you":** Ellie Silverman, "Ninalee Craig: The Woman Made Famous by the 'American Girl in Italy' Photos," *The Independent*, May 9, 2018, independent.co.uk/news/obituaries/ninalee-craig-dead-american-girl-italy-famous -photos-a8337071.html.

99 **After Robert Doisneau's *The Kiss*:** By 1995, sales of the poster version of *American Girl in Italy* numbered 250,000. Shaun Considine, "The Making of a Classic," in *American Girl in Italy: The Making of a Classic* (New York: Howard Greenberg Gallery, 2005).

99 **"It's not a symbol":** Howard Greenberg Gallery, Announcement of the Exhibition "Ruth Orkin: Jinx Allen in Florence," 16 September–22 October, 2005, https://community.today .com/parentingteam/post/at-age-88-the-american-girl-in-italy-wrote-this-message-to- my-8-year-old-son.

99 **At another exhibition:** Howard Greenberg Gallery, Announcement of the Exhibition "Ruth Orkin: Jinx Allen in Florence," 16 September–22 October, 2005, https://www.howard greenberg.com/storage/app/media/Exhibition%20Files/Orkin%202005%20PR.pdf.

99 **In 2017, a Philadelphia restaurant:** Michael Klein, "Restaurant Removes Iconic Image after Sexism Outcry," *Philadelphia Inquirer,* November 16, 2017, https://www.inquirer.com/philly/blogs/the-insider/gran-caffe-laquila-to-remove-iconic-orkin-photo-after-sexism-outcry-20171116.html.

100 **she "clutched at herself":** Richard Sandomir, "Ninalee Allen Craig, at the Center of a Famous Photograph, Dies at 90," *New York Times,* May 4, 2018, nytimes.com/2018/05/04/obituaries/ninalee-allen-craig-center-of-a-famous-photograph-dies-at-90.html.

101 **"The idea for this picture":** Orkin, *A Photo Journal,* 90.

101 **"Art is always difficult":** Teju Cole, "A Too-Perfect Picture," *New York Times,* March 30, 2016, nytimes.com/2016/04/03/magazine/a-too-perfect-picture.html.

103 **"Walking about Florence":** Shaun Considine, "Candid or Contrived? The Making of a Classic," *New York Times,* April 30, 1995, nytimes.com/1995/04/30/arts/art-candid-or-contrived-the-making-of-a-classic.html.

105 **And in fact, a few:** David Schonauer, "An Image of Innocence Abroad," *Smithsonian,* October 2011, smithsonianmag.com/travel/an-image-of-innocence-abroad-72281195/.

105 **"Italy was spread out":** "L'Italia era dispiegata davanti a me. Non c'erano tanti turisti ancora. In cima alla Torre di Pisa ero da sola. Anche la Cappella Sistina era quasi vuota. Non mi ricordo quanto sono rimasta seduta a guardare il soffitto." "La ragazza con gli occhi addosso: Compie 60 anni lo scatto '*An American Girl in Italy,*'" *Quotidiano Nazionale,* August 22, 2011, quotidiano.net/cultura/2011/08/22/566735-ragazza_occhi_addosso.shtml.

13. A Sparrow Flies into a Hall

119 **"For what is all of":** Francesco Petrarca, "Invective against a Detractor of Italy," *Invectives,* ed. and trans. David Marsh, I Tatti Renaissance Library II (Cambridge, MA: Harvard University Press, 2003), 416 (Latin), 417 (English).

119 **For he felt that by:** "It grieves me to go further; for the scepter and dignity of the empire which was founded by us with such effort will be stolen by outsiders of Spanish and African descent." Petrarca, *Africa,* ed. Nicola Festa, Edizione nazionale di Petrarca I (Florence: Sansoni Editore, 1926), 2.274–76.

122 **These questions felt especially relevant:** Francis Fukuyama, "The End of History?" *The National Interest,* no. 16 (1989): 3–18. Fukuyama subsequently nudged his hypothesis into a broader and more confident theory no longer in need of a question mark in his book *The End of History and the Last Man* (New York: Free Press, 1992).

122 **Even though Herodotus is:** Cicero, *On the Republic. On the Laws,* trans. Clinton W. Keyes. Loeb Classical Library 213 (Cambridge, MA: Harvard University Press, 1928), 300-1, https://doi.org/10.4159/DLCL.marcus_tullius_cicero-de_legibus.1928.

14. Ithaca

134 **In search of guidance:** Keith Sidwell, *Reading Medieval Latin* (Cambridge: Cambridge University Press, 1995), 2.

135 **"Fewer and fewer students":** Sidwell, *Reading Medieval Latin,* ix.

15. Living Latin

142 **He is working for his:** For some details of Reginald Foster's biography, I have relied on Alexander Stille's rich profile "Latin Fanatic: A Profile of Father Reginald Foster," *American Scholar* 63, no. 4 (1994): 497–526.

143 **One Vatican Latinist called Reginald:** John Byron Kuhner, "The Vatican's Latinist," *New Criterion* 35, no. 7 (March 2017), https://newcriterion.com/issues/2017/3/the-vaticans-latinist.

148 **As Anne Carson has said:** Anne Carson, "The Art of Poetry, No. 88," interview by Will Aitken, *Paris Review* 171 (Fall 2004), https://www.theparisreview.org/interviews/5420/the-art-of-poetry-no-88-anne-carson.

151 **"We advanced step by step"**: Saint Augustine, *Confessions,* trans. Vernon J. Bourke (Washington, DC: Catholic University of America Press, 1953), 9.10.24.

152 **"We just barely touched Wisdom"**: St. Augustine, *Confessions,* ed. L. Verheijen. Corpus Christianorum Series Latina, 27 (Turnhout: Brepols, 1981), 9.10.24.

17. The Past Is a Great Din

169 **On the wall above:** Dante Alighieri, *The Divine Comedy: Paradiso,* trans. Allen Mandelbaum (Berkeley: University of California Press, 1984), 33.145.

18. Winter Will Melt Away

174 **"Come, see your Rome"**: "Vieni a veder la tua Roma che piagne / vedova e sola, e dì e notte chiama: / Cesare mio, perché non m'accompagne?" Dante Alighieri, *The Divine Comedy: Purgatorio,* trans. Allen Mandelbaum (Berkeley: University of California Press, 1980), 6.112–14.

174 **In these impassioned passages:** Dante, *Purgatorio,* 6.77 and 6.89, respectively.

177 **By the 1310s, residents numbered:** Ronald G. Musto, *Apocalypse in Rome: Cola di Rienzo and the Politics of the New Age* (Berkeley: University of California Press, 2003), 24–25.

178 **In the expanse of the Colosseum's:** I am indebted to Philip Graham for reminding me of this marvelous tidbit. Also, Robert Brentano, *Rome Before Avignon: A Social History of Thirteenth-Century Rome* (Berkeley: University of California Press, 1990), 13.

21. The Holy Roman Alpine Club

205 **As I munch on:** Piero Ledda, *In cerca di guai: Ossia come rischiare la pelle senza alcun pericolo e sentirsi liberi legandosi ad una corda,* 1st ed. (Rome: Edizioni Grafema, 1998), 217.

208 **"A few tens of people"**: Piero Ledda, *In cerca di guai: Ossia come rischiare la pelle senza alcun pericolo e sentirsi liberi legandosi ad una corda,* 2nd ed. (Perugia: Porzi Editoriali, 2006), 20.

22. Vatican Library

214 **Beginning in about 1000 CE:** Richard Krautheimer, *Rome: Portrait of a City, 312–1308* (Princeton, NJ: Princeton University Press, 2000), 310.

221 **Royal seat of priests:** "Regalis sedes sacerdotiii / Origo armorum et legum / Mater fidei et exemplorum / Amicorum et regum auxilium." My translation. Giovanni Cavallini dei Cerroni, comments on Valerius Maximus, *Facta et dicta memorabilia,* MS *Vat. Lat.* 1927, fol. 12r, Biblioteca Apostolica Vaticana, Vatican City.

221 **"Note the excellence"**: "Nota excellentiam huius littere R que Romam designat." My translation.

222 **Bartolus had condemned:** Bartolus of Sassoferrato, *"Tractatus de regimine civitatis,"* in *Politica e diritto nel Trecento italiano: Il 'de tyranno' di Bartolo di Sassoferrato (1314–1357),* ed. Diego Quaglioni (Florence: Leo Olschki, 1983), 2.65–74, p. 152. My translation.

223 **"Note against Nicola"**: Cavallini, *Facta et dicta,* fol. 44v.

24. If Only I Could Live in Their Times

246 **One Florentine visitor described:** "I Romani, che già furono del mondo signori, e cche dierono le leggi e' costumi a tutti, erano stati gran tempo sanza ordine o forza di stato popolare, onde loro contado e distretto si potea dire una spilonca di ladroni, e gente disposta a mal fare." Matteo Villani, *Cronica, con la continuazione di Filippo Villani,* ed. Giuseppe Porta, 2 vols. (Parma: Fondazione Pietro Bembo, 1995), 9:51.

246 **A contemporary chronicler, known:** Anonimo Romano, *The Life of Cola di Rienzo,* trans. John Wright (Toronto: Pontifical Institute of Mediaeval Studies, 1975), 31.

247 **Among Cola's tasks:** Ronald G. Musto, *Apocalypse in Rome: Cola di Rienzo and the Politics of the New Age* (Berkeley: University of California Press, 2003), 57.

247 **"My heart was all inflamed"**: Petrarch, *Sine Nomine* 7, quoted in *The Revolution of Cola di Rienzo*, ed. Mario Emilio Cosenza, 3rd ed. (New York: Italica Press, 1996), 4.

247 **"If only I could live"**: Anonimo Romano, *Life of Cola di Rienzo*, 31.

248 **"Read whenever you have"**: Petrarch, *Epistolae variae* 48, "Hortatoria," quoted in Cosenza, ed., *Revolution of Cola di Rienzo*, 20.

249 **By reviving Rome, Cola dreamed**: Musto, *Apocalypse in Rome*, 120–26.

250 **"With his little coat"**: Anonimo Romano, *Life of Cola di Rienzo*, 32.

251 **Dressed in layers of ethereal**: Anonimo Romano, *Life of Cola di Rienzo*, 36.

251 **Just beside the tablet**: Musto, *Apocalypse in Rome*, 113–17.

252 **He called himself "Nicholas"**: Musto, *Apocalypse in Rome*, 137–42.

253 **"Italy, which only recently"**: Petrarch, *Epistolae Variae* 48, "Hortatoria," quoted in Cosenza, ed., *Revolution of Cola di Rienzo*, 16–18.

253 **He also informed Cola**: Petrarch, *Epistolae Variae* 38, quoted in Cosenza, ed., *Revolution of Cola di Rienzo*, 40.

253 **Not so for Stefano**: Musto, *Apocalypse in Rome*, 151.

253 **The Ordinances of 1347**: These are described in detail in Musto, *Apocalypse in Rome*, 143–45.

255 **"All Rome was happy"**: Quoted in Musto, *Apocalypse in Rome*, 176.

255 **In a remarkable speech**: The translated text of Cola's speech is quoted in full in Musto, *Apocalypse in Rome*, 180–81.

255 **The papal vicar, stunned**: Anonimo Romano, *Life of Cola di Rienzo*, 72–73.

256 **Among those few conspicuously absent**: Musto, *Apocalypse in Rome*, 188–89.

257 ***"Per ti, tribuno"***: Anonimo Romano, *Cronica*, ed. Giuseppe Porta (Milan: Adelphi, 1991), 140. Translation from Anonimo Romano, *Life of Cola di Rienzo*, 75.

257 **Cola gifted each nobleman**: Musto, *Apocalypse in Rome*, 207–11.

258 **"I have cut off"**: Anonimo Romano, *Life of Cola di Rienzo*, 87.

258 **A few days after the battle, Cola**: Cola's letter to the Florentines, November 20, 1347, quoted in Musto, *Apocalypse in Rome*, 228.

258 **Now he would also lose Petrarch**: Quoted in Musto, *Apocalypse in Rome*, 241.

259 **In a stunning display**: Quoted in Musto, *Apocalypse in Rome*, 252.

259 **Exchanging the laurel leaves**: Musto, *Apocalypse in Rome*, 253.

259 ***You shall leave everything***: Dante, *Paradiso*, 17.55–60.

261 **But this time, instead**: Anonimo Romano, *Life of Cola di Rienzo*, 150.

261 **Someone tore off Cola's cloak**: Anonimo Romano, *Life of Cola di Rienzo*, 151.

26. Checklist

288 **This rock was born**: Alex Maltman, "The Tangled World of Tuff, Tufa, Tufo, and Tuffeau," *World of Fine Wine* 26 (2017): 116. An edited version of this piece is available at: worldoffinewine .com/news-features/tuff-tufa-tufo-tuffeau-vineyard-soil.

35. Sacred Grove

331 **Why delve into the "scandal"**: "Uno scandalo che dura da diecimila anni" was the original subtitle for Elsa Morante's novel *La Storia*.

331 **Or excavate the "one single"**: Walter Benjamin, "Theses on the Philosophy of History," in *Illuminations: Essays and Reflections*, ed. Hannah Arendt, trans. Harry Zohn (New York: Schocken Books, 1985), 257.

332 **"Because it's there"**: "Climbing Mount Everest Is Work for Supermen," *New York Times*, March 18, 1923, nytimes.com/1923/03/18/archives/climbing-mount-everest-is-work-for-supermen -a-member-of-former.html.

332 **For, as he wrote, "when":** Friedrich Nietzsche, "On the Uses and Disadvantages of History for Life," *Untimely Meditations*, trans. R. J. Hollingdale (Cambridge: Cambridge University Press, 1987), 95.

332 **Germany, as he saw it:** Nietzsche, "On the Uses," 60.

333 **The environmental historian Bathsheba Demuth:** Bathsheba Demuth, "On the Uses of History for Staying Alive," *The Point*, July 12, 2020, thepointmag.com/examined-life/on-the-uses-of-history-for-staying-alive/.

333 **"Only if history can endure":** Nietzsche, "On the Uses," 95–96.

36. BEATRICE

337 **Dante invoked her:** I am particularly indebted to Professors Teodolinda Barolini and Joan Ferrante, and Columbia University's Digital Dante project for my reading of Beatrice.

A NOTE ON THE TYPE

Pietro Bembo (b. 1470) was a Venetian scholar, poet, and essayist. Widely recognized for his command of Latin and Greek, he served as Latin secretary to Pope Leo X and, later, as cardinal. Bembo also contributed substantially to the development of the Italian vernacular. His 1525 grammatical treatise *Prose della volgar lingua* codified Italian grammar and orthography and eventually furthered Dante's project of making the Tuscan dialect Italy's foremost literary language. His primary literary models for Tuscan poetry and prose were not Dante, however, whose literary style he considered uneven, but Petrarch and Giovanni Boccaccio. Bembo was active in literary circles and was noteworthy for his interactions with many learned women.